The Reality of God

AND OTHER ESSAYS

The Reality of God

AND OTHER ESSAYS

Schubert M. Ogden

1817

Published in San Francisco by

Harper & Row, Publishers

New York Hagerstown San Francisco London

"The Temporality of God" first appeared in *Zeit und Geschichte, Dankesgabe an Rudolf Bultmann zum 80. Geburtstag,* ed. Erich Dinkler. Copyright © 1964 by J. C. B. Mohr, Tübingen.

"What Does It Mean to Affirm, 'Jesus Christ Is Lord'?" was originally published under the title "The Lordship of Jesus Christ: The Meaning of Our Affirmation" in *Encounter,* Autumn, 1960. Copyright © 1960 by Christian Theological Seminary.

First Harper & Row paperback edition published in 1977.

Library of Congress Catalog Card Number: 66-20783
ISBN: 0-06-066351-0

The text of this book is printed on 100% recycled paper.

77 78 79 80 81 10 9 8 7 6 5 4 3 2 1

To

My Colleagues at Perkins School of Theology
who have shared in these
theological essays

Contents

Preface to the Paperback Edition

The title essay in this volume was originally prepared as the 1965 Merrick Lectures at Ohio Wesleyan University. When I was invited to give these lectures, I resolved almost at once that their theme should be what seemed to me then, even as it still seems to me, to be the central problem of Christian theology. Of course, I am even more aware now, some twelve years later, of the perils involved in attempting to treat so immense a problem in so short a space. But I am also convinced that events have vindicated my decisions both to do the lectures and to publish them essentially as they were originally given. Indeed, considering the response the book has received since its publication in 1966 (and, in German translation, in 1970), I think I may claim that the title essay has achieved the modest goal I then set for it—namely, to give notice of a possible alternative to the more conventional approaches to the problem of God and thus to make a difference to the ongoing discussion. Even today, I regret to admit, this discussion is still hampered by the untenable assumptions that one can affirm Christian faith in God only in the terms of classical theism and that one can be wholeheartedly secular only by accepting the claims of modern secularism. But I seem to see signs that these assumptions no longer have anything like as firm a hold, and it is gratifying to think that my essay, in this new edition, will go on with its wonted work of exposing them for what they are.

Beyond this, I remain convinced that oversimplification is not the only threat to good theology. Too often, the complexity of more extensive treatments of a theological problem serves only to obscure its essentially simple structure as most persons in fact confront it. This is perhaps especially likely to happen today in the case of the problem of God, which developments in modern Western history have managed to reduce for many of us to the simplicity of a few crucial questions. There is, first of all, the question of the problem itself, of its proper clarification and formulation, which, as in most cases, is the point where many attempted solutions already disqualify themselves from further consideration. Then, there is the question of a possible solution, which, in this case, is really two questions: (1) as to the bases in our common human experience for talking about the reality of God at all; and (2) as to the conceptuality or system of fundamental concepts in which that reality is most adequately conceived and understood. My readers will have no trouble recognizing that it is just these questions that provide the formal structure of the title essay. My hope, therefore, is that they will also readily discover in the essay answers to questions they themselves are asking and that this directness of communication will in part make up for an admitted insufficiency of development in the answers themselves. At the same time, I would remind them that the essay is exactly that—an essay, which will more likely serve their good if its limitations are not forgotten.

It was partly from my own sense of these limitations that I did not issue the title essay alone, but rather in the context of several additional essays, some of which had previously appeared in other books and theological journals. Treating as they do of a number of systematic problems from prolegomena to eschatology, these other essays fill in some of the gaps left by the first and further illustrate the way of doing theology which it exemplifies. The more important reason for publishing them here, however, was that they, too, are all variations on the one theme of the reality of God. Their presence in the volume thus serves to underscore by way of example what I have often stated as a precept—that this theme is, in the last analysis, the *sole* theme of all valid Christian theology, even as it is the *one* essential point to all authentic Christian faith and witness.

This leads to a brief comment on what, in retrospect, now seems to me the most serious difficulty in the book's main argument for the reality of God. The observation has sometimes been made that the least rationalized step in each of Aquinas's famous "five ways" is the last minor premise, which he expresses in some such statement as "And this all men call God." I am now convinced, as a result of critical discussion of my book, that I myself am open to the same kind of implied criticism. For my argument in the second section of the title essay that basic confidence in the meaning of life is, at least implicitly, faith in God is valid only insofar as the word "God" is used in the completely general sense in which I use it in that argument, to mean the objective ground of our basic confidence in reality itself. The difficulty with so using the word, however, especially in a context in which the issue, finally, is the truth of Christian theism, is that this issue is made to appear a good deal simpler than it is. The burden of theistic argument is to show that theism's constitutive concept "God" is not only *a* way of conceptualizing the ground of our faith in the worth of life but also the *only* way, in the sense of being the most appropriate way in which this can be done. For this reason, to establish "the reality of God" in the distinctively theistic sense of that phrase logically requires that one establish more than "the reality of faith" and its objective ground.

Readers will recognize, I think, that I was by no means unaware of this in originally working out my argument. Nevertheless, they should know that I feel the force of the objection that, by introducing the term "God" as I do, without sufficiently distinguishing my more general use of it from the distinctive sense it has for theism, I tend more to obscure the logic of my argument than to clarify it.

At the same time, I must say that none of the criticisms I have seen has shaken my conviction that the only point I intend to make by that argument is validly made. To ask about the reality of God is not possible at all except in terms of the mode of reasoning established by our basic confidence in the worth of life. But because such confidence is a necessary presupposition not only of religion but of human existence as such, the question of God is implicitly asked and answered by all that we think or say, and it must also be asked and answered explicitly by any metaphysics whose business it is to analyze the basic presuppositions of all our thought and speech. Thus, in this as in all other truly radical questions, the only issue there is any point in discussing is not whether but in what sense—not whether we have confidence in life's meaning, but in what terms, theistic or some other, we can most appropriately conceptualize and account for it. To this extent, I should agree with Paul Tillich that the God who is the content of "absolute faith" is not "the God of theism." Because the God in whom we unavoidably believe is "the God who transcends the God of the religions," he remains as the ground of our basic confidence even when the claims of theism and Christianity are questioned or denied.[1]

I shall not repeat what I have said in earlier prefaces in acknowledging the special help I received in connection with this book. But I do feel obliged to express once again my gratitude to the various publishers and editors who have kindly allowed me to reissue the essays originally appearing in their books or journals: to the University of Chicago Press, publisher of the *Journal of Religion*, in which "What Sense Does It Make to Say, 'God Acts in History'?" and "Theology and Objectivity" first appeared in January, 1963, and July, 1965, re-

1. Paul Tillich, *The Courage to Be* (New Haven: Yale University Press, 1952), pp. 182–190.

spectively; to Herr Paul Siebeck, in which volume, *Zeit und Geschichte, Dankesgabe an Rudolf Bultmann zum 80. Geburtstag*, ed. Erich Dinkler (Tübingen: J. C. B. Mohr, 1964), "The Temporality of God" was originally published; to Professor Ronald E. Osborn, editor of *Encounter*, in the Autumn, 1960, issue of which "What Does It Mean to Affirm, 'Jesus Christ Is Lord'?" appeared under the title, "The Lordship of Jesus Christ: The Meaning of Our Affirmation"; to Professor Paul Davies, editor of the *McCormick Quarterly*, whose special supplement of January, 1965, first included "Myth and Truth"; and to Abingdon Press, publisher of *Religion in Life*, from which some of the paragraphs in my article, "Beyond Supernaturalism," in the Winter, 1963–64, issue, have been used here (in altered form) in Section 3 of the title essay.

S. M. O.

Dallas, Texas
August, 1977

Whenever it abandons a system of thought, humanity imagines it has lost God.

The God of "classical ontology" is dead, you say? It may be so; but it does not worry me overmuch. . . . And if "classical ontology" disappeared, it was surely because it did not correspond adequately with being. Nor was its idea of God adequate for God. The mind is alive, and so is the God who makes himself known to it.

"God is dead!" or so at least it seems to us . . . until, round the next bend in the road, "we find him again, alive." Once again he makes himself known, in spite of all that we have left behind on the road, all that was only a viaticum for one stage of our journey, all that was only a temporary shelter till we had to make a fresh start. . . . And if we have really progressed along the road, we shall find God himself greater still. But it will be the same God. *Deus semper major*. And once again we shall move on in his light.

God is never left behind among the dross. . . . In whatever direction we go, he is there before us, calling to us and coming to meet us. . . .

HENRI DE LUBAC, *The Discovery of God*, p. 167.

The Reality of God

AND OTHER ESSAYS

I

ɣ

The Reality of God

1. THE PROBLEM OF GOD TODAY

One of the obvious conclusions to be drawn from the latest developments in Protestant theology is that the reality of God has now
become the central theological problem. This statement may seem
odd, since, as popularly understood, theology is nothing if not, in
Richard Hooker's words, "the science of things divine,"[1] and therefore an unending struggle with just this problem. The fact remains
that for much of the theology of the first half of our century the
reality of God was not its one great theme.

For a complex of reasons that need not be gone into here, the most
influential Protestant theologians of the last generation focused their
thinking on other themes. There were, of course, exceptions, and I do
not wish to imply that the theological work of this period was either
lacking in express treatments of the problem of God or is without
significant bearing on its eventual solution. Neither implication could
be supported by the evidence, and I should question in principle
whether any thinking about the distinctive meaning of faith in Jesus
Christ (with Karl Barth) or about the nature and destiny of man
(with Reinhold Niebuhr) could fail to be relevant to this central
problem of theology. Rightly understood, the problem of God is not
one problem among several others; it is the only problem there is.
Hence all our thinking, on whatever theme and whether properly
theological or not, is of some, at least indirect, relevance to clarifying
and solving it. Even so, the reality of God need not become directly
thematic in our reflections, and even when it does, it may not be their

[1] *Works,* Vol. I, ed. John Keble, Oxford: Clarendon Press, 7th ed., 1888, p.
374.

one pre-eminent and all-determining theme. This is evident from the Protestant theology between the two world wars, when pronounced tendencies toward either christological or anthropological concentration removed the problem of God from the center of theological thinking.

Lately, however, the scene has shifted, and this problem is now very much to the fore. At once symbolizing and, to an extent, summarizing this change is one of the most remarkable books produced by the Protestant theology of the present generation: John A. T. Robinson's *Honest to God*.[2] Although the argument of this book bears on almost all the basic issues of Christian theology, its one all-controlling concern is with the possibility and meaning of an honest faith in God in our time. This became evident immediately from the responses that greeted the book and is fully documented by the summary of the whole discussion since made available in the follow-up volume, *The Honest to God Debate*.[3] Yet, significantly, Robinson expressly disavows that his proposals are in any way original and offers his little book as simply "an attempt at communication."[4] That his disavowal is more than false modesty is at once apparent from the content and character of his proposals themselves. *Honest to God* stands squarely in the main movement in Protestant theology since World War II, and there is ample reason for its constant appeals to the work of Dietrich Bonhoeffer, Rudolf Bultmann, and Paul Tillich. Indeed, the main importance of Robinson's book lies in clearly focusing the one demand on which the contributions of these three thinkers all converge and in popularizing a program of theological reconstruction such as is necessary to respond to their demand.

And this brings us directly to the initial task of the present essay. If we are to deal with the problem of God responsibly, we must first of all understand the problem in its current form. A promising way to achieve such understanding is simply to ask why the reality of God has now become of central theological concern. Given a clear answer to this question, we should also be able to discern the present shape of the problem of God itself and thus be in a position to take the next

[2] London: SCM Press Ltd., 1963. For a discussion of the significance of this book for our present problem, see my article, "Beyond Supernaturalism," *Religion in Life*, Winter, 1963–64, pp. 7–18.

[3] Ed. John A. T. Robinson and David L. Edwards, London: SCM Press Ltd., 1963.

[4] *Honest to God*, p. 21.

steps toward its possible solution. Accordingly, we must now inquire as to the reasons for the recent change in Protestant theology just described.

The first of these reasons we already touched on in what was said about the importance of *Honest to God*. Robinson, I suggested, has rightly sensed that the three theologians whose influence has recently become determinative—Bonhoeffer, Bultmann, and Tillich—all agree in making one basic demand on contemporary theology. If we ask now as to the exact content of this demand, one reply is the insistence common to these thinkers that theology today must be in the strict sense postliberal. This reply, naturally, requires clarification, because the word "postliberal," like other words of its type, admits of diverse interpretations. But, since such labels are certain to be used, theological responsibility can never consist in eschewing them, but only in so clarifying their meaning that they serve rather than hinder a fuller understanding of the issues.

It is commonly recognized that the driving concern of the representative liberal theologians of the nineteenth century was with the meaning and truth of historic Christian faith, given the changed conditions of a distinctively modern cultural situation. Sensing that the Protestant orthodoxy of the previous two centuries had been decisively challenged by the criticisms of the Enlightenment, they undertook a comprehensive theological reappraisal directed toward assimilating the legitimate motives in these criticisms, while yet making possible an appropriate formulation of Christian faith. For a long time, the historiography of this period tended to disregard the second element in the liberals' concern, presenting their work as simply the expression in the area of religion of the general liberalizing movement typical of the nineteenth century. But recent studies, benefiting from greater perspective and more inclined to be sympathetic, have succeeded in exposing the one-sidedness of such presentations.[5] They have made clear that liberal theology was, in fact, an authentic expression of the Christian faith, an eloquent testimony that the word which God has addressed to mankind in Jesus Christ should and can be heard even by the modern man who fully affirms his modernity. No less evident is that there was a distinctively Protestant

[5] See, e.g., Christoph Senft, *Wahrhaftigkeit und Wahrheit, Die Theologie des 19. Jahrhunderts zwischen Orthodoxie und Aufklärung*, Tübingen: J. C. B. Mohr, 1956; and, for the later liberal development in America, Kenneth Cauthen, *The Impact of American Religious Liberalism*, New York: Harper & Row, 1962.

inspiration behind the decision and outlook of the liberal theologians. In affirming, as they did, the proper autonomy and validity of secular methods of knowledge (thereby insisting, for example, that historical-critical research be applied even to Scripture), they but reaffirmed in their own situation the fundamental decision of the Protestant Reformers as expressed in the watchword, *sola gratia—sola fide*.[6]

The difficulty, however—and about this there is also general agreement—is that the liberals were on the whole unsuccessful in implementing their concern. In seeking a formulation of the Christian faith which would respect all that was valid in modern man's understanding of himself and his world, they too often proceeded uncritically and thus failed also to respect the distinctive claims of faith itself. In many instances, to be sure, the trouble lay in their perforce having to make use of conceptualities that obscured their real intentions. Recall, for example, Schleiermacher's definition of religion in terms of "feeling" (*Gefühl*) or the attempt by Wilhelm Herrmann and others to conceptualize the existential understanding of faith as "experience" (*Erlebnis*). Yet, important as it is to recognize this, it by no means accounts for the splendid failure that was liberal theology. It remains true that the liberals' courageous pursuit of an inescapable theological task led to a certain compromising of essential Christian truth.

That we today clearly recognize this is perhaps our principal debt to the creative theological movement of the first half of our century, which reacted so sharply against liberal theology. This movement has led to a fresh sense for the authentic witness of Holy Scripture and of the Reformers, and has impressed upon us that this witness can no more be brought into an easy harmony with the modern age than it can be assimilated to any other. Furthermore, it is impossible to dismiss the theologians responsible for these insights as if they were concerned merely to restore the *status quo ante* liberal theology of the seventeenth and eighteenth centuries. One must never forget that the movement conventionally spoken of today as "neo-orthodoxy" was, in its beginnings, an attempt at self-criticism from *within* the ranks of liberal theology. From its first great expressions—Karl Barth's *Römerbrief*[7] and, in America, Reinhold Niebuhr's *Moral Man and Immoral Society*[8]—the old orthodoxy could derive but scant encour-

---

[6] Cf. Gerhard Ebeling, *Word and Faith,* trans. J. W. Leitch, Philadelphia: Fortress Press, 1963, pp. 17–61, especially p. 55.

[7] Bern: G. A. Bäschlin, 1919; 2d ed., 1922.

[8] New York: Charles Scribner's Sons, 1932.

agement, because of their tacit acceptance of much that the liberal theologians had sought to achieve. At the same time, the new movement was not lacking in certain reactionary tendencies, and, as it developed, the liberals' characteristic concern with the meaning and truth of Christianity in a modern setting was more and more displaced by another interest. Especially through the influence of Barth's later work in *Die kirchliche Dogmatik*,[9] the theological task came to be viewed as entailing a radical separation of Christian faith and modern culture, and many Protestant theologians once again assumed a deliberately dogmatic stance.

Thus, although the main theological development between the two world wars was in a sense postliberal, it was so only in a rather loose sense. The new movement definitely succeeded in breaking the hold of liberal theology. But this it did, at least in some of its representatives, less by providing a more adequate solution to the problem with which the liberals had struggled than by exposing the inadequacy of their achievements and disregarding the seriousness of the problem itself. The result was that, while some of the distinctive claims of Christian faith were rediscovered and reasserted, the question of the meaning and truth of these claims for men living in a modern secular world was for the most part not even clearly posed, much less effectively answered.

Since the Second World War, however, the tendencies toward reaction in Protestant theology have been arrested, and a new direction has become increasingly evident. With the emergence into prominence of Tillich in America and Bultmann and Bonhoeffer on the Continent, the question of the meaning and truth of theological assertions, given a modern situation, is once again being recognized as a serious question. Hence the original concern of Protestant liberalism is finding renewed expression; and, because this is so, the theology these three thinkers have projected as the task of our generation is in the exact sense a postliberal theology.

Another way of characterizing this change is to say that, primarily through the work of these men, Protestant theologians today have once more been made aware of their inescapable apologetic task. Here, too, there are dangers of misunderstanding, since the word "apologetic" is likewise ambiguous. Moreover, while Tillich expressly designates his theology as "apologetic," Bultmann generally resists the designation and understands the word only in a pejorative sense.

[9] Zollikon-Zürich: Evangelischer Verlag, 1932–59.

Yet, despite this obvious difference, both thinkers, together with Bonhoeffer, so conceive the theologian's responsibility as to include the task for which "apologetic" would still appear to be the best word. They insist that the terms of theological adequacy are always set not only by the faith which the theologian must seek to express appropriately, but also by the existence of man himself, to whom the theologian must try to express that faith understandably. This insistence assumes that Christian faith is not utterly alien to man, whatever his historical situation, but rather is his own most proper possibility of existence, which can and should be understandable to him, provided it is so expressed as to take his situation into account. I should say it is this assumption which, in some form or other, provides the minimal condition for all properly apologetic theology. If this is so, the use of the word "apologetic" in the present context is easily defended. Whether we use the word or not, this assumption, along with the conception of theological responsibility following from it, is just what is now being reasserted by the leading figures in Protestant theology.

This fact by itself, however, hardly explains why it is the problem of *God,* instead of any number of other problems, that has now emerged as of crucial importance. Therefore, we must press our inquiry still further and consider a second reason for this development. That reason, too, as we shall see, has to do with a certain alteration in our more recent history; only now the fact to be observed is not an immanent shift within Protestant theology itself, but a fundamental change that has become ever more apparent in our larger cultural situation.

The most succinct way to describe this change is to say that, when contemporary Western man is judged by some of his more creative self-expressions, his outlook no longer seems merely secular, but appears to have become increasingly secularistic. In saying this, one must, of course, depend on a distinction usually obscured in our ordinary language. We commonly use the adjectives "secular" and "secularistic," like the nouns "secularity" and "secularism," interchangeably, without observing any difference of meaning between them. Yet, for some time, it has been fairly common among theological students of the historical process known as "secularization" to insist that our ordinary usage at this point has to be refined if it is not to trap us in serious misunderstandings.[10] Thus Friedrich Gogarten,

[10] See C. H. Ratschow's article in *Religion in Geschichte und Gegenwart,* Vol. V, ed. Kurt Galling, Tübingen: J. C. B. Mohr, 3d ed., 1961, pp. 1288–96.

for example, holds that we must distinguish between "two fundamentally different kinds of secularization," for only one of which we
should use the term "secularism."[11] Since I, too, believe that accur-
ate analysis demands some such distinction, I venture to speak of the
change we must now try to understand as one from a secular to a
secularistic outlook—or, as we may also say, from secularity to
secularism. I should perhaps add that the following discussion is in
no way intended as an exhaustive analysis of this important change.
My sole purpose is to illustrate its essential character sufficiently to
provide what is necessary for the argument of this essay.

It is now a commonplace that the outlook of most men today who
have been shaped by modern Western culture is more or less deeply
determined by the scientific picture of the world. Ever since the
seventeenth century, science and technology have been effecting such
a radical transformation in our understanding of ourselves and our
environment that even contemporary common sense includes an at
least tacit acceptance of the world picture correlative with the
scientific method.[12] Whenever, then, modern men have become
reflectively self-conscious, they have for generations typically
affirmed this method and picture as defining the horizon within which
knowledge of the world and its phenomena must be obtained. Thus
the pursuit of such knowledge has long since become, in the sense of
the word intended here, a wholly "secular" affair. Any attempt by
religious or ecclesiastical authorities to control the pursuit by imposing heteronomous criteria of truth has been consistently repudiated in
the name of the autonomy of scientific method throughout the whole
field to which it properly applies. Furthermore, all assertions which
ostensibly have reference to this field, from whatever source and
however long accepted, have been referred to this method and judged
to be true only when they have met the criteria implicit in it.

Herein, of course, is the reason for "the warfare of science with
theology" which entered its decisive phase a century ago.[13] Because
so many traditional theological assertions have at least appeared to

---

[11] *Verhängnis und Hoffnung der Neuzeit, Die Säkularisierung als theolog-
isches Problem,* Stuttgart: Friedrich Vorwerk Verlag, 2d ed., 1958, pp. 142 f.
Cf. also Gabriel Vahanian, *The Death of God: The Culture of Our Post-
Christian Era,* New York: George Braziller, 1961, pp. 60–78.

[12] See the discussion of so-called "common sense" in Stephen Toulmin and
June Goodfield, *The Fabric of the Heavens,* London: Hutchinson & Co. Ltd.,
1961, pp. 15–22.

[13] See Andrew D. White, *A History of the Warfare of Science with
Theology in Christendom,* New York: D. Appleton & Co., 1896.

make scientific claims—and have been interpreted accordingly by both their defenders and their attackers—they have naturally been subjected to scientific criticism, only to prove unacceptable when judged by these criteria. Hence theologians have been forced to make such distinctions as that between "history" and "myth," which has gradually come to be regarded as necessary if theology is still to be a responsible undertaking. Even today, it is true, there are theologians who fail to take this distinction seriously, and, as Bultmann points out, it is a *testimonium paupertatis* for our theological situation that the demand for demythologizing has yet to meet with universal acceptance.[14] But, if anything seems certain, it is that this state of affairs cannot continue. The scientific world picture is here to stay and will assert its rights against any theology, however imposing, that conflicts with it. So far as his knowledge of the world is concerned, modern man long ago opted for the method of science and therewith decided irrevocably for secularity.

Accompanying this decision, however, was always another possibility, which was occasionally realized throughout the whole modern period, only to emerge more recently as the option apparently favored by ever larger numbers of Western men. For many cultured persons today, the general scientific method is not only the sole means for obtaining knowledge about the world disclosed by our senses, but this kind of knowledge is the only knowledge there is. The classic expression of this outlook in reflective philosophical terms is the position generally known as logical positivism, with its dogmatic claim that there are but two kinds of significant statements.[15] Aptly named "Hume's fork," since it goes back to a famous passage in David Hume's *Enquiry Concerning Human Understanding,*[16] this claim holds that all meaningful assertions are divided between either the tautologies of formal logic and mathematics or putative statements of fact that can be falsified by ordinary sense experience. The force of the claim, therefore, is to restrict all knowledge of "how things are" to the general type of knowledge of which modern science

[14] H. W. Bartsch (ed.), *Kerygma und Mythos,* Vol. I, Hamburg: Herbert Reich-Evangelischer Verlag, 2d ed., 1951, pp. 23 f. (English translation by R. H. Fuller in H. W. Bartsch [ed.], *Kerygma and Myth,* New York: Harper & Row, 2d ed., 1961, p. 12).

[15] See especially Alfred Jules Ayer, *Language, Truth and Logic,* London: Victor Gollancz Ltd., 1936; 2d ed., 1946.

[16] *Enquiries Concerning the Human Understanding and Concerning the Principles of Morals,* ed. L. A. Selby-Bigge, Oxford: Clarendon Press, 2d ed., 1902, p. 165.

is the refined and fully developed form. Since its original promulgation, this positivistic dogma has been extensively criticized and reformulated, and most philosophers who currently invoke it exhibit a keener sense for our different uses of language than did its first proponents. At the same time, the dogma is still widely accepted, and, even where efforts are made to limit its force, it has a curious way of reasserting itself.[17]

More important is that the basic standpoint for which this dogma is but the conceptually precise formulation has come to be shared by many persons who are by no means professional philosophers. For them, exactly as for their more reflective spokesmen, the issue is no longer whether the theologian can make assertions that conflict with science, but whether he can make any meaningful assertions at all. They reason that, if the kind of knowledge represented by science is the only knowledge there is, then the putative assertions of theology, so far as empirically unverifiable, can hardly make good their claim to cognitive meaning. Such reasoning, it seems to me, can no longer be considered merely secular, but must be distinguished by the different adjective "secularistic." It is one thing to affirm the validity of the scientific method and to insist on its complete autonomy within the field where it alone logically applies. But it is clearly something different to affirm that this method is the only valid means to knowledge we have, because it circumscribes the limits of the whole cognitive sphere. The first affirmation, I hold, is entirely of a piece with the legitimate *secularity* of modern culture. The second, on the other hand, is an integral element in that *secularism* which appears to have become ever more widely prevalent among contemporary Western men.

The shift from a secular to a secularistic outlook with respect to knowledge provides one illustration of the second important change that has led to our present situation. It would be easy to trace the same change in the other spheres of culture where parallel shifts have also become apparent. But, for the present, it will be sufficient briefly to note how morality, too, has become for many persons today utterly secularistic.

---

[17] A perfect illustration of this is the argument of W. H. Walsh, *Metaphysics,* London: Hutchinson & Co. Ltd., 1963. Although Walsh effectively blunts Hume's fork by adducing the distinct logical class of "categorial principles" (pp. 154–60), his denial that these principles have any but a "prescriptive," noninformative character, and hence his further denial of "ontology," clearly presuppose Hume's distinction.

Throughout most of Western history, man's action, like his knowledge, was kept within definite bounds by religious or ecclesiastical authority. The official standards of moral conduct were either set or sanctioned by the will of God as interpreted in the teachings of the church. By the seventeenth century, however, the process of secularization had led to several attempts to develop a wholly secular ethic. As with so many other ventures toward secularity, these first attempts reached a rich culmination in the philosophical work of Immanuel Kant.

Indeed, nothing was more important to Kant than "the autonomy of the will as the supreme principle of morality."[18] By this he meant that man as a moral agent is bound to reject any effort to subject his action to moral laws or maxims which are not his own legislation as rational will. What makes any course of action morally obligatory is not that it is grounded, say, in the will of God, but that it is demanded by the "categorical imperative" implicit in man's own practical reason. Therefore, Kant sharply repudiated the views of "theological moralists" as a form of "heteronomy," which is "opposed to the principle of duty and to the morality of the will."[19] In doing so, however, he had no intention of affirming a morality without religious faith. On the contrary, he was convinced that it is just when one grasps the autonomy of moral action that the essential function of religion can be rightly understood. We can give an adequate account of our moral experience only by appealing to certain basic presuppositions or "postulates," which together make up the content of a "rational faith." Thus Kant held that we must not only presuppose our own freedom and responsibility as moral agents, but also postulate our subjective survival of death and the reality of God as the ultimate ground and guarantor of a morally reasonable world.

It is only by comparison with a secular moral philosophy such as Kant's that one can mark the fundamental difference in moral outlook that has become increasingly apparent in our own century. Kant's deep conviction that morality, while wholly autonomous, nevertheless "leads ineluctably to religion"[20] now strikes many a

---

[18] Critique of Practical Reason and Other Writings in Moral Philosophy, ed. and trans. Lewis W. Beck, Chicago: The University of Chicago Press, 1949, p. 97 (Foundations of the Metaphysics of Morals, Sec. II).

[19] Ibid., p. 144; cf. pp. 146–52 (Critique of Practical Reason, I, 1, i).

[20] Religion Within the Limits of Reason Alone, trans. T. H. Green and H. H. Hudson, New York: Harper & Row, 2d ed., 1960, p. 5.

person as hopelessly unconvincing. In its place, one more and more encounters the claim not only that the sole standards of conduct are those implicit in human action itself, but that such action realizes no will to good beyond the merely human and neither requires nor admits of any transcendent justification.

It is true that contemporary discussions of morality often reveal a deeper and more discriminating understanding of man's nature than was possible for even as tempered a rationalism as Kant's. Especially through the writings of existentialist philosophers, we have recovered the insight that man is, first of all, an existing self or person, whose primary moral task is the realization in himself and others of an authentic personal existence. We now recognize that *what* we do is in a sense less important than *how* we do it and that "existential norms" like freedom, openness, and love are finally regulative of such traditional virtues as wisdom, prudence, and justice.[21] Hence the educated man of today is almost certain to be concerned with more than the earlier secular causes of disseminating knowledge and advancing men's social and economic well-being. He is also typically interested in the new task of preserving a measure of personal authenticity against the pressures toward conformity of a technological civilization. In fact, this whole development in our ethical perspective and, more generally, in our view of man's nature and destiny is so significant that it seems justified to speak of a distinctively postmodern phase in the over-all evolution of modern culture.

But, significant as this development is, it is neither the only nor the most far-reaching change in contemporary morality. This is evidenced by the fact that the very postmodern deepening of our moral understanding has as often as not found explicitly secularistic expression. Some of its most eloquent and influential statements, indeed, are those of avowedly atheistic writers such as Jean-Paul Sartre and Albert Camus. The thought of these men is clearly informed by a view of human conduct and of the human condition which, in its realism and tragic sense, cannot but recall many of the basic insights of classical Christian anthropology. And yet, in every case, these insights are present in their writings in a completely secularistic form, so that faith and sin, say, are the wholly immanent possibilities of man's self-understanding which Sartre designates respectively as "good faith" and "bad faith." Also significant in this connection is the way recent theological analyses of the nature of man and of moral

[21] Cf. John Wild, *The Challenge of Existentialism*, Bloomington, Ind.: Indiana University Press, 1955, pp. 250–72, especially pp. 258 ff.

action are frequently appropriated by persons who quite reject the theistic framework in which theologians present them. Thus, for instance, Reinhold Niebuhr's profound anthropological and ethical reflections have been extremely influential on historians, political theorists, and practical statesmen, as well as on Protestant theologians. But who would deny that many who have assimilated these reflections are still far from in any way sharing Niebuhr's own robust version of historic Christian faith?[22]

For these and other reasons, one is led to see the most fundamental change in contemporary thinking about morality, not in a certain postmodern deepening of ethical insight, but in an ever-growing secularism in moral outlook. In their understanding of action, as in their view of knowledge, numbers of men today are no longer content merely to affirm the autonomy and importance of their life in the world, but deny unequivocally that this world in any way points beyond itself.[23]

By now it should be evident that it is this secularistic denial in its several different forms which explains why the problem of God in particular has become central for Protestant theology. Such a denial is by its very nature the negation of God's reality, the claim, in Nietzsche's words, that "God is dead."[24] Therefore, because the denial is now so often heard, any theologian made newly sensitive to his apologetic task cannot but find his whole endeavor concentrated on a single point. His hearers have become concerned primarily with one question, to which they expect him and his colleagues to give a forthright reply: whether, if the word "God" as Christians use it has any meaning at all, the sentences in which it occurs somehow express assertions capable of being true.

[22] Cf. Morton White's remarks about those whom he calls, tellingly, "atheists for Niebuhr" (*Religion, Politics, and the Higher Learning,* Cambridge: Harvard University Press, 1959, pp. 117 f.). It is only fair to add that, if Niebuhr's anthropological concentration has proved to have its dangers, the same is true of the "christological concentration" of Karl Barth. This is well brought out by the title under which a book by one of Barth's students, Paul M. van Buren's *Secular Meaning of the Gospel* (New York: The Macmillan Co., 1963), was reviewed in the *Christian Century* (October 2, 1963, pp. 1208 f.): "There Is No God and Jesus Is His Son"!

[23] The *Vorgeschichte* of this change, especially as regards morality, in the metaphysical rebellion of the nineteenth century is traced with unusual insight by Henri de Lubac, *The Drama of Atheist Humanism,* trans. E. M. Riley, New York: Sheed & Ward, Inc., 1951.

[24] *The Joyful Wisdom,* trans. Thomas Common, London: George Allen & Unwin Ltd., 1910, p. 168.

If this conclusion is correct, our inquiry has indeed led us beyond an answer to our initial question. Not only have we discovered why the problem of God has now become of central importance, but, true to our expectation, we have also learned how this problem presents itself to us today. We have learned, in short, that our age, as Gerhard Ebeling has said, is "the age of atheism"[25]—that, if the reality of God is still to be affirmed, this must now be done in a situation in which, on an unprecedented scale, that reality is expressly denied.

To accept this finding, however, may seem to leave the theologian with an insoluble problem. Either he must continue to affirm God's reality, thereby flatly contradicting the atheistic assumptions of a growing number of his contemporaries; or else he, too, must accept these assumptions and thus surrender what has generally been regarded as the foundational claim of Christian faith. The striking thing about some of the latest developments in Protestant theology is that we are now being told even by certain theologians that this dilemma is inescapable. To be sure, the proposal of a "theology without God" (at least in anything like the sense of "God" in our religious heritage) is hardly new. Already a generation and more ago, experiments along this line were made not only by some important philosophers, but by several liberal or modernist theologians as well. In some cases—I am thinking especially of George Santayana's *Reason in Religion*,[26] John Dewey's *Common Faith*,[27] and Henry Nelson Wieman's *Source of Human Good*[28]—the results were exceedingly fruitful and are still deserving of the most serious consideration. But, until quite recently, at any rate, this general way of disposing of the problem of God has failed to resonate with any but a small minority of Protestant theologians. For this reason, the proposals which certain new voices are now advocating are bound to attract attention. In keeping with the postliberal concern of much recent theology, these theologians have resolved to take full responsibility for the meaning of their utterances in our present situation. At the same time, because they themselves regard secularistic assumptions as simply given, they

[25] "The Message of God to the Age of Atheism," *Oberlin College Bulletin,* January, 1964, pp. 3–14.

[26] New York: Charles Scribner's Sons, 1905. See also Santayana's magnificent essay in *Obiter Scripta,* New York: Charles Scribner's Sons, 1936, pp. 280–97.

[27] New Haven: Yale University Press, 1934.

[28] Chicago: The University of Chicago Press, 1946.

conclude that the affirmation of God's reality must be surrendered if there is to be anything like a tenable contemporary theology.

This conclusion has been drawn with the greatest clarity and consistency by Paul M. van Buren in *The Secular Meaning of the Gospel*. Van Buren argues that the attitudes of contemporary men are in every respect "secular" and that no presentation of the Christian witness can hope to be understandable which fails to reckon with this fact. Actually, what he means by the word "secular" is just the outlook I have distinguished here as secularistic. In his terms, "secular" refers to an essentially positivistic understanding of the scope of knowledge, as well as to a conception of moral action that is exclusively humanistic. Terminology aside, however, van Buren is insistent that the outlook typical of men today makes any meaningful assertions about God impossible. "The empiricist in us finds the heart of the difficulty not in what is said about God, but in the very talking about God at all. We do not know 'what' God is, and we cannot understand how the word 'God' is being used."[29] Therefore, our only real option is simply to abandon any claim for God's reality and give ourselves to interpreting the gospel in completely secularistic terms.

Strange as it may seem, van Buren holds that this choice is not only made necessary by our situation, but is also permitted as possible by the gospel itself. Indeed, he finally assures us that the reality of God can be completely denied without in any way doing violence to the real meaning of the Christian witness. But with this assurance his proposal ceases to carry conviction and begins to appear as a not altogether ingenuous *tour de force*. However absurd talking about God might be, it could never be so obviously absurd as talking of Christian faith without God. If theology is possible today only on secularistic terms, the more candid way to say this is to admit that theology is not possible today at all.

Similar judgments are, of course, constantly being passed by theological reactionaries, and there are many who regard a theology even on secular terms as out of the question. But the two cases, I am convinced, are at the crucial point totally unlike. Faith in God of a certain kind is not merely an element in Christian faith along with several others; it simply *is* Christian faith, the heart of the matter itself. Therefore, the very thing about the expressions of faith in Scripture and tradition which makes a properly *secular* interpretation of them possible and even necessary also makes a *secularistic* the-

[29] *Op. cit.*, p. 84.

ology impossible. The issue here is indeed either/or, and all talk of a Christianity *post mortem dei* is, in the last analysis, neither hyperbole nor evidence of originality but merely nonsense.[30]

The question, then, is whether there can be another formulation of our problem that does not utterly exclude its possible solution. I believe one can formulate the problem differently and that other recent developments in philosophy as well as theology support this conviction. The clue to such a formulation lies in the lesson we all should have long since learned from the outcome of the original liberal theology. We noted above that the liberal theologians too often proceeded uncritically in appropriating the insights of their contemporary culture. Failing to discriminate between the legitimate motives in these insights and other motives that have subsequently been superseded, they foreclosed certain options for defining, and thus solving, their problem. But this is the very danger that also threatens our work today, as is evident from the procedure of those who would base Christian theology on the secularistic premise that God is dead. Their assessment of our cultural situation is completely undiscriminating in simply assuming that secularism is an essentially unified and internally consistent outlook. It is possible, naturally, that an analysis of secularism might show this assumption to be justified. But, as I shall now try to indicate, there are good reasons for doubting this, and it is important that these reasons be carefully examined. If the secularistic outlook of our day is so self-consistent that we must simply accept or reject it, then the prospects for theology are dim indeed.

We saw earlier that secularism differs from secularity solely at the point of its negations. The typical secularist not only affirms himself and the world in their significance and proper autonomy, but also denies any transcendent reality in which the secular order has its ultimate ground and end. Thus, with respect to knowledge, for example, the secularist is sure to be either a lay or a professional positivist. Not content to assert the validity of scientific statements, he goes on to deny that, with the exception of the purely analytic truths of logic and mathematics, any other kind of statements can make good on their cognitive claims.

Interestingly, however, this denial seems wholly unjustified in terms of the only criteria it itself admits as possible. It is certainly not a statement of fact that could ever be empirically falsified; nor can

[30] See below, pp. 84–90, 159 ff.

one plausibly contend that it is an analytic statement with a logical or mathematical kind of truth. If, on the other hand, one treats it simply as a postulate, as some positivists have tried to do, he must then deal with substantial objections to accepting it. Some of the best work by contemporary philosophers of ordinary language makes clear that restriction of the scope of knowledge exclusively to the empirically falsifiable derives no support whatever from our actual usage.[31] This by itself, of course, hardly establishes the validity of the metaphysical and theological knowledge that positivists wish to deny. Yet it does expose the basis of their denial to be arbitrary, and so dispels the notion that positivism has any self-evident logical force.

I shall attempt to show below (Section 2) that a somewhat similar criticism may be made of the secularist's treatment of morality. It should then become even clearer that his unqualified denials are neither required by, nor consistent with, his positive affirmations. But, even now, having seen some of the well-known difficulties of a positivistic view of knowledge, we may say that these denials are something genuinely additional in the secularist's position. They are a second, wholly negative element, whose validity in itself and in relation to the first or positive element in his position is clearly an independent question.

That this is so would, I am sure, be much more commonly recognized but for one important fact. Historically regarded, modern secularism is the most extreme expression of a centuries-long reaction against the classical metaphysical-theological tradition of the Western world. Although its denials typically take an unqualified form—for example, *"All* talk of God is meaningless"—what makes them seem far from arbitrary is their effectiveness against *this* particular tradition and its ways of thinking and talking about God. In other words, the plausibility of the secularist's negations is a function of the all but complete dominance of our cultural heritage by a total metaphysical-theological outlook, to which our experience and thought as secular men are indeed sharply opposed.

Most of us today, even if we are secularists, are determined in our thinking about God by a common intellectual tradition that has served throughout Western history for the conception of his reality. Broadly speaking, this tradition is that usually referred to as the *philosophia perennis* or "Christian philosophy," whose crowning

---

[31] See especially Stephen Toulmin, *The Uses of Argument,* Cambridge: Cambridge University Press, 1958; cf. also below, pp. 88 f., 110 ff.

achievement is a supernaturalistic theism uniquely combining elements of classical Greek philosophy with religious insights derived from the Hebraic-Christian Scriptures. For centuries, this traditional theism has been in the process of breaking down under the cumulative weight of experiences and reflections that run counter to its basic premises. Yet, remarkably enough, even where these premises are denied, they continue to exert an influence scarcely less profound than where they are still affirmed. Indeed, their atheistic critics commonly pay them the supreme tribute of being the only theistic premises there are, since to overcome them is supposed to be sufficient to "overcome theism" altogether. Because the defenders of the premises, for their part, suppose the very same thing, the unqualified claim of the attackers is bound to seem plausible, even if it is actually an arbitrary and highly debatable assumption.

This is all the more so because there is, in fact, an irreconcilable opposition between the premises of this supernaturalistic theism and the whole direction of our experience and reflection as secular men. Thus, for one thing, commitment to secularity entails acceptance of logical self-consistency as one of the necessary conditions for the truth of any assertion. And yet, as some three hundred years of careful criticism have shown, the main assertions of classical theists are utterly incapable of satisfying this condition. This is evident, for example, from traditional theological discussions of the creation of the world. Theologians usually tell us that God creates the world freely, as the contingent or nonnecessary world our experience discloses it to be. This assertion is also made necessary because it offers the only really credible construction of the account of creation in Holy Scripture. At the same time, because of their fixed commitment to the assumptions of classical metaphysics, theologians also tell us that God's act of creation is one with his own eternal essence, which is in every respect necessary, exclusive of all contingency. Hence, if we take them at their own word, giving full weight to both of their assertions, we at once find ourselves in the hopeless contradiction of a wholly necessary creation of a wholly contingent world.

In a similar way, supernaturalists have traditionally maintained that the end of man is to serve or glorify God through obedience to his will and commandments. And yet the God whom we are thus summoned to serve is, in the last analysis, so conceived that he can be as little affected by our best actions as by our worst. As *actus purus,* and thus a statically complete perfection incapable in any respect of further self-realization, God can be neither increased nor diminished by what we do, and our action, like our suffering, must be in the strictest sense wholly indifferent to him.

This second antinomy may serve to indicate that it is by no means its theoretical incoherence alone that explains why traditional theism is unacceptable to secular men. There is the even more important consideration of its existential repugnance.[32] If what we do and suffer as men in the world is from God's perspective wholly indifferent, that perspective is at most irrelevant to our actual existence. It can provide no motive for action, no cause to serve, and no comfort in our distress beyond the motives, causes, and comforts already supplied by our various secular undertakings. But, more than that, to involve ourselves in these undertakings and to affirm their ultimate significance is implicitly to deny the God who is himself finally conceived as the denial of our life in the world. Small wonder that countless men have concluded with Ludwig Feuerbach that "the question of the existence or non-existence of God is the question of the non-existence or existence of man."[33] True, classical theists' statements about God do not add up to a consistent negation of our secular involvements. They generally contend not only that God is the metaphysical Absolute, whose only relation to the world is wholly external, but that he is also the loving heavenly Father revealed in Jesus, who freely creates the world and guides it toward its fulfillments with tender care. The difficulty, however, as we noted above, is the obvious incoherence of these two contentions, which both deny and affirm that God's relation to the world is real and that he is relevant to its life because it is relevant to his. Thus, even at best, supernaturalism offers but uncertain support for our affirmation as modern men of the importance of the secular; and, at worst, it so

[32] This existential motive in contemporary atheism is rightly emphasized by Henri de Lubac (*op. cit.,* pp. 3–7, 27–35, 61–73) and other Roman Catholic students of the matter like John Courtney Murray (*The Problem of God: Yesterday and Today,* New Haven: Yale University Press, 1964, pp. 77–121, especially p. 95). The weakness in their analyses, however, is that they never really free themselves from the assumption that Christian faith in God and supernaturalistic theism are indissolubly connected, and thus fail to do justice both to atheism's theoretical motives (as is particularly true of Murray) and to what is legitimate in the existential motive itself. De Lubac does concede that "the principle which inspired [the great systems of rebellion—namely, the assertion of man's dignity and freedom] was not devoid of nobility" (*op. cit.,* p. 34). But he nowhere seems to realize just what this principle implies nor does he anywhere so much as question whether a truly Christian affirmation of the greatness of man can ever be reconciled with the premises of classical theism.

[33] Quoted by Henri de Lubac, *op. cit.,* p. 27.

undercuts this affirmation that many of us have no choice but to reject it once we have clearly grasped its implications.

Given no more than has been said, this conclusion may well appear rash; and it will indeed be necessary to confirm it at a later stage in the argument (Section 3). But we should already be able to understand why the secularist's unqualified denial of God is so widely accepted despite its questionable logical force. Because most of us assume that the reality of God stands or falls with the classical theistic scheme for conceiving it, our rejection of that scheme in the name of secularity seems to leave us with nothing but complete secularism. In this, of course, we are the victims of an illusion—of imagining that in abandoning a "system of thought" we have also lost the reality of God himself. What is really warranted by a secular affirmation is not the unqualified denial of the secularist, which is itself problematic, but the more restricted denial logically implied by that affirmation. We are justified not in rejecting God as such, but in casting aside the supernaturalistic conception of his reality, which is in fact untenable, given our typical experience and thought as secular men.

Significantly, it is this formulation of our problem, rather than the one offered by van Buren and others, which has also been proposed by the leading postliberal theologians. As Robinson summarizes the matter, the real problem of theology today is that Christian faith "is moulded, in the form we know it, by a cast of thought that belongs to a past age—the cast of thought which, with their different emphases, Bultmann describes as 'mythological,' Tillich as 'supranaturalist,' and Bonhoeffer as 'religious.' "[34] One may object, no doubt, that Robinson here, as well as elsewhere, tends to minimize the differences between his three mentors. But his main point, at least, is surely right: for each of them the problem now confronting us is posed, not by the death of God, but by the demise of a "cast of thought," of some particular conceptuality through which the witness of Christian faith has traditionally been expressed. The point I would emphasize is that the major obstacle to real progress in dealing with the problem of God is the supernaturalistic theism of the metaphysical tradition. Thus my own way of responding to the demand of these thinkers that theology today be fully postliberal is to seek a conception of God's reality in which the inadequacies of this traditional theism can be overcome.

[34] *Honest to God*, p. 123.

These same theologians have all made important contributions to just this end, if only by avoiding crude formulations of the problem and pointing us to our real task. Even so, it is necessary, in my judgment, to press still further along the lines they have laid down if we are to reach an adequate solution to our problem. This is so because none of these thinkers has, for various reasons, been in a position to exploit fully the resources for theological construction made available by contemporary philosophy. Specifically, they have all failed to appreciate the emergence in our time of a distinct neo-classical alternative to classical metaphysics and philosophical theology. The fact is, however, that certain philosophers have recently posed the question of theism in a wholly new setting, which relativizes all the answers conventionally given to it. They have shown that for philosophy, at any rate, supernaturalism is far from the only theistic position and that God can be so conceived as to avoid its inadequacies, while doing even greater justice to the insights of our religious heritage. Therefore, in Section 3 of this essay, I wish to make use of these philosophical resources to outline a new theism through which Protestant theology may more nearly approach a solution to the problem of God's reality.

But here we may profitably remind ourselves that no theistic scheme, however adequate, can alone be sufficient to solve this problem. The only way any conception of God can be made more than a mere idea having nothing to do with reality is to exhibit it as the most adequate reflective account we can give of certain experiences in which we all inescapably share. This, too, it seems to me, is a conclusion that forces itself upon us out of our modern situation. We have slowly learned through our actual history that no assertions are to be judged true, unless, in addition to being logically consistent, they are somehow warranted by our common experience, broadly and fairly understood. But one thing, it would appear, in which almost all of us today share is just our experience as modern, secular men: our affirmation of life here and now in the world in all its aspects and in its proper autonomy and significance. My conviction is that it is in this secular affirmation that we must discover the reality of God in our time. The adequate response to secularistic negations will not be made by a supernaturalism that is no longer tenable or by a naturalism that uncritically accepts the same negations. It will be made, rather, by an integral secularity—a secularity which has become fully self-conscious and which therefore makes explicit the faith in God already implied in what it itself affirms.

2. THE REALITY OF FAITH

The task before us in the remainder of the essay is to test the reasonableness of this conviction. And to that end, I now wish to claim that for the secular man of today, as surely as for any other man, faith in God cannot but be real because it is in the final analysis unavoidable.

I realize that to support this claim is a large undertaking and that the most which can be done in this essay is to suggest some of the steps in a possible argument. Equally clear to me is that there are many for whom such an argument will seem doomed from the start. After all, numbers of our contemporaries seem to get along quite well with no belief in God whatever; and there are the others whom I have called secularists who expressly deny any such belief. To hold that even these persons cannot finally avoid faith in God is to imply that men may be wholly mistaken about the real scope or direction of their own beliefs.

Yet, dubious as this implication may seem, the claim I am making has one obvious merit that the theologian, at least, should find hard to deny: it is the only claim completely consistent with Christian faith in God itself. By its very character, Christian faith so understands God that everyone must in some sense believe in him and no one can in every sense deny him. Were one to object to this on the ground that it is radically otherwise with all the other objects of our belief and knowledge, he would simply beg the central theological question. The whole point is that God *is* radically different from everything else we experience, and one of the implications of this difference is the peculiar character of the question of God itself.

Just this, indeed, is the real import of the famous ontological argument for God's existence first worked out by Anselm of Canterbury.[35] The widespread notion that the purpose of this argument is merely to establish one more fallacious inference from idea to reality does as little credit to the acumen of Anselm's critics as it is unfair to

[35] See especially Charles Hartshorne, "What Did Anselm Discover?" *Union Seminary Quarterly Review,* March, 1962, pp. 213–22; also Alvin Plantinga (ed.), *The Ontological Argument,* Garden City, N.Y.: Doubleday & Co., Inc., 1965.

the saint himself. His point was not that *any* idea provides the warrant for such an inference, but that it *is* warranted by the idea of God implicit in Christian faith. He discovered, in other words, that this idea, alone among others, has a peculiar logical character that exempts it from the law otherwise pertaining to the relation of essence and existence. To be able to conceive *what* God is, is also to know *that* he is; and from this it follows that no one can be utterly without faith in his reality, since as the necessary existent he must somehow be experienced in anything that is so much as even possible.

The only way to avoid this conclusion is to attack Anselm's argument at the one point for which he did fail to provide sufficient justification—namely, to show that we cannot really conceive even the idea of God because it is by its very nature a meaningless idea. But this line of attack, which has become the favorite of many positivistic critics,[36] has the corresponding merit of at least recognizing the radical character of the issue. If it could be successfully followed up, the conclusion would not be simply that some men believe in God, although they happen to be in error, but that no man, not even one who speaks of God with the greatest passion, really believes in him after all. In that event, it would be those who affirm God's reality, not those who deny it, who would be quite mistaken as to what they themselves in fact believe. Such an attack, incidentally, provides striking confirmation that critics of faith in God often contribute more than its defenders to a clear grasp of the real question. Whether the positivist is right or wrong, he undoubtedly presents the kind of challenge that the Christian theologian has every reason to respect.

Therefore, if the claim I have to support is questionable—and, of course, it is—it is not any more questionable than Christian faith in God itself. Unless God is somehow real for every man, he is not genuinely real for any man. To take exception to this statement is not merely to quarrel with the vagary of one or more theologians, but to call in question the very meaning of faith in God as attested down through the Christian tradition.

Does this mean, then, that Christians are committed to the proposition "There are no atheists," that the distinction between faith and unfaith in God is simply false? No, it does not mean that, but means, rather, that the theologian is bound to exercise caution in interpreting this distinction. There is no question that the difference between faith

[36] See, e.g., J. N. Findlay's essay in Alvin Plantinga (ed.), *op. cit.,* pp. 111–22.

and unfaith is both real and important and that the word "atheism" has a legitimate and irreducible meaning. However, everything turns on understanding the difference aright and so defining the word as to take account of its proper uses.

The crucial point is that unfaith, like faith, is a phenomenon occurring at two essentially different levels of human life. At the deepest level, it is not a matter of self-conscious disbelief, but is a more or less conscious misunderstanding of one's own existence as a person. It is, one may say, an atheism in the bottom of the heart, instead of merely an atheism in the top of the mind.[37] Christian theology has recognized time and again that this existential denial of God in one's heart is by far the more serious denial of him and that it is quite compatible with a flawless orthodoxy in one's reflective beliefs. One may affirm God's reality with one's mind as well as one's lips, and yet deny his reality by actually existing as a godless man.

But how are we to understand this existential godlessness? Is it something utterly negative and empty, implying the complete absence of faith in God? This, clearly, is the conventional view, and there are theological interpretations that reinforce it. Yet reflection discloses that the phenomenon of unfaith is more complex. The truth about it is better suggested by the statement of H. Richard Niebuhr that the negative forms of faith such as distrust and disloyalty "are to positive faith as minus 1, not 0, is to plus 1, or as error, not ignorance, is to the life of reason."[38] In other words, unfaith is not the absence of faith, but the presence of faith in a deficient or distorted mode. It is, as Scripture universally declares, faith in God in the perverted form of *idolatry*. "The idea of God," Henri de Lubac writes, "cannot be uprooted because it is, in essence, the Presence of God in man. One cannot rid oneself of that Presence. Nor is the atheist a man who has succeeded in doing so. He is only an idolater who, as Origen said, 'refers his indestructible notion of God to anything rather than to God himself.' "[39]

Only here, too, we must guard against a common misunderstanding. It is easy to suppose that idolatry means the diversion of faith wholly away from God himself to some merely nondivine thing

---

[37] Cf. John Baillie, *Our Knowledge of God,* New York: Charles Scribner's Sons, 2d ed., 1959, pp. 47–104.

[38] *Radical Monotheism and Western Culture,* New York: Harper & Row, 1960, pp. 41 f.

[39] *The Discovery of God,* trans. Alexander Dru, London: Darton, Longman & Todd Ltd., 1960, pp. 180 f.

falsely identified as divine. Actually, however, it is less that the idolater simply identifies the nondivine thing as God than that he regards it as having a unique significance as a symbol or sacrament of God's presence. His idol is for him the indispensable evidence of God's power and favor, and so, while his trust is indeed in God, it is not whole, but is finally divided between God himself and the idol. For this reason, the real issue of faith at the deepest, existential level is never *whether* we are to believe in God, or even, as is sometimes said, *what* God we are to believe in; the issue, instead, is *how* we are to believe in the only God in whom anyone can believe and in whom each of us somehow must believe. And here there are but the two possibilities clarified once for all by the Protestant Reformers: either we are so to believe in God that we finally place our trust in him *alone;* or else we are so to believe in him that we divide our ultimate trust by placing it in part in some idol alongside him.

Because there is always this second possibility, the word "atheism" has a perfectly proper use with respect to the deeper level of man's existential self-understanding. Although, at this first level, faith in God in some mode is unavoidable, this in no sense precludes that such faith may take the perverted form of idolatry in one or another of its innumerable variations.[40]

This, however, is not the only use of the term "atheism." There is also the godlessness of the mind in which the reality of God is denied at the level of full self-consciousness. As a matter of fact, it is this reflective denial of God that is most frequently intended in the usual discussions of atheism. The atheist, as commonly understood, is the man who explicitly disbelieves in God and whose expressions of disbelief are taken as sufficient evidence that his is also the deeper godlessness of the heart. From what has been said, it is clear that this may well be a mistaken inference. One may grant that reflective atheism is indeed an enemy of existential faith and that it inevitably tends to pervert the heart as well as the mind. But it is always possible in a particular case that no real correlation exists between

[40] It also follows that Charles Hartshorne is mistaken when he says that the differences between those who do and do not believe in God's existence are "*all* differences between implicit and explicit knowledge and admission" (*The Logic of Perfection and Other Essays in Neoclassical Metaphysics,* La Salle, Ill.: Open Court Publishing Co., 1962, p. 110; my italics). Although Hartshorne is correct that the very idea of God entails that "Implicitly everyone knows (or at least feels) the divine existence" (*ibid.*), it is by no means necessary that this implicit knowledge (or feeling) be in every case authentic. To maintain otherwise is to succumb, however unintentionally, to an intellectualistic misunderstanding of faith.

the reflective denial of God and the existential affirmations by which the person in question actually lives. Furthermore, nothing automatically guarantees consistency even between the different types of one's fully conscious beliefs. It is perfectly conceivable that one can explicitly deny God, even while implicitly affirming him in yet other things one reflectively affirms.

The reason for this is that faith in God can be present at the level of self-conscious belief only in terms of some theistic scheme. Any such scheme is always only more or less appropriate to the faith of which it is the reflective account and is subject to judgment by the standards generally applicable to conceptualities—notably, logical self-consistency and congruence with experience, broadly construed. This means that one may reject a particular theistic scheme without necessarily rejecting the faith for which it claims to account, or, for that matter, every conceivable form of reflective theism. It is evident that much so-called "atheism" down through our intellectual history has really involved nothing more than this kind of reflective rejection. It has not been a disbelief in God as such but has been a refusal to accept some conceptual scheme in which faith in God has found expression. Thus a figure like Spinoza is for the theists of his own day an atheist, whereas, in the eyes of the romanticist Novalis, he is *ein Gottbetrunkener Mensch*. I suggested above (Section 1) that it is in this light that we should also view the secularistic denial of God in our own time. The real force of this denial is not to exclude faith in God altogether, but to make fully explicit the incompatibility between our experience as secular men and the supernaturalistic theism of our intellectual tradition.

Still, the fact that the secularist usually claims more than this for his denial reminds us of an important truth. It makes clear that, at the second level of self-conscious belief also, the distinction between faith and unfaith must in some sense be acknowledged. Men try, at least, to avoid reflective belief in God and, in some cases, completely to deny him.

The question we must now consider is whether such attempts are, as I believe, finally bound to fail. No doubt the most convincing reason for thinking they can succeed is the argument typically developed by the positivistically-minded philosopher. Unlike the atheist of an earlier generation, the positivist of today does not merely challenge the *truth* of assertions about God, but presses the logically prior question whether such assertions even have *meaning*. Secure in his confidence that meaningful statements are restricted either to the tautologies of mathematics and logic or to statements of fact that are empirically falsifiable, he seeks to show that religious language has no valid cognitive use whatever. Hence the case he presents for the denial of God is a formidable one indeed. It is so formidable, in fact, as at last to eliminate one important traditional approach sometimes adopted by Christian theologians. If the issue is whether assertions about God are even meaningful, it will hardly do to reply—as many have done and are still doing—that such assertions rest solely on the basis of faith in a special revelation. Obviously, not even faith can assert something as true which is in principle lacking in any genuine meaning.[41] In consequence, the only way the positivist's criticism can be met is by showing that there are religious assertions which are, after all, meaningful; and this is something no merely fideistic approach which appeals exclusively to special revelation is in a position to show.[42]

[41] This has been convincingly demonstrated in the recent paper by Kai Nielsen in *New Theology, No. 1,* ed. Martin E. Marty and Dean G. Peerman, New York: The Macmillan Co., 1964, pp. 131–49. I should perhaps add that this much of Nielsen's argument stands even if one rejects, as I do, the positivistic conclusion that Nielsen himself apparently wishes to draw. For a lucid and more inquiring demonstration of the same point, see Peter Alexander, "The Difficulties Which the Scientist Experiences in Accepting Theological Statements," *Christian Scholar,* September, 1955, pp. 206–18.

[42] Hence the serious limitation of Helmut Gollwitzer's in many ways instructive book, *Die Existenz Gottes im Bekenntnis des Glaubens,* München: Christian Kaiser Verlag, 1963 (English translation by J. W. Leitch in Helmut Gollwitzer, *The Existence of God as Confessed by Faith,* Philadelphia: The Westminster Press, 1965; cf. also Gollwitzer's pamphlet, *Gottes Offenbarung und unsere Vorstellung von Gott,* München: Christian Kaiser Verlag, 1964). Like his mentor, Karl Barth, Gollwitzer proposes to accept no criterion of meaning and truth save the Christian revelation, and thus is unable to show whether any of his claims even have sense (see especially the extreme statements in the special appendix to the English translation, pp. 247–53). On the other hand, his concern to avoid any existentialistic reduction of theology merely to anthropology is completely justified and confirms the formulation of the problem of God given in this essay. This is not to say that his allegation of such reduction in the case of Herbert Braun and others is fully convincing. One constantly senses in his argument, as, indeed, in Braun's reply (in Erich Dinkler [ed.], *Zeit und Geschichte, Dankesgabe an Rudolf Bultmann zum 80. Geburtstag,* Tübingen: J. C. B. Mohr, 1964, pp. 399–421), a deficiency of philosophical resources, which makes a clarification of the real alternatives impossible. At the same time, Gollwitzer's criticisms are often perceptive and fair (especially, I think, in the case of Bultmann) and quite avoid the crudeness and banality apparent in Wilhelm Knevels, *Die Wirklichkeit Gottes, Ein Weg zur Überwindung der Orthodoxie und des Existentialismus,* Stuttgart: Calwer Verlag, 1964.

Significantly, something like this is being at least suggested, if not shown, by other philosophers who, like the positivist, also approach the problem of God through the analysis of language. Many so-called analytic philosophers, to be sure, share an essentially positivistic understanding of cognition, and so seek to interpret language referring to God as having some wholly noncognitive use or uses. It is not surprising, therefore, that theistic philosophers and theologians have often looked upon analytic philosophy as more of a threat than a resource. But, as has been noted, there are other linguistic philosophers whose work has quite different implications. It not only is free of any positivistic narrowness, but even contributes toward making clear why the positivist's account of our uses of language can never be accepted without qualification. Since there seems little doubt that the general analytic approach to philosophical and theological problems will continue to be influential, I want to proceed with my argument by entering into discussion with one of these nonpositivistic analysts of religious language. Such a procedure promises to be all the more fruitful because this particular analyst has outlined a position strikingly similar to one to which I was first led from a quite different background and approach.

The philosopher to whom I refer is Stephen Toulmin, whose direct consideration of religious language is confined, so far as I am aware, to one suggestive chapter in his book, *An Examination of the Place of Reason in Ethics*.[43] As its title indicates, the main purpose of this book is to clarify the kind of argument, and thus the logical principles, that are implicit in our reasoning as moral agents. This Toulmin seeks to do by rigorously following the general method of the philosopher of ordinary language, that is, by discovering the meaning of our moral or ethical discourse through examining the uses to which we put it in everyday situations of moral decision. Distinctive of his approach, however, is the larger setting in which he places this analysis of our ethical reasoning; and it is with this setting, in three of its main elements, that we must here concern ourselves.

In the first place, Toulmin argues against what he speaks of as "too narrow a view of the uses of reasoning," by which he means the positivistic assumption that "a mathematical or logical proof or a scientific verification can be the only kind of 'good reason' for any statement."[44] Contrary to this assumption, "the uses of argument" (to quote the title of another of Toulmin's books referred to earlier)

[43] Cambridge: Cambridge University Press, 1950.
[44] *Ibid.*, p. 46.

are actually many, and questions of truth, falsity, and rational justification are as relevant in ethics, aesthetics, and even theology, as in mathematics and the sciences. The proof of this is the way we use language in all these different fields. "Speech is no single-purpose tool. It is, in fact, more like a Boy Scout's knife (an implement with two kinds of blade, a screw-driver, a corkscrew, a tin-and-bottle opener, a file, an awl, and even a thing for taking stones out of horses' hooves); and, further, it is one which we continually shape and modify, adding new devices (modes of reasoning, and types of concepts) to perform new functions, and grinding old ones afresh, in the light of experience, so that they shall serve their old, familiar, well-tried purposes better."[45] It is this "full variety of purposes for which speech is used" that makes clear "the versatility of reason," and thus confutes, along with certain other views, the positivistic limit on the scope of cognition.

In the second place, Toulmin holds that we must always understand both our language and the reasoning of which it is the expression in relation to the larger reality of life to which they belong. The different uses of language, like the different kinds of argument, arise in function of the various situations and activities of human existence in the world. Thus science, for instance, has its origin in the everyday situation where one is suddenly surprised by a phenomenon that his previous experience had not led him to anticipate. It is to deal with this situation and the question it poses that the whole enterprise of scientific explanation comes to be. From its simplest to its most complex forms, such explanation functions "to bring our past experience to bear upon our present and future explanations, in such a way as to 'save appearances' and turn the unexpected, as far as possible, into the expected."[46] Therefore, the logic of scientific language and reasoning, including the criteria or standards of judgment governing them, is the logic implicit in this special function. Insofar as any statement or argument enables us so to understand our experience as to predict particular future events, and thus avoid unpleasant and maybe even dangerous surprises, it to that extent fulfills its original human purpose and is scientifically valid.[47]

[45] *Ibid.*, p. 83.

[46] *Ibid.*, p. 88.

[47] It is the emphasis on *understanding* which keeps Toulmin's theory of science from being narrowly or one-sidedly pragmatic. See his discussions in *The Philosophy of Science: An Introduction*, London: Hutchinson & Co. Ltd., 1953; and especially *Foresight and Understanding: An Enquiry into the Aims of Science*, London: Hutchinson & Co. Ltd., 1961.

In a parallel way, Toulmin argues, we may understand the logic of our moral language and reasoning. Here the underlying life activity is man's pursuit of desires or interests in a social context in which each of his fellows is similarly engaged. Since this multiple pursuit of interests creates a state of potential conflict and poses questions as to how one is to act or what he is to do, moral reasoning emerges in order to cope with the situation and thereby facilitate our moral decisions. Its function, accordingly, is "to correlate our feelings and behaviour in such a way as to make the fulfilment of everyone's aims and desires as far as possible compatible."[48] This it seeks to do by one or the other of two somewhat different kinds of argument. In most cases, it simply refers the various possible courses of action to the moral rules or laws evolved by the relevant community for governing human behavior in the kind of situation in question. In these cases, the "right" thing to do is the thing sanctioned by the prescribed rules, and the valid moral argument is the one that establishes this conclusion. In other cases, however, where the prescribed rules conflict with one another or do not apply or are themselves in need of rational justification, a different kind of argument becomes necessary. Its major premise is not any particular rule or law, but the ultimate moral principle implicit in the situation of human action as such—namely, that the "right" action or rule is the one which maximizes the realization of men's several desires while minimizing their frustration. According to Toulmin, the whole apparatus of our moral language, from single concepts like "right" and "duty" up to fully developed ethical theories, arises so as to make possible these two kinds of argument. And, as in the case of science, the criteria of moral reasoning, like the norms of moral action itself, are wholly secular and autonomous, in the sense of being standards already implied in the activity and situation of men's pursuit of their vital interests.[49]

Yet Toulmin maintains, in the third place, that there is an important sense in which science and morality alike point beyond themselves. Although both enterprises have their bases in specific human purposes, which include certain kinds of reasoning while excluding

[48] *An Examination of the Place of Reason in Ethics,* p. 137.

[49] It is worth noting that much the same kind of analysis of our moral experience was worked out years ago by William James in *The Will to Believe and Other Essays in Popular Philosophy,* New York: Longmans, Green & Co., 1897, pp. 184–215. The parallel extends so far, in fact, that James, too, insisted that, in the sphere of morality, reason, as Toulmin puts it, "marches upon faith."

others, they nevertheless are not completely self-contained. The evidence for this is a phenomenon to which Toulmin refers as the "limiting question."[50] Sometimes in a chain of moral reasoning, for example, we reach the point where the question demanding an answer looks like a moral question, and yet clearly is not, since no strictly moral statement or argument could ever answer it. Thus someone may ask, "But why ought I to keep my promise anyway?" If he continues to press this question even after he has been referred to the prescribed rule that promises are always to be kept or has been shown that such practice alone makes for the maximum harmonization of men's interests, then he is no longer asking a properly moral question. He is not asking why he should keep his promise rather than not keep it, but, provided he is not simply confused, is asking the limiting question of why he should do anything moral at all. To this question, no moral reasoning as such can in the nature of the case give an answer. And yet it is a question that can and does arise precisely in connection with one's life and thought as a moral agent.

Questions of the same general type, Toulmin believes, also arise at the boundaries of scientific explanation. But, since the logic of the questions there is the same as at the limits of moral reasoning, we need not consider them further. The important point is that it is to the category of limiting questions that Toulmin proposes to assign questions properly regarded as religious. The purpose of "religion," he holds, and thus of the kind of language and reasoning that can be called "religious" or "theological," is to give answers to the questions that naturally arise at the limits of man's activities as moral actor and scientific knower.

But why are these limiting questions natural? Is there here, too, some actual situation in human life that tends to give rise to them? As might be expected, Toulmin's answer is affirmative; and, in considering the way he develops it, we come to the heart of his analysis of religious language.

Men, he claims, are faced by a much more profound problem than those that give rise to either scientific explanation or ethical argument. Our uncertainty about the future is not such, finally, as to be allayed by our being able to predict particular events, nor are we really free to act simply because we know we should do this instead of that. Our distress, rather, is "at once more general and deeply rooted" and is, in fact, the very distress expressed in the limiting

50 An Examination of the Place of Reason in Ethics, pp. 204 ff.

questions of Pascal: " 'When I consider the briefness of my life, swallowed up in the eternity before and behind it, the small space I fill, or even see, engulfed in the infinite immensity of spaces which I know not, and which know not me, I am afraid. . . . Who has set me here? By whose order and arrangement have this place and this time been allotted me? . . .' "[51] In short, the fact that we exist as men at all means that we are faced by a total threat to a meaningful existence. Our most serious problem is that of accepting ourselves and the world, of pursuing scientific knowledge and embracing moral duty, in spite of conditions that make for the profoundest uncertainty about what the future finally holds. Toulmin is not very specific as to just what is to be included among these conditions. But I think we may assume from his obvious fondness for Pascal (as well as, incidentally, for Tolstoy and Dostoevsky) and from the tone of his discussion that what he has in mind are the finitude and death—or, more generally, the "boundary situations"—which existentialist philosophers have focused as the defining elements of *la condition humaine*. At any rate, men, as Toulmin sees them, are sufficiently threatened by their actual life situation that they are moved by a deep "desire for reassurance, for a general confidence about the future."[52] And so there arise the limiting questions in which this desire finds explicit expression.

Religion in its various forms is an attempt to answer these limiting questions at the level of self-conscious belief, thereby providing the needed reassurance. As such, it is directly relevant to our activities of explaining the world scientifically and making concrete moral decisions. As Toulmin puts it, "Over those matters of fact which are not to be 'explained' scientifically [like the deaths on their birthdays of three children in one family], the function of religion is to help us to resign ourselves to them—and so feel like accepting them. Likewise, over matters of duty which are not to be justified further in ethical terms, it is for religion to help us embrace them—and so feel like accepting them."[53] Given this function of religion, Toulmin argues, there is no reason to hold with the positivist that all answers to the religious question are necessarily invalid or that there are no rational criteria whereby the better among them can be distinguished from the worse. Religious language also has its logic, and this logic permits the general cognitive distinctions of valid and invalid, true and false, as

[51] *Ibid.*, pp. 209 f.
[52] *Ibid.*, p. 216.
[53] *Ibid.*, pp. 218 f.

surely as do the different logics appropriate respectively to science and ethics. This is so because religious and theological language, too, is firmly grounded in our actual life, and arises in response to questions that likewise prescribe the standard by which answers to them may be judged. They prescribe the standard, namely, that a good religious answer "will give us a reassurance which will not be disappointed; will allay our fear of 'the eternity before and behind the brief span' of our lives, and of 'the infinite immensity' of space; will provide comfort in the face of distress; and will answer our questions in a way which will not seem in retrospect to have missed their point."[54]

I have analyzed Toulmin's position in some detail because it has the most direct bearing on the claim I wish to defend. In order now to clarify its precise relevance, I propose to consider rather more closely two of its central points, from which I shall then draw what seems to me the necessary conclusion.

There is, first, the point that the function of religious assertions is to provide "reassurance." As we know from our everyday experience, to reassure someone is simply to restore to him an assurance or confidence which, for some reason or other, he seems to have lost. And this can be done only in the one way suggested by the word "re-assure" itself, namely, by assuring *again,* by re-presenting assurance. This would seem to indicate that religious assertions can serve to reassure us only because they themselves are the re-presentation of a confidence somehow already present prior to their being made. But is this a judgment that Toulmin would permit us to make?

---

[54] *Ibid.,* p. 212. Toulmin continues with sentences that also deserve to be quoted: "Now, provided that the answers given are good answers, by this sort of standard, what logical justification can there be for dismissing them? Of course 'theological' and 'religious' questions and answers . . . are on quite a different footing, as a matter of logic, from scientific and ethical arguments, questions and answers. But it is only if we suppose that religious arguments pretend (say) to provide exact knowledge of the future—so competing with science on its own ground—that we can be justified in attempting to apply to them the logical criteria appropriate to scientific explanations; and only if we do this that we have any grounds for concluding (with Ayer) that 'all utterances about the nature of God are nonsensical,' . . . or (with Freud) that religion is 'an illusion.' . . . Provided that we remember that religion has functions other than that of competing with science and ethics on their own grounds, we shall understand that to reject all religious arguments for this reason is to make a serious logical blunder—an error as great as that of taking figurative phrases literally or of supposing that the mathematical theory of numbers (say) has any deep, religious significance."

I believe it is. Implied, at least, by his whole analysis is a recognition that religious assertions, like ethical and scientific ones, have a properly re-presentative character. As we have seen, these three kinds of assertion are all alike in being securely grounded in our actual existence as human beings. Each comes to be to enable us to answer a basic question that naturally arises out of our life itself. Like all questions, however, these basic questions, whether scientific, moral, or religious, rest on certain presuppositions, in the sense that, in asking them at all, we already take for granted that some things are the case. Thus, in pursuing any scientific inquiry, for instance, we assume that the world of events of which we are a part is so ordered that our experience of phenomena in the past and the present warrants our having certain expectations for the future. This is apparent from what we always find ourselves doing whenever our particular expectations turn out to have been mistaken: we undertake so to revise our understanding of our experience that any unexpected phenomena can henceforth be expected. In a similar way, our typical moral questions invariably rest on definite assumptions—for example, that some course of action open to us ought to be adopted and that it should be a course which, so far as possible, promotes the maximum realization of all relevant interests. So it is that we do not ordinarily ask *whether* there are good actions or even *what* the standards are by which all our actions must be judged; we ask, instead, for a rational justification of what we are actually to think and do in deciding between the courses of action concretely open to us.

So, too, with our religious question or questions. If Toulmin is right, in religious inquiry also, the real issue is never the issue of *whether*—of whether there is some ground in reality for "a general confidence about the future." Nor, for that matter, is it the purpose of such inquiry to determine *what,* in principle, must be the nature of that ground. To the contrary, we cannot so much as ask the religious question without presupposing not only that a ground of confidence is somehow real, but also that it is such as, in Toulmin's words, to make possible "a reassurance which will not be disappointed."

In this sense, the answers to the religious question, in the form of particular religious assertions, have a strictly re-presentative character. They are not so much the *cause* of our general confidence that existence is meaningful as its *effect.* By this I mean that the various "religions" or "faiths" of mankind, including what may be called the "Christian religion," are one and all expressions or re-presentations of a yet deeper faith that precedes them. Logically prior to every particular religious assertion is an original confidence in the meaning and worth of life, through which not simply all our religious answers, but even our religious questions first become possible or have any sense. Hence the different historical religions, again including Christianity, can be thought of only as several attempts at a more or less self-conscious understanding of this original confidence. They are the results, one may say, of *fides quaerens intellectum,* of that original faith itself in its search for a more fully conscious understanding of its own nature. As such, naturally, the several religions also exercise a formative function in relation to the confidence of particular individuals and communities. But Toulmin seems to me exactly right in describing this function as that of providing *re*-assurance. Because all religions are by their very nature re-presentative, they never originate our faith in life's meaning, but rather provide us with particular symbolic forms through which that faith may be more or less adequately re-affirmed at the level of self-conscious belief.

The second of Toulmin's points which repays closer consideration is that religious assertions, in thus providing reassurance, are directly relevant to both our scientific explanations and our moral thought and action.[55] Since religious questions are typically limiting questions, which arise precisely at the boundaries of such activities as science and morality, the answers to them set forth in religious assertions cannot but have a bearing on these activities themselves. Thus—to take the single example of morality—religion has a most important relation to our life as moral agents. As Toulmin expresses it, "Ethics provides the *reasons* for choosing the 'right' course: religion helps us to put our *hearts* into it."[56] In reassuring us that our

[55] This is a far-reaching difference between Toulmin's analysis and another very good one, which provides independent confirmation of his other main points by a much more elaborate argument: William A. Christian, *Meaning and Truth in Religion,* Princeton: Princeton University Press, 1964. Like Toulmin, Christian rightly insists on analyzing the logic of religious language in the context of "a general logic of inquiry which becomes specified in various ways when specific interests (for example, scientific, moral, or religious interests) prompt us to ask questions of various sorts" (*ibid.,* p. 3). Unlike Toulmin, however, Christian fails to see that the religious sort of question is not simply parallel or co-ordinate to the scientific and moral sorts, but, since it is related to them as a sort of limiting question, is also fundamental to them. This is evident from the rather different use to which Christian puts the phrase "limiting question" (see *ibid.,* pp. 84 ff., 262 f.).

[56] *An Examination of the Place of Reason in Ethics,* p. 219.

life is, after all, worth while, religious assertions speak to the question arising at the limits of morality itself, of why we should do anything moral at all. They tell us, in effect, that because our existence as such is finally meaningful—or, as Ludwig Wittgenstein once suggested, because we are absolutely safe and nothing can injure us, whatever happens[57]—we are free to pursue the right as we see it and need not succumb to cynicism or despair.

Yet, if religious assertions have this kind of moral relevance, it plainly seems to follow that the original confidence they re-present is itself the necessary condition of all our moral action. We must ask, in other words, whether we could make any moral choices whatever, unless we could, to some extent at least, put our hearts into them— unless we were, in some slight degree, already confident of their long-term significance, whatever happens. How Toulmin himself would answer this question is not completely clear. At one point, he concedes that particular religious beliefs can hardly be morally necessary, since "though religion may help some people to put their hearts into virtue, many people can do so without religion."[58] But he then goes on to argue that one may say much the same about the moral dispensability even of ethics; it is also possible to act morally without the self-consciousness about our actions in which ethical reflection properly consists. This, however, seems to me to leave the important question still unanswered, and, so far as I can see, Toulmin nowhere adequately speaks to it. Even if one grants that no religion as such is necessary to moral action, it is another question altogether whether we can make any moral choice at all without the under-girding confidence in life's meaning which it is religion's function to re-present. In my judgment, one must answer this question negatively if he is to accept Toulmin's analysis of religious language. The

---

[57] See Norman Malcolm, *Ludwig Wittgenstein: A Memoir,* London: Oxford University Press, 1958, p. 70. According to Malcolm, Wittgenstein once read a paper on ethics in which he reported having sometimes had "the experience of feeling *absolutely* safe. I mean the state of mind in which one is inclined to say 'I am safe, nothing can injure me, *whatever* happens.' " In my judgment, there is a definite connection between this experience and the other one Wittgenstein reported in the same paper, and which also found expression in his famous statement in the *Tractatus Logico-Philosophicus* (London: Kegan Paul, Trench, Trubner & Co. Ltd., 1922, p. 186): "Not *how* the world is, is the mystical but *that* it is." Both experiences are of the reality and significance of our existence as such, whence arise the limiting questions that religious assertions seek to answer.

[58] *An Examination of the Place of Reason in Ethics,* p. 220.

conclusion seemingly implied by all he says is that morality is unavoidably dependent on faith, regardless of its independence of the particular religions in which such faith finds expression.

But, whatever the route by which one reaches this conclusion, it is, I hold, both basic and inescapable. In any analysis which is in the least convincing, our moral life, like our science and all our other undertakings, can never be represented as wholly self-contained. Always presupposed by even the most commonplace of moral decisions is the confidence that these decisions have an unconditional significance. No matter what the content of our choices may be, whether for this course of action or for that, we can make them at all only because of our invincible faith that they somehow make a difference which no turn of events in the future has the power to annul.

This is not to say that any particular re-presentation of this faith in the form of some religion is a necessary condition of our moral action. I agree fully with Toulmin that claims to this effect are unconvincing and would insist that they can have no place in a responsible apologetic theology. If any religion, whether Christianity or another, is in some sense "necessary," this can hardly be because without it men would be utterly unable to be moral. Furthermore, I accept as proven that many putative religious beliefs which have been widely touted as essential to morality are not really thus essential at all. This seems to me true, for example, of the conventional beliefs in subjective immortality and in a wholly external scheme of supernatural rewards and punishments. Both of these beliefs I consider highly questionable, and that in large part because of what I can only describe as their moral crudity. I suspect not only that one can be moral without them, but that it is hard to be truly moral on any other terms. But the point for which I am arguing is not the moral importance of any particular religion or set of religious beliefs. Rather, I am arguing for the much more fundamental point that moral thought and action are existentially possible only because their roots reach down into an underlying confidence in the abiding worth of our life. The one thing for which none of us can rationally decide, whatever his particular choices, is the eventual nullity of any of his decisions. Even the suicide who intentionally takes his own life implicitly affirms the ultimate meaning of his tragic choice. This is why Alfred North Whitehead voices a faith common to us all when he says that "the immediate facts of present action pass into permanent significance for the Universe. The insistent notion of Right and Wrong,

Achievement and Failure depends upon this background. Otherwise every activity is merely a passing whiff of insignificance."[59]

In sum, to be moral at all is always to beg the basic question to which the religions of mankind are more or less adequate attempts to express the answer. And the proof of this, as Toulmin helps us see, is that it is to just this question that we find ourselves driven when we follow our moral reasoning itself to its final limits.

It will be recalled that the question with which we approached Toulmin's analysis of religious language was whether attempts to avoid explicit belief in God or to deny his reality altogether are, in the last analysis, bound to fail. Given the conclusion at which we have now arrived, we have taken a first important step toward answering this question. We have at least learned that no reflective inventory of the existential beliefs by which we actually live, as illustrated by our moral beliefs, can pretend to be successful which fails to take account of our basic confidence in the abiding worth of our life. But, if we are to answer our question as we actually formulated it, we must obviously take the further step of seeing the essential connection between the reality of our existential faith in the worth of life and what is properly meant by the word "God." Why there is such a connection ought to become evident once we understand the conditions under which this word is rightly used.

I hold that the primary use or function of "God" is to refer to the objective ground in reality itself of our ineradicable confidence in the final worth of our existence. It lies in the nature of this basic confidence to affirm that the real whole of which we experience ourselves to be parts is such as to be worthy of, and thus itself to evoke, that very confidence. The word "God," then, provides the designation for whatever it is about this experienced whole that calls forth and justifies our original and inescapable trust, thereby meaning existentially, as William James once said, " 'You can dismiss certain kinds of fear.' "[60] From this it follows that to be free of such fear by

[59] Paul A. Schilpp (ed.), *The Philosophy of Alfred North Whitehead,* New York: Tudor Publishing Co., 2d ed., 1951, p. 698.

[60] *Some Problems of Philosophy: A Beginning of An Introduction to Philosophy,* New York: Longmans, Green & Co., 1911, p. 62; cf. also Paul Weiss, *The God We Seek,* Carbondale, Ill.: Southern Illinois University Press, 1964, p. 3, where God is said to be "the being who remains steadfast when all else gives way."

existing in this trust is one and the same thing with affirming the reality of God.

It might be objected that this analysis of "God" in terms of our trust in life's meaning fails to establish that the word has any referent independent of our trust itself. A critic could hold that God merely appears real to us, given our unavoidable belief in him, while the word "God" actually has no reference to an objective reality. But, despite the seriousness with which this objection is often taken, it is not, I believe, particularly impressive. It rests on a failure to observe the peculiar conditions that govern our use of the word "real" and the other terms related to it.

Here, too, Toulmin provides a clarifying insight. " 'Reality,' in any particular mode of reasoning," he tells us, "must be understood as 'what (for the purposes of this kind of argument) is relevant,' and 'mere appearance' as 'what (for these purposes) is irrelevant.' And, since these purposes differ from case to case, that which is, say, 'aesthetic reality' may yet be, for physics, 'mere appearance.' "[61] "Real," in other words, is a term which, like "true" and several other terms of logical assessment, has both (as Toulmin elsewhere calls them[62]) a "field-invariant force" and "field-dependent standards." Although the *meaning* of "real" is constant—"what for the purposes of some mode of reasoning is relevant," or, as James proposed, "what we in some way find ourselves obliged to take account of"[63]—the *criteria* governing its use are, by that very meaning, variable. But this means that, whenever we ask about the "reality" of something, we must always presuppose *some* mode of reasoning, some way of taking account of things through questions and answers, even to ask about its reality with any meaning. Then, if we are to avoid disputes that are in the nature of the case nonadjudicable, we must take pains to see that the mode of reasoning we presuppose permits us to decide the issue of this particular thing's reality. Were we to dispute the claim of the scientist, for instance, that the sun at sunset is not red but "really yellow," we would simply show that our own everyday criteria of "reality" are different from those which he as a scientist quite properly takes for granted. Once we presuppose the mode of reasoning proper to religion, however—and not to presuppose it is to leave religious issues in principle undecided—the question whether

61 *An Examination of the Place of Reason in Ethics*, p. 114.
62 *The Uses of Argument*, p. 38; cf. also below, pp. 111 f.
63 *Some Problems in Philosophy*, p. 101.

God is real at once becomes pointless. This is because, as was explained above, "God" is the very meaning of "reality" when this word is defined in terms of our basic confidence in the significance of life and the kind of questions and answers such confidence makes possible. We may indeed inquire how the ground of our confidence is most appropriately understood or conceived, and whether any among the historical religions is justified in claiming to be its decisive representation or revelation. But to question whether the word "God" as here analyzed refers to anything objectively real is not, I believe, a sensible inquiry. If the religious mode of reasoning is once assumed, there is no point in even raising this question; and, if such reasoning is not assumed, we can never hope to answer it.[64]

The upshot of the discussion—to take once again the example of morality—is that any reflective account of our moral experience that tries simply to avoid talking about God must be, at the least, essentially fragmentary. By this I mean that, when "God" is understood in accordance with the preceding analysis, such an account cannot but imply any number of assertions for which it declines to take responsibility. Since, as we have seen, all our moral choices unavoidably beg the question of basic confidence in the worth of life, that question

[64] I should perhaps explain why the premise of this argument does not seem to me to entail the "metaphysical neutralism" that Toulmin himself may wish to draw from it. Even if one holds that "reality" has different uses correlative with the different kinds of criteria that may warrant our using it, this does not require one to grant that these different uses are all merely parallel or co-ordinate to one another, with none being fundamental in relation to the rest. Indeed, on Toulmin's understanding of religion, it seems clear that the religious use of "reality"—or, in other words, what I mean by "God"—is necessarily presupposed by its other uses both in science and ethics (see above, p. 34, n. 55). In any case, I myself hold that it is thus presupposed and see nothing in the above argument that would require one to hold otherwise. Equally left open by the argument is whether there may not be a certain overlapping of our at least ostensibly different modes of reasoning, and so also of the different senses of the word "reality." Metaphysical reasoning, for example, may—and I maintain does—overlap with religious or theological (see below, pp. 93 f.). I would also mention that another and, in my judgment, essentially similar way of analyzing "reality" is suggested by Martin Heidegger's reflections on the transcendental correlation of "thinking and being" (*Denken und Sein*). Heidegger's attempts, first, at a "fundamental ontology" of human existence and then, later, at a "thinking of thinking" have also aimed, in their way, at an analytic of "the uses of reasoning" and thus at clarification of "the manifold sense of being." See especially William J. Richardson, *Heidegger: Through Phenomenology to Thought,* The Hague: Martinus Nijhoff, 1963; and Otto Pöggeler, *Der Denkweg Martin Heideggers,* Pfullingen: Günther Neske Verlag, 1963.

must also be begged, though now at the level of self-conscious belief, by any wholly nontheistic theory of morality. This is not to say that such a theory may not be within its limits both true and important. It is perfectly possible that its treatment of our moral experience may be in many respects illumining. Still, at best, it must be profoundly inadequate if it is put forward as in any sense a complete or exhaustive account of that experience. The characteristic deficiency of all nontheistic moral theories is that they leave the final depth of morality itself utterly unillumined. Although they may well focus our moral action and the immanent standards by which it is governed, they fail to render at all intelligible the underlying confidence and its transcendent ground in which our moral activity, as our life generally, actually has its roots.

Often enough, this failure is not lacking in a certain irony. Proponents of nontheistic moral theories typically pride themselves on their right to give a fully rational account of man's moral experience. Nothing in this experience, they contend, is to be left merely at the level of unexamined belief or tradition, but must be raised to the level of complete self-consciousness. Ironically, however, this demand for rationality is not extended to the basic confidence that all our moral experience necessarily presupposes. Hence, for all their vaunted "humanism," such theories are, in truth, deficiently humanistic. While they may cast a bright light on the foreground of morality, they leave what Whitehead calls its "background" wholly obscure. They allow the original faith in which all our moral action is finally based to remain a merely nonreflective, quasi-animal kind of faith.

But this inherent incompleteness is a minor failing compared with that of the second kind of moral outlook, where the reality of God is denied altogether. Here the essential inadequacy of the position is nothing less than outright antinomy or self-contradiction. If all our moral thought and action rest on an underlying confidence in the final meaning of life, then we are implicitly affirming such confidence, together with its transcendent ground, in all that we think and do. Therefore, it is logically impossible utterly to deny this ground of confidence without explicitly contradicting the implication of morality itself. And so it is that all secularistic or atheistic accounts of our moral experience are characteristically caught in an inescapable dilemma. Insofar as they do justice at all to the presuppositions of our moral questions and answers—that some course of action ought always to be chosen and that the right course is one meeting the greatest number of relevant needs—they are forced to make affirmations that conflict with their sweeping atheistic denials. On the other hand, to the extent that they press these denials—denying, say, that there is any ground for the permanent significance of our choices or for the authority of moral standards—their accounts lose all touch with our actual moral experience and tend increasingly to become morally nihilistic.

Illustrations of this essential inconsistency are easy to find in the writings of representative postmodern atheists.[65] One of the most instructive of these is Albert Camus' notion of the "absurd hero," which is developed in detail in his early book, *Le mythe de Sisyphe*.[66] According to Camus, the whole character of human life is determined by its essential absurdity, by the unclosable gap between our demand for rationality, practical as well as theoretical, and "the unreasonable silence of the world." Thus we must live without any guarantee that our own actions or the human enterprise as such are finally worth while. Nevertheless, Camus insists that the only fitting response to this absurdity is heroic resistance against it, which includes an absolute lucidity about our condition, together with an affirmation of our life in spite of its ultimate meaninglessness. Indeed, in Camus' later writings, this response of resistance comes to embrace a profoundly humanistic ethic of love and concern for all mankind. He exhorts us time and again to throw ourselves into the struggle for man against everything in nature or history that would impair his unforfeitable dignity.[67]

But, intriguing as this notion of the absurd hero doubtless is, it can hardly define a real possibility, whether for thought or for existential choice. If all our actions are in principle absurd, the act of heroically resisting their absurdity must also be absurd. It, too, is *ex hypothesi* a totally meaningless response and can be supposed not a bit more fitting than the various attempts to flee from absurdity that Camus so unsparingly condemns. Or, to take the other side of the dilemma,

[65] For an extended critique of Jean-Paul Sartre's position on this point, see below, pp. 126–34.

[66] Paris: Gallimard, 1942 (English translation by Justin O'Brien in Albert Camus, *The Myth of Sisyphus and Other Essays*, New York: Alfred A. Knopf, Inc., 1955). The one quotation in the text below is from the English translation, p. 28.

[67] See especially the collection of shorter writings translated by Justin O'Brien in Albert Camus, *Resistance, Rebellion, and Death*, New York: Alfred A. Knopf, Inc., 1960.

insofar as resistance for the sake of man *is* a meaningful act—is somehow fitting as the alternatives to it are not—the absurdity of our existence cannot be as unrelieved as was originally alleged.

That Camus himself was by no means unaware of this inconsistency is apparent from his later work.[68] There is also not the least question that he profoundly believed in the significance of our moral choices and that this belief came more and more to predominate in his mature reflections. As he once confessed, "In the darkest days of our nihilism, I sought only for reasons to lead beyond the nihilism."[69] But just for this reason, those who have given us the most discerning studies of his thought have seen in it, especially toward the end, the clear signs of a genuine, if scarcely conventional, religious faith. They have felt compelled to conclude that his "quarrel with God" is marked by "inaccurate firing," and is really effective not against faith in God as such, but against a supernaturalistic theism with which that faith ought never to be simply identified.[70]

Thus the answer to our initial question would seem to be that faith in God is finally unavoidable even at the level of self-conscious belief. If we are to give a reflective account of our experience at all, the only alternatives to some form of theism, properly understood, are inventories of our beliefs that are either essentially fragmentary or else shot through with self-contradiction. The reason for this is that belief in God's reality proves to be inescapable at the deeper level of our actual existence. This is the conclusion to which we are led by an analysis of religious language like that offered by Toulmin. It helps us to see, first, that such analysis is possible only if we grant an original

[68] See *L'homme révolté*, Paris: Gallimard, 1951 (English translation by Anthony Bower in Albert Camus, *The Rebel: An Essay on Man in Revolt*, New York: Alfred A. Knopf, Inc., 1956).

[69] "The Riddle," *Atlantic Monthly*, June, 1963, p. 85.

[70] See especially the sensitive study by Nathan A. Scott, *Albert Camus*, New York: Hillary House Publishers Ltd., 1962, pp. 18 f., 89, 95 ff. The phrases quoted above are cited by Scott from R. W. B. Lewis, *The Picaresque Saint: Representative Figures in Contemporary Fiction*, Philadelphia: J. B. Lippincott Co., 1959, p. 78. As to Lewis' effort to show that the God whom Camus declares dead is "a God who in fact had not been alive very long; he had been created in the polemics of Martin Luther" (*ibid.*, p. 79; cf. pp. 301 f.), I find it most unconvincing. The positive influence of Luther in the development of humanism—even, indeed, of our modern "this-worldliness"—is too well established to be dismissed so highhandedly. Furthermore, boast of its "theocentric humanism" as he may, Lewis must reckon with the fact that some of Thomism's most astute contemporary critics have found the metaphysical premises of its doctrine of God profoundly anti-humanistic.

confidence in the ultimate significance of life as the basis of all our religious questions and answers. Because the function of religious assertions is to speak to our question for re-assurance, we are forced to view them less as the creators than as the creatures of existential faith in God's reality. But this kind of analysis makes clear, second, that religious assertions thus have the greatest relevance for such other of our life activities as morality and scientific explanation. This is because the basic question to which these assertions are intended to provide the answer is a limiting question which arises at the boundaries of these same activities. From this, then, one can only conclude that faith in God as the ground of confidence in life's ultimate meaning is the necessary condition of our existence as selves.

In arguing here for this conclusion, to be sure, I have limited our consideration to the single example of morality. But this has been done solely for the sake of simplifying the argument, not because of any preference on my part for a so-called "moral proof of the existence of God." It would be equally possible to argue that our scientific reasoning, also, naturally leads us to ask limiting questions which have their presupposition in existential faith in the reality of God. Therefore, the claim whose reasonableness I have tried at least to suggest is that not simply our morality, but our existence as such and in *all* its undertakings is a standing testimony to God's reality. This, as I believe, is the only really essential "proof of God's existence"—that we are selves at all only because of our existential faith in him and that, in consequence, such faith must also be affirmed self-consciously if the reflective inventory of our beliefs is to be both complete and consistent.[71]

[71] On the matter of the proofs of God's existence as they may be developed by the philosopher or the theologian, I would add that I consider such proofs to be both necessary and important—in their proper place. That place, as I see it, is the secondary place of reason or reflection generally, whether in philosophy or in theology. This means that the proofs of God, as Maurice Blondel expressed it, "are not so much an invention as an inventory, not a revelation so much as an elucidation, a purification and a justification of the fundamental beliefs of humanity" (quoted by Henri de Lubac, *The Discovery of God,* p. 64, n. 10, who himself offers a superb treatment of this whole question). The philosopher who, more than any other contemporary thinker, seems to me not only to have understood the place of the proofs, but also to have developed them most adequately is Charles Hartshorne (see especially *Man's Vision of God and the Logic of Theism,* New York: Harper & Brothers, 1941, pp. 251–341; and *The Logic of Perfection,* pp. 28–117). For further discussion, see my essay, "Theology and Philosophy: A New Phase of the Discussion," *Journal of Religion,* January, 1964, pp. 1–15.

3. TOWARD A NEW THEISM

If belief in God is thus unavoidable, reflectively as well as existentially, we may draw two obvious inferences of the greatest importance for the problem of this essay.

First of all, we may say that modern secular man, with his characteristic affirmation of our life in the world in its proper autonomy and significance, is in a peculiarly good position to discover the reality of God—nay, has already made that discovery, at least implicitly. If we exist as selves at all only because of a confidence in the final worth of our existence, the more consistently and emphatically we affirm that worth, as is the wont of secularity, the more clearly we evince our faith in that to which the word "God" refers.

Of course, in saying this, we are challenging an assumption widely shared by both those who expressly affirm God's reality and those who do not. Nothing is so typical of defensive interpreters of Christian faith, Protestant as well as Catholic, as the claim that modern man's decision *for* secularity has been a decision *against* faith in God. These theologians maintain that a secular affirmation of man and his several autonomous undertakings is a sign of "worldliness" and so stands condemned as the great apostasy of the modern age.[72] We should not be surprised, then, that those who have made this affirmation have generally supposed themselves to be rejecting religious faith. They have taken the word of their theological critics and construed their affirmation as godless rebellion.[73] Yet, despite—or, perhaps, just because of—this suspicious agreement between opposing points of view, we have good reason to stand by our inference. Secularity as such, as distinct from secularism, is simply the emphatic affirmation that man and the world are themselves of ultimate significance. Hence, by the logic of the preceding argument, it implies the equally emphatic affirmation of God as the ground of that

[72] Such a view is evident, I fear, even in as informed a historical interpretation as John Courtney Murray's (*op. cit.*). So far as I can see, Murray acknowledges almost nothing in the "godlessness" either of "modernity" or of the "post-modern age" except "apostasy," "betrayal," etc.

[73] Cf. Dietrich Bonhoeffer, *Letters and Papers from Prison*, ed. Eberhard Bethge and trans. R. H. Fuller, London: SCM Press Ltd., 1953, p. 146.

significance. Far from being the great defection from God—at any rate, as "God" has been defined here—secularity is actually an expression of profound faith in him.

And this leads directly to the second inference: secularism, in the sense of the express and unqualified denial of God, is not the friend of a secular affirmation but its enemy. Here, too, however, the inference is important largely because it is much more commonly denied than affirmed. Just as it is usually supposed that faith in God is identical with accepting supernaturalistic theism, so it is also generally assumed that secularity and secularism are one and the same. Yet we are now able to recognize that this assumption, widespread as it is on both sides of the theistic discussion, has to be rejected. Not only are the secularist's sweeping negations not required by secularity, they actually serve but to stultify it.

To be sure, secularism is something more than these negations, even though they are its defining characteristic. Together with his atheistic denial, the secularist also intends to make a humanistic affirmation. But the truth of the matter is that he denies God *and* man—or, since his position is in principle self-stultifying, he at best affirms neither except ambiguously. Insofar as he denies God as the ground of confidence in life's meaning—and this is the import of his unqualified negations—he implies a denial of the meaning of human life itself. That the secularist typically ignores this implication ought never to mislead us, although it should, naturally, deter us from attributing to him a nihilistic intention he does not share. It ought, instead, to give us all the more reason to challenge his sweeping denials—and that, not because of our adherence to some traditional form of theistic belief, but because of his own intention to affirm man, which is undercut by those denials. Just to the extent that any of us is serious in his secular affirmation and knows what he is about, he must find all secularistic outlooks unacceptable. They do not simply fail to support this affirmation, but are in the last analysis deeply repugnant to it.

And yet, important as these two inferences are, they can be given their rightful place only if they are set alongside another conclusion equally inescapable. This must be stated the more emphatically because it is so often disregarded by apologists for theistic belief. Certain theologians would be quick to agree that belief in God *is* the implication of a serious secular affirmation and that secularism, in consequence, is really antagonistic to modern man's own deepest concerns. Thus Henri de Lubac, for example, has brilliantly argued that atheistic humanism arose from "a tragic misunderstanding" and has led not to man's emancipation and fulfillment, but to his "dissolution."[74] But, having made this point, de Lubac proceeds simply to assume the validity of traditional supernaturalistic theism, without seeing that atheism's misunderstanding was in part "tragic" just because of the conception of God against which it rebelled. He does say, to be sure, that the world which atheists "spew forth has often no right to call itself Christian in any but a purely sociological sense, and the God they reject is all too often a mere caricature of the God we worship."[75] Even so, he nowhere so much as questions whether the God of classical theism is not also a caricature of the God of Christian piety and whether atheists may not perhaps be fully justified in refusing adherence to *that* God. On the contrary, he insists "There is nothing that should be changed in [Christianity], nothing that should be corrected, nothing that should be added . . . ";[76] and, in another context, he assures his readers that there is nothing in his treatment of the problem of God "which has not been borrowed from the double treasure of the *philosophia perennis* and Christian experience."[77] My view is that this procedure, frequently followed as it is, is totally unwarranted and can serve only to perpetuate the tragic misunderstanding between the Christian witness to God and the legitimate concerns of modern man. I agree fully with de Lubac's point that "Man without God is dehumanized."[78] But I am quite certain that this point will never strike home for the secular man of today so long as God is conceived as he is by traditional theism.

The reason for this, as was indicated in Section 1, is that this older form of theism is fundamentally opposed to a truly secular decision and outlook on life. So basic is its opposition, in fact, that I should say it, too, is the enemy rather than the friend of secularity. Whether one may say this is, naturally, debatable, since supernaturalism, like secularism, is in principle an inconsistent and self-stultifying position. Elements in it support a secular affirmation, and there can be little doubt that such appeal as it still has for many contemporary men is to be accounted for by this fact. Still, one must be equally clear that its other and more essential elements are completely antagonistic to

[74] *The Drama of Atheist Humanism,* pp. 3–7, 27–35.
[75] *Ibid.,* p. 34.
[76] *Ibid.,* p. 72.
[77] *The Discovery of God,* p. 194.
[78] *Ibid.,* p. 186.

modern man's concerns. Consequently, if supernaturalism is to be called the friend of these concerns, it is the same kind of treacherous or, at least, unreliable friend that secularism also might be said to be. This conclusion we may now confirm in the following way.

We have seen that the only God whose reality is implied by a secular affirmation is the God who is the ground of confidence in the ultimate worth or significance of our life in the world. Given this affirmation, God must be so conceived that his being this ground of confidence is rendered as intelligible as possible. This requires, in turn, that our conceptuality, or system of fundamental concepts, enable us to think of his nature as defined by two essential characteristics.

First, God must be conceived as a reality which is genuinely related to our life in the world and to which, therefore, both we ourselves and our various actions all make a difference as to its actual being. To speak of a ground of significance or worth except as involving such relatedness is logically impossible. If, for instance, I have no real relation to a certain historical happening, so that it makes no difference whatever to my actual thoughts and actions, then such significance as it may have cannot be explained by referring to me as the ground of that significance. Should it prove to be significant at all, this can only be because someone else is so related to it as to be genuinely affected by it. Of necessity, therefore, the ground of the significance of our life has to be a supremely relative reality. God must enjoy real internal relations to all our actions and so be affected by them in his own actual being.

But, second, we can think of God only as a reality whose relatedness to our life is itself relative to nothing and to which, therefore, neither our own being and actions nor any others can ever make a difference as to its existence. Here it is important to understand a distinction between existence and actuality, which is one of the distinctions quite obscured in the metaphysical tradition. A person or thing may properly be said to "exist," provided the essential characteristics by which he or it is defined are somehow actualized. Thus I exist, for example, so long as the complex of traits designated by my proper name at all the stages of my life history is realized in some state or other of actual relations to my fellow human beings and to the larger natural environment. This is to say that my existence as such has to be distinguished from any of these actual states taken simply by itself. I exist as the person I essentially am—whether as actually young or old, sick or well, in relation to these particular persons or to those. "Existence," in short, properly functions as an abstract constant always implying "actuality" as an abstract variable. Hence, to say that anything "exists" requires that the variable "actuality" have *some* specific value. Yet the mere attribution of existence to something in no way specifies what that value is—any more than the statement "John is married" discloses the identity of the woman who bears John's name.

Now the second essential requirement of secular faith is that the *existence* of its ground, as distinct from that ground's *actual being,* be conceived as in the strictest sense nonrelative or absolute. Unless the ground of our life's significance exists absolutely, relative to no cause or condition whatever, that significance itself could not be truly ultimate or permanent, and so could not be the object of an unshakable confidence.

Thus the only conception of God more or less clearly implied in a secular affirmation is intrinsically two-sided or dipolar.[79] It conceives God as at once supremely relative and supremely absolute, thereby explicating both essential elements in a secular faith in the ultimate worth of our life.

To recognize this, however, is to see at once that secular faith and supernaturalistic theism must be unalterably opposed. The whole character of traditional theism is defined by an essential one-sidedness or monopolarity. As it conceives God, he is so far from being the eminently relative One that he is denied to be really related to our life at all. He is said to be a reality which is in every respect absolute and whose only relations to the world are the purely nominal or external relations of the world to him. Thus Thomas Aquinas tells us: "Since therefore God is outside the whole order of creation, and all creatures are ordered to Him, and not conversely, it is manifest that creatures are really related to God Himself; whereas in God there is no real relation to creatures, but a relation only in idea, inasmuch as creatures are referred to Him."[80] Accordingly, the attributes or perfections by which the nature of God is classically defined—pure

[79] The distinction between "dipolar" and "monopolar" forms of theism is worked out in detail in Charles Hartshorne and William L. Reese, *Philosophers Speak of God,* Chicago: The University of Chicago Press, 1953. This is one of the reasons why this book achieves something like a Heideggerian "dismantling" (*Destruktion*) of the history of philosophical theology.

[80] *Summa Theologica,* Vol. I, trans. Fathers of the English Dominican Province, New York: Benziger Brothers, Inc., 1947, p. 66 (*Ia,* 13, 7, *in corpore*).

THE REALITY OF GOD

actuality, immutability, impassivity, aseity, immateriality, etc.—all
entail an unqualified negation of real internal relationship to anything
beyond his own wholly absolute being.

True, these so-called "metaphysical attributes" do not exhaust the
predications of classical theists in speaking of God. Following the
mythological representations in Holy Scripture, they also speak of
God as the heavenly Father or King, whose relations to man and his
other creatures seem anything but purely nominal or external. As the
eminent personal or social being, God freely creates and judges all
things and in his mercy so acts as to bring them to their final end of
sharing in his own eternal life. To this extent, then, one must admit
that classical theism does give the appearance of offering a dipolar
conception of God's nature. But that this is finally more than an
appearance cannot, I believe, be convincingly argued.

To begin with, the traditional theist typically treats the mythological representations of God in Scripture as "anthropomorphisms"
which the philosopher and theologian must critically interpret. The
scriptural designation of God as Father, for instance, is said to
predicate of him a "mixed perfection," which we may rightly understand only as a metaphor. God is not "eminently" but merely "virtually" Father, so the word "Father" in this case has to be taken
symbolically and construed in terms of the other so-called "simple
perfections," which alone can be properly predicated of God with
respect to the "thing signified" (*res significata*). One may insist,
rightly, that with this much of the supernaturalist's position no
theist is likely to disagree. It lies in the very nature of mythological
portrayals of God that they should misrepresent him. Because their
terms and categories are those whose proper use is to express our
ordinary sense experience, they cannot represent the ground of our
life's significance except inappropriately. In this sense, at least,
demythologizing is a task that any theism, old or new, must somehow
accept and try to carry out.[81]

However, the difficulty with the old theism's demythologizing is
that it does not really *interpret* the scriptural myths, but rather
eliminates them. If God, according to Scripture, is the eminent Thou
or Person who both knows the world and loves it, supernaturalism
permits him to do neither unless the words "know" and "love" are
given meanings exactly opposite to those we ordinarily understand.
This is unmistakably the case, for example, in Aquinas' interpretation

[81] See below, pp. 104–9, 117 ff.

of the divine knowledge.[82] Aquinas' general theory of knowledge is in the broad sense realistic, and so he holds that, in all ordinary cases of knowing, it is the subject or knower who is really related to the object known, not *vice versa*. The object's relation to the subject is not real but "logical," something purely external to the object itself. Hence it would seem that, in the relation which constitutes God's knowing of the world, it is God as subject who is really relative, while the world as object is nonrelative or absolute. Aquinas, however, draws precisely the opposite conclusion: it is the world as known that is really related to God as its wholly absolute knower!

In similar ways, supernaturalists have interpreted all the other relative perfections of God which are so prominent in the scriptural representations of his nature. And in each case, the result has been just what one would expect: although God is spoken of as if he were also the eminently relative One, the cash value of such speaking, once it is critically interpreted, is that God is the metaphysical Absolute, nothing more. The fully justified assertion that God is not literally related to the world (if by "literal" is meant in the same way as we are related to it) proves on examination to mean that he is literally not related to the world. Consequently, any impression that supernaturalism is dipolar in its conception of God is finally deceptive. Its unqualified denial that God could still be God and yet be really related to anything beyond himself betrays a fundamental "monopolar prejudice" in its whole hermeneutical procedure, which requires that Scripture's most characteristic designations of God be completely emptied of meaning.

One must grant that supernaturalists have never simply abandoned these scriptural designations, but rather have continued to affirm them, together with the denial that God is in any sense a genuinely relative reality. In fact, in the case of many Protestant theologians, for whom the influence of Scripture has been greater than that of Greek metaphysics, the stress on God as wholly absolute has often enough receded behind an emphasis on just those divine perfections that entail relativity. But, true as this is, it hardly qualifies the conclusion for which I am arguing. It merely makes clear that supernaturalism, at best, is a maze of inconsistencies which we must pronounce unacceptable in proportion to the strength and clarity of our secular affirmation. As long as God must be conceived, finally, as not really related to our life in the world, any speaking of him that

[82] *Op. cit.*, pp. 72–86 (*Ia*, 14, 1–16). Cf. the extended critique by Hartshorne and Reese in *Philosophers Speak of God*, pp. 119 f., 131 ff.

seems to imply such relationship can do little more than increase our difficulties with the whole conception. To our acute sense of the existential repugnance of the idea it adds the burden of puzzlement at insoluble antinomies and contradictions—as when we are asked to believe, say, that God's love is so tender that he marks the fall of a sparrow, though all the while he remains the νόησις νοήσεως of Aristotle, utterly unmoved by the motions of the world. Classical theists claim, of course, that it is not contradiction that here confronts us, but "mystery." Yet, ever since the profound criticisms of Spinoza (though he, too, evinces the same monopolar prejudice), this claim has ceased to be plausible to many of the best Western minds. In their eyes, the so-called "mystery" has been unmasked as logical confusion, which makes supernaturalism all the more incredible as a reflective account of our experience.

The deeper reason for modern man's alleged "atheism," however, has not been the theoretical incoherence of the traditional theistic conception. Rather, as I have tried to indicate, the more important reason is that this conception cannot but seem repugnant to anyone who has a truly secular attitude toward our life in the world. If, when all mythological representations are interpreted as symbols, we must conceive God as nothing other than the Absolute of classical philosophy, then the reality of God is continually called in question by the very existence of secular man. The whole point of secularity is its emphatic affirmation that our life here and now in space and time, in nature and history, is of ultimate significance. Yet it is just this affirmation that a wholly absolute God renders otiose. Since nothing whatever can make the least difference to such a God, all our strivings and sufferings also must be ultimately indifferent. From the perspective of the Absolute, which alone enjoys ultimate reality, what we do or fail to do can neither add nor detract in any permanently significant way. God's perfection is in every sense statically complete, an absolute maximum, so we can no more increase him by our best efforts than diminish him by our worst. Then, so far as our sufferings are concerned, the wholly absolute God can provide no consolation, no sense of peace, in the midst of our distress. Because he remains completely unaffected by the ills that befall us, he is, as Camus has charged, the eternal bystander whose back is turned to the woe of the world.

It is mainly because supernaturalism is in these ways existentially repugnant that it is, in the last analysis, irreconcilable with secularity. Simply by deciding to be secular, one implicitly repudiates the conception of God whereby that decision is finally robbed of any force. For a time, no doubt, this repudiation need not become explicit and may even seem unnecessary, what with the inconsistencies in which supernaturalism is typically entangled. But, sooner or later, the conclusion must be faced that the God conceived by this form of theism cannot be the God of secular man.

To some degree, philosophers and theologians have long since recognized this to be true. Much of modern philosophy, from Spinoza down through Hegel and the other idealists of the nineteenth century, has been an attempt to supplant supernaturalism by a more attractive and credible account of our experience.[83] In Protestant theology also, announcements of "the end of theism" are by no means original with the present generation. Already with Schleiermacher, classical theism was definitely abandoned for an outlook that, in all essentials and regardless of its author's intention, is quite close to Spinoza's pantheism. Around the turn of the century, James and others also proposed conceptions of a "finite God," which, while theistic in basic motive, were nevertheless designed to overcome the inadequacies of supernaturalism, existential as well as theoretical.[84] Such conceptions subsequently played a role in certain expressions of liberal Protestantism, notably in the version of so-called "personalism" worked out by Edgar S. Brightman.[85] More recently, as we noted earlier, several thinkers in the vanguard of Protestant theology have attempted to go "beyond supernaturalism" as the necessary condition of an adequate theology for our time. Of this development, the position set forth in Robinson's *Honest to God* is both a symbol and a convenient summary.

Yet, significant as this all is in supporting the demand I am here making for a new Christian theism, it does not mean that Protestant theologians have already succeeded in meeting this demand. One of the most frequently expressed reactions to the leading postliberal theologians is that they are long on criticisms of supernaturalism, but short on an adequate constructive alternative. Sometimes, very likely,

[83] Cf. Walter Schulz's essay in *Der Gottesgedanke im Abendland,* ed. Albert Schaefer, Stuttgart: W. Kohlhammer Verlag, 1964, pp. 89–108. The other contributions to this symposium are also relevant to the problem of the present essay.

[84] In addition to James' *Will to Believe,* pp. 1–215, see especially his later formulation in *A Pluralistic Universe,* New York: Longmans, Green & Co., 1909.

[85] See especially *The Problem of God,* New York: Abingdon Press, 1930.

this reaction is little more than a defense against the unsettling effects of new ways of thinking. But it would be a mistake, in my judgment, to suppose that the constructive efforts of Bultmann, Bonhoeffer, and Tillich are free of any but minor defects. It seems clear to me that the work of all of these men exhibits one fundamental weakness that will have to be corrected if supernaturalism is really to be overcome. This weakness may be described as an inadequacy in fundamental concepts, which takes one or the other of two different forms. Either the conceptuality these theologians employ is insufficiently developed, so that what they mean when they speak of God is left obscure and uncertain, or else their conception of God is still determined by the same metaphysical-theological premises by which the supernaturalism they seek to transcend is itself determined. It will be instructive now, before proceeding to outline a possible alternative, to consider briefly both forms of this conceptual inadequacy.

Some of the most arresting passages in Bonhoeffer's *Letters and Papers from Prison* are those in which he speaks of "a suffering God" as at once "the God of the Bible" and the positive alternative to the God of traditional religion and metaphysics.

The God who makes us live in this world without using him as a working hypothesis is the God before whom we are ever standing. Before God and with him we live without God. God allows himself to be edged out of the world and onto the cross. God is weak and powerless in the world, and that is exactly the way, the only way, in which he can be with us and help us. . . . only a suffering God can help. To this extent we may say that the process . . . by which the world came of age was an abandonment of a false conception of God, and a clearing of the decks for the God of the Bible, who conquers power and space in the world by his weakness. This must be the starting point for our "worldly" interpretation.[86]

Again, Bonhoeffer writes:

"Christians range themselves with God in his suffering; that is what distinguishes them from the heathen." . . . That is the exact opposite of what the religious man expects from God. Man is challenged to participate in the sufferings of God at the hands of a godless world.

He must therefore plunge himself into the life of a godless world, without attempting to gloss over its ungodliness with a veneer of religion or trying to transfigure it. He must live a "worldly" life and so participate in the suffering of God. He *may* live a worldly life as one emancipated from all false religions and obligations. To be a Christian does not mean

[86] *Op. cit.,* p. 164.

to be religious in a particular way, to cultivate some particular form of asceticism (as a sinner, a penitent or a saint), but to be a man. It is not some religious act which makes a Christian what he is, but participation in the suffering of God in the life of the world.[87]

On the face of it, the God of whom Bonhoeffer here speaks seems to be a radically different reality from the wholly absolute God of traditional theism. Indeed, as a God who allows us to be utterly free and responsible and is of help to us exactly and only by suffering our autonomous decisions, he appears to be just the eminently relative One, whom we have identified as the only God of a secular faith. The difficulty, however, is that it is impossible to be certain of this, given no more than Bonhoeffer ever tells us. All his statements about God, expressed as they are in concrete language that is obviously meta-phorical, cry out for a conceptual clarification that he nowhere pro-vides. Hence one can never be sure whether God as he views him is to be conceived as really related to the world and affected by it in his very being, or whether, as for supernaturalism, all the talk about God's suffering our actions is merely symbolic and not finally to be taken seriously. I realize, naturally, that Bonhoeffer's proposals in these letters are at best hints and suggestions which he was never given the opportunity to work out. The fact remains that what he offers in the way of a constructive statement about God is so insufficiently developed conceptually that it presents no clear alterna-tive to the traditional theism it is intended to supplant.

In the case of Tillich, on the other hand, it is a second form of conceptual inadequacy that invites criticism. Unlike Bonhoeffer—and, in a different way, Bultmann as well[88]—Tillich has developed a conception of God that, with all its modern elements, has something of the same metaphysical scope and depth as that of classical theism. In doing this, his intention, as he expresses it, has been to go "beyond naturalism and supranaturalism."[89] By this he means that an ade-quate doctrine of God must overcome both pantheism and traditional theism, while still doing justice to the legitimate motive in each posi-tion. Accordingly, it must represent God as "self-transcendent," as

[87] *Ibid.,* p. 166.

[88] Bultmann's treatment of the problem of God is considered in some detail below, pp. 170 ff. See also my essay in William L. Reese and Eugene Freeman (eds.), *Process and Divinity: The Hartshorne Festschrift,* La Salle, Ill.: Open Court Publishing Co., 1964, pp. 493–513.

[89] *Systematic Theology,* Vol. II, Chicago: The University of Chicago Press, 1957, pp. 5–10.

the all-inclusive ground of whatever exists, which yet infinitely transcends the beings of which it is the ground. In developing his doctrine,
however, Tillich continues to assume with classical theists that the
fundamental concept in terms of which God must be conceived is that
of absolute, unchanging "being." Hence he holds that God is not *a*
being, but "being-itself," which is completely beyond all relativity and
change and therefore—except for this one dubiously literal assertion—can be thought of and spoken about only symbolically. Tillich
sharply objects, to be sure, to the implication of the words, *"only*
symbolically." Yet, as careful criticism of his position has shown, the
implication has its point.[90] While God as what Tillich calls "creative
life" is symbolically, though not literally, relative and changing, God
as "being-itself" (or in some places, even, "the absolute") is not only
symbolically, but also *literally non*relative and chang*eless*.[91]

Consequently, far from going beyond the alternatives of supernaturalism and naturalism, Tillich's position actually remains sus-
pended uncertainly between them. If he stresses the theistic motive of
God's transcendence of other beings, then, since "being-itself" literally excludes all relativity and change, God is in the strictest sense
something merely alongside other beings, related to them only externally. If, on the other hand, Tillich emphasizes the motive of God's all-
inclusiveness, the same reason requires that the relativity and change
which we experience in beings other than God be ultimately unreal,
and so his doctrine becomes indistinguishable from a Spinozistic
pantheism.

The purpose of these criticisms is in no sense to do justice to the
important contributions of Tillich and Bonhoeffer toward a new
theism. Their point, instead, is simply to indicate why, even where the
task of developing such a theism has been most clearly seen and
resolutely accepted, it still has not been adequately accomplished.
Because the understanding of God that these theologians present is
either left conceptually undeveloped or is itself decisively shaped by
the concepts of classical metaphysics, they fail to set forth an
alternative in which supernaturalism is in principle overcome. Of

[90] See Charles Hartshorne's essay in Charles W. Kegley and Robert W.
Bretall (eds.), *The Theology of Paul Tillich,* New York: The Macmillan Co.,
1952, pp. 164–95.

[91] Cf. *Systematic Theology,* Vol. I, Chicago: The University of Chicago
Press, 1951, p. 270. For the use of the term "the absolute" to refer to God, see
p. 239, also pp. 235, 242. In his reply to Hartshorne (Charles W. Kegley and
Robert W. Bretall [eds.], *op. cit.,* p. 331), Tillich says, puzzlingly enough, "for
many years I have avoided the term 'absolute' with reference to God."

course, no theologian can ever be wholly successful in securing concepts suitable to his purposes. The problem of the adequate conceptuality—or, as Bultmann puts it, of the " 'right' philosophy"[92] —is the perennial problem of any theology aspiring to an adequacy always beyond its grasp. Moreover, because the concepts available in a given situation are always a matter of the theologian's historical destiny, he is often forced to express his intentions within limits that make their adequate expression impossible. Yet, for the very same reason, he is also sometimes given opportunities for constructive statement which, provided he recognizes and lays hold of them, enable him to achieve a degree of adequacy denied to his predecessors.

I hold that ours today is the second kind of situation and that Protestant theology now has at its disposal just the conceptual resources which make a relatively more adequate Christian theism a possibility. Among the most significant intellectual achievements of the twentieth century has been the creation at last of a neoclassical alternative to the metaphysics and philosophical theology of our classical tradition. Especially through the work of Alfred North Whitehead and, in the area usually designated "natural theology," of Charles Hartshorne, the ancient problems of philosophy have received a new, thoroughly modern treatment, which in its scope and depth easily rivals the so-called *philosophia perennis*.[93] It is my belief that the conceptuality provided by this new philosophy enables us so to conceive the reality of God that we may respect all that is legitimate in modern secularity, while also fully respecting the distinc-

---

[92] H. W. Bartsch (ed.), *Kerygma und Mythos*, Vol. II, Hamburg: Herbert Reich-Evangelischer Verlag, 1952, pp. 191–95 (English translation by R. H. Fuller in H. W. Bartsch [ed.], *Kerygma and Myth*, New York: Harper & Row, 2d ed., 1961, pp. 191–96).

[93] The most complete and technical formulation of Whitehead's metaphysics is given in *Process and Reality: An Essay in Cosmology*, New York: The Macmillan Co., 1929. The others of his many writings of greatest relevance for the problem of this essay are *Religion in the Making*, New York: The Macmillan Co., 1926; *Adventures of Ideas*, New York: The Macmillan Co., 1933, especially Part III; and *Modes of Thought*, New York: The Macmillan Co., 1938. In addition to the works of Hartshorne already referred to, see especially *Beyond Humanism: Essays in the New Philosophy of Nature*, Chicago: Willett, Clark & Co., 1937; *The Divine Relativity: A Social Conception of God*, New Haven: Yale University Press, 1948; and *Reality as Social Process: Studies in Metaphysics and Religion*, Glencoe, Ill.: The Free Press, 1953. For a discussion of the contribution of Martin Heidegger's *Sein und Zeit*, Halle: Max Niemeyer Verlag, 1927, to the same end, see below, pp. 144–63.

tive claims of Christian faith itself. In the rest of the essay, I shall try to give the reasons for this belief.

The starting-point for a genuinely new theistic conception is what Whitehead speaks of as "the reformed subjectivist principle."[94] According to this principle, we can give an adequate answer to the metaphysical question of the meaning of "reality" only by imaginatively generalizing "elements disclosed in the analysis of the experiences of subjects." In other words, the principle requires that we take as the experiential basis of all our most fundamental concepts the primal phenomenon of our own existence as experiencing subjects or selves.

To adhere to this requirement is to be led ineluctably to a distinctly different kind of metaphysics and philosophical theology from those of the classical tradition. As not only Whitehead, but also Heidegger and others have made clear, the characteristics of classical philosophy all derive from its virtually exclusive orientation away from the primal phenomenon of selfhood toward the secondary phenomenon of the world constituted by the experience of our senses. It assumes that the paradigmatic cases of reality are the objects of ordinary perception—such things as tables and chairs, and persons as we may know them by observing their behavior—and from these objects it constructs its fundamental concepts or categories of interpretation. The chief of these categories is that of "substance" or "being," understood as that which is essentially nontemporal and lacking in real internal relations to anything beyond itself. Insofar as the self is focused by classical philosophy, it, too, is interpreted in these categories and thus conceived as a special kind of substance. As soon, however, as we orient our metaphysical reflection to the self as we actually experience it, as itself the primal ground of our world of perceived objects, this whole classical approach is, in the Heideggerian sense of the word, "dismantled" (*destruiert*). Whatever else the self is, it is hardly a substance which, in Descartes' phrase, "requires nothing but itself in order to exist,"[95] nor is it altogether without intrinsic temporal structure. To the contrary, the very being of the self is relational or social; and it is nothing if not a process of change involving the distinct modes of present, past, and future.

[94] *Process and Reality*, pp. 252 f.
[95] *The Philosophical Works of Descartes*, Vol. I, trans. E. S. Haldane and G. R. T. Ross, Cambridge: Cambridge University Press, 1911, p. 239 (*Principles of Philosophy*, LI).

To exist as a self, as each of us does, is always to be related, first of all, to the intimate world constituted by one's own body. What I think and feel has its most direct effects on my own brain cells and central nervous system, and thence on the rest of the organism in which I as a self am incarnate. Likewise, what most directly affects me as a conscious subject is just the incredibly complex state of that same organism in which I as a self participate by immediate sympathetic feeling. By means of my body, then, I am also affected by, and in turn affect, the larger whole of things beyond myself. But, whether directly or indirectly, I am really related to an encompassing society of other beings and am a self at all only by reason of that real relatedness. No less constitutive of my selfhood is its essential temporality. I know myself most immediately only as an ever-changing sequence of occasions of experience, each of which is the present integration of remembered past and anticipated future into a new whole of significance. My life history continually leads through moments of decision in which I must somehow determine what both I and those with whom I am related are to be. Selecting from the heritage of the already actual and the wealth of possibility awaiting realization, I freely fashion myself in creative interaction with a universe of others who also are not dead but alive.

If we begin by taking the self as thus experienced as paradigmatic for reality as such, the result is a complete revolution of classical metaphysics. It thereupon becomes clear that real internal relation to others and intrinsic temporality are not "mixed perfections" peculiar to finite beings such as ourselves, but "simple perfections" inherent in the meaning of "reality" in the most fundamental use of the word. In consequence, the chief category for finally interpreting anything real can no longer be "substance" or "being" (as traditionally understood), but must be "process" or "creative becoming," construed as that which is in principle social and temporal. Whatever is, is to be conceived, in the last analysis, either as an instance of, or an element in, such creative becoming and thus as somehow analogous to our own existence as selves.

By *this* "analogy of being," however, God, too, must be conceived as a genuinely temporal and social reality, and therefore as radically different from the wholly timeless and unrelated Absolute of traditional theism. This is not to say that God is to be thought of as only one more instance of creative becoming alongside all the others. As we saw earlier (Section 2), the idea of God cannot be thought at all unless that to which it refers is in all ways truly supreme, a unique reality qualitatively different from everything else. But this may all be granted, indeed, insisted upon, even though one still maintains that God must be conceived in strict analogy with ourselves. The whole point of any *analogia entis* is to enable one to think and speak of God in meaningful concepts, while yet acknowledging that those concepts apply to him only in an eminent sense, which is in principle different from that intended in their other uses. All that a valid method of analogy requires is that the eminence attributed to God really follow from, rather than contradict, the positive meaning of our fundamental concepts as given them by experience. Just this, of course, as we saw from Aquinas' interpretation of the divine knowledge, the classical practice of analogy is unable to do. Because it rests on the premise that God can be in no sense really relative or temporal, it can say that he "knows" or "loves" only by contradicting the meaning of those words as we otherwise use them.

On neoclassical premises, this difficulty, along with innumerable others, is at last removed.[96] God is now conceived as precisely the unique or in all ways perfect instance of creative becoming, and so as the one reality which is eminently social and temporal. Instead of being merely the barren Absolute, which by definition can be really related to nothing, God is in truth related to everything, and that through an immediate sympathetic participation of which our own relation to our bodies is but an image. Similarly, God is no longer thought of as utterly unchangeable and empty of all temporal distinctions. Rather, he, too, is understood to be continually in process of self-creation, synthesizing in each new moment of his experience the whole of achieved actuality with the plenitude of possibility as yet unrealized.

This implies, naturally, that God is by analogy a living and even growing God and that he is related to the universe of other beings somewhat as the human self is related to its body. And yet, just as surely implied is that God is even in these respects the truly eminent or perfect reality, whose unsurpassability by others is a matter of principle, not simply of fact.[97] If God is the *eminently* temporal and

---

[96] See below, pp. 156 f.

[97] This is commonly overlooked by critics of neoclassical theism. Thus, for instance, John Macquarrie (*Twentieth Century Religious Thought: The Frontiers of Philosophy and Theology, 1900–1960,* New York: Harper & Row, 1963, p. 277) questions whether a conception of God such as Whitehead's and Hartshorne's is "satisfying *religiously*," since God "becomes to some extent a God who is 'on his way,' so to speak, a God who in one way or another is not yet complete in his perfection, a natural God rather than a supernatural God."

changing One, to whose time and change there can be neither beginning nor end, then he must be just as surely the One who is also eternal and unchangeable. *That* he is ever-changing is itself the product or effect of no change whatever, but is in the strictest sense changeless, the immutable ground of change as such, both his own and all others. Likewise, the notion that God is not utterly immaterial or bodiless ("without body, parts, or passions"), but, on the contrary, is the *eminently* incarnate One establishes a qualitative difference between his being and everything else. The human self, as we noted, is incarnate in the world only in a radically inferior fashion. It directly interacts with little more than its own brain cells, and so is always a localized self, limited by an encompassing external environment. As the eminent Self, by radical contrast, God's sphere of interaction or body is the whole universe of nondivine beings, with each one of which his relation is unsurpassably immediate and direct. His only environment is wholly internal, which means that he can never be localized in any particular space and time but is omnipresent. Hence, just because God is the *eminently* relative One, there is also a sense in which he is strictly absolute. His being related to all others is itself relative to nothing, but is the absolute ground of any and all real relationships, whether his own or those of his creatures.

Macquarrie's question, like the vagueness of his language ("to some extent," "so to speak," "in one way or another"), betrays that he has missed the point of the neoclassical view of God. That point is not that God is growing and therefore is "a God who is not or who is not yet completely perfect," but that "growing" is itself a wholly positive conception, of which, as of *all* positive conceptions, God is the eminent or perfect exemplification. In other words, the new theism asserts that God *is* "completely perfect" *in whatever sense these words have any coherent meaning* and then questions whether the old use of the words is not, in part, meaningless. It asks, for example, whether the very idea of *actus purus,* of the simultaneous actualization of *all* (even incompossible) possibilities of being and value, is not an incoherent idea, given what we mean by "actuality" and "possibility." If its answer to this question is correct, then a God who is, in the right sense, "on his way" could not be less, but only infinitely more perfect than a God who is "pure actuality," since the latter could be at most merely nonsense. In fairness to Macquarrie and others, however, it must be admitted that even the most careful neoclassical theists have sometimes made their point in a misleading way—as when they have said that God "is perfect and complete in some respects, but not in all" (Charles Hartshorne, *Reality as Social Process,* p. 155). Although, in context, the meaning of such a statement ought to be clear, it nevertheless reinforces a classical conception (and, by the new theist's lights, a total misconception) of what "perfection" alone can properly mean. This is hardly the first case, however, where an attempt to make a radically new philosophical point has been in part betrayed by the very conceptions it wishes to overcome.

In its way, therefore, a neoclassical conception of God's reality incorporates all the "metaphysical attributes" on which classical theists alone insist. For it, too, God is in a literal sense "eternal," "immutable," "impassive," "immaterial"—in brief, the metaphysical Absolute. The difference, however—and it is radical—is that God is now conceived not as simply identical with the Absolute, but as the supremely relative Self or Thou who includes the Absolute as the abstract principle of his own concrete identity. In other words, the traditional attributes of God are all reconceived on the analogical basis provided by our own existence as selves. Just as in our case, our defining characteristics are but abstract elements in our concrete experiences, so in the case of God, his attributes are really only abstractions. As such, they define that sense of his eminence or perfection which is indeed statically complete, an absolute maximum. But, because they are in themselves nothing more than abstractions, they are far from constituting the whole of his perfection. That, to the contrary, is nothing merely abstract, but something unimaginably concrete: the ever new synthesis into his own everlasting and all-embracing life of all that has been or ever shall be.

Such, in its main outlines, is the new theism I am proposing. From a classical standpoint, the principal objection to it is almost certain to be that it is not really theism at all, but simply another form of an untenable pantheism. After all, it even goes so far as to conceive God as having a body and as therefore necessarily dependent on a world of other beings.

To this objection, I reply that if the view I have outlined is to be called "pantheism," it is nevertheless at one point significantly different from the views of Spinoza, Hegel, Schleiermacher, Royce, and others, which have also been called by that name. The conventional assumption that the pantheism of these thinkers and the old theism are logically contradictory of one another obscures the fact that both conceptions rest on the same metaphysical premises. They share, namely, a common monopolar denial that God can be in any way conceived as genuinely temporal or related to others.[98] Given this denial, one is unavoidably faced with two choices, of which the positions of Aquinas and Spinoza respectively may be taken to be representative. Either one must conceive God with Aquinas as wholly external to the world, something merely alongside it, and so but part of a whole somehow including God and the world together; or else

[98] Cf. the development of this point by Hartshorne and Reese in *Philosophers Speak of God,* pp. 1 ff.

one must say with Spinoza that it is God who includes the world, but only so as to make the world itself wholly necessary and our experience of its contingency and dependence an illusion. When faced with this dilemma, classical theists typically treat the absurdities of their own position as "mystery" and exploit those of the pantheist's as doing at least as much violence to our actual experience. Thus Frederick C. Copleston, in discussing this very issue, assures us that "Obviously, we are here in the region of mystery; in the region of contradiction, some would say," and then goes on to conclude: "Pantheism does nothing to diminish the difficulties which may be thought to accompany theism. It involves one in denying or explaining away or in falsifying the foundation from which all our metaphysical reflections must start, namely, the real multiplicity of distinct finite things with which we are acquainted in experience."[99] The truth, however, is that neither of the traditional choices offers the least hope of permitting us to solve what another Roman Catholic theologian has recently called "the central problem of Christian philosophy—the problem of the coexistence and coagency of the infinite and the finite, the necessary and the contingent, the eternal and the temporal, the absolute and the relative."[100]

But, on the dipolar view of God outlined here, this "problem of synthesis" seems at last to have found a solution—and that in a way which is as far removed from classical pantheism as from its traditional theistic alternative. By conceiving God as infinite personal existence or creative becoming, one can assert God's independence of the actual world (in his abstract identity) without saying he is wholly external to it, and one can affirm his inclusion of the actual world (in his concrete existence) without denying that the world as actual is completely contingent and radically dependent on him as its sole necessary ground. This is to say that, on the new conception, the real motive of the traditional doctrine of *creatio ex nihilo a deo,* which is the theological point at issue in any warranted rejection of pantheism, can be fully expressed. What is at stake in that doctrine (as even Aquinas in a way saw) is not the claim that God once existed in lonely isolation, as the Creator of no actual world of creatures. Its point, rather, is to deny, against all forms of metaphysical dualism, that there is any being or principle save God alone which is the necessary ground of whatever exists or is even possible. This denial,

---

[99] *Aquinas,* Harmondsworth: Penguin Books Ltd., 1955, pp. 139, 141.
[100] John Courtney Murray, *op. cit.,* p. 92.

however, is an essential implication of the new theism, as surely as it ever was of the old. Although, for the new view, one cannot meaningfully claim that God was ever without *some* actual world of creatures, any such world was itself created "out of nothing," in the sense that there once was when it was not. Its real potentiality, of course, lay in the conjoint actuality of God and of the creatures constituting the precedent actual world (or worlds). But to suppose that this in any way denies *creatio ex nihilo* can appeal to no valid theological warrant and runs the risk of involving obvious absurdity besides. After all, children do have parents; and classical theism itself has always been insistent (however incoherently) on the real agency of "secondary causes." Furthermore—and this is the essential point— no actual world with which God ever co-operates in creating a new world is in any sense necessary or eternal. It, too, was once his completely free, contingent creation, so that his prerogatives of strict necessity and eternity of existence are shared by him with no one, but belong to him alone.[101]

In sum, the point at which the new theism most obviously differs from the old is the very point at which it is also utterly different from what is properly called "pantheism"—namely, its insistence that reality as such and, to an eminent degree, God are by their very natures temporal and social. Because of this insistence, the new view discloses the older conceptions to be related logically not as contradictories, but as mere contraries, to which it is in each case the real contradictory or alternative.

There is ample reason, therefore, to dismiss the charge of pantheism and to claim that the new conception is in its way genuinely theistic. But just as evident and, to my mind, considerably more important is that it is a way of conceiving God's reality which is able to do justice to modern secularity. Indeed, the preceding exposition

---

[101] Since the new theism has sometimes been designated, especially by Hartshorne, as "panentheism," it is of interest to note what is said of this term in Karl Rahner and Herbert Vorgrimler, *Kleines theologisches Wörterbuch,* Freiburg: Herder Verlag, 1961, p. 275: "This form of pantheism does not intend simply to identify the world and God monistically (God = the 'all'), but intends, instead, to conceive the 'all' of the world 'in' God as his inner modification and appearance, even if God is not exhausted by the 'all.' The doctrine of such a 'being-in' of the world in God is false and heretical when (and *only* when) it denies the creation and the distinction of the world from God (not only of God from the world). . . . Otherwise it is a challenge to ontology to think the relation between absolute and finite being both more exactly and more deeply (i.e., by grasping the reciprocal relation between unity and difference which increase in the same degree)."

should have made clear that this form of theism offers a full reflective explication of the understanding of God which is present at least implicitly in any serious affirmation of the secular. We saw that, although such an affirmation necessarily rests on an equally emphatic affirmation of God's reality, the only God it thus affirms is the dipolar ground of the ultimate significance of our life in the world. It is just such a God, however, whom the premises of a neoclassical metaphysics enable and even require us to conceive. Given these premises, God both may and must be thought of as the eminently relative One who makes possible "a general confidence about the future," an assurance of the final worth of our life which will not be disappointed.

Thus we may at last render really intelligible our deep conviction as modern men that it is our own secular decisions and finite processes of creative becoming which are the very stuff of the "really real" and so themselves somehow of permanent significance. Because God himself is most immediately affected by all that we are and do, the future for which we ultimately live our lives is neither merely our own nor that of others as limited as ourselves, but also the unending future of God's own creative becoming, in which we are each given to share. It is his self-creation that is the ultimate cause advanced or retarded by all our lesser causes and their issues; and the motive finally inspiring our own decisions as men, in relation to one another and to all our fellow creatures, is so to maximize the being and joy of the world as to increase as fully as we can the concrete perfection of his everlasting life. So, too, are our sufferings at last conceivable as having the nature and importance our secularity prompts us to claim for them. No longer must they be thought of as ultimately indifferent, as secularism and supernaturalism alike imply; nor need we heed the pantheist's discouraging word that they are the wholly necessary parts of what James once described, characteristically, as "one vast instantaneous co-implicated completeness."[102] Rather, our sufferings also may be conceived as of a piece with a reality which is through-and-through temporal and social. They are the partly avoidable, partly unavoidable, products of finite-free choices and, like everything else, are redolent of eternal significance. Because they, too, occur only within the horizon of God's all-encompassing sympathy, they are the very opposite of the merely indifferent. When they can be prevented, the responsibility for their prevention may now be realized in all its infinite importance; and, when they must be borne with, even that

[102] *A Pluralistic Universe*, p. 322.

may be understood to have the consolation which alone enables any of us to bear them.

Only slightly less important is that the new theism is also free of the incoherence, of the antinomies and contradictions, that make the old supernaturalism incredible to the modern mind. As we saw, the reason for this incoherence is the classical metaphysical denial that God can be in any sense temporal and relative, which stands in stark contradiction to Scripture's representation of God as the eminent Self or Thou. But, with the new metaphysical premises, by contrast, there is no longer any basis for such a contradiction. While the new theism does indeed conceive God as both absolute and relative, it so understands these two aspects of his nature that they may be seen to be complementary, instead of contradictory. By completely reversing the classical procedure and thinking of God as, first of all, the eminently relative One, the new view construes God's absoluteness as simply the abstract structure or identifying principle of his eminent relativity. It is thereby able to show what could never be shown by classical theism, how the Thou with the greatest conceivable degree of real relatedness to others—namely, relatedness to *all* others—is for that very reason the most truly absolute Thou any mind can conceive. It can similarly show how maximum temporality entails strict eternity; maximum capacity for change, unsurpassable immutability; and maximum passivity to the actions of others, the greatest possible activity in all their numberless processes of self-creation.

I cannot develop the details of this demonstration, to make clear how with this, so to speak, great reversal, the main antinomies of traditional theism—including the allegedly insoluble problem of evil—are all capable of resolution. But I trust it is clear at least in principle why the new theism can overcome the theoretical incoherence which also precludes supernaturalism as a live option for secular man.

There remains the question, crucial for Protestant theology, whether this new view can also do justice to the faith in God's reality decisively re-presented in Jesus Christ. Granted that it is a form of theism which seems possible for secular man, does it also make possible, as I believe, a distinctively *Christian* theism?

Let us be clear from the outset that no answer to this question can ever be completely convincing. What we are given to understand of Christ is always dependent in part on our own concepts, so any attempt to justify those concepts always tends to be circular. We may simply read out of revelation a warrant for the conceptions we first had to read into it in order to understand it at all. Nevertheless, in this, as in any other process of interpretation, it is possible to reach judgments that are at least relatively sure. Some conceptualities clearly seem more appropriate than others to the witness to God in Christ which is given in Holy Scripture.

If the argument of this essay is correct, the concepts taken over by Christian theologians from classical metaphysics can only be pronounced inadequate when judged by *this* criterion of appropriateness. From the standpoint of theology's total concern and task, the objection to supernaturalism is not simply that it is an impossible conception for contemporary men, but that it also makes impossible an appropriate theological witness to the God of Jesus Christ. By conceiving God as, first of all, the metaphysical Absolute, traditional theists completely reverse the priority of Scripture, thereby creating a totally different theological problem. Now the question becomes the one endlessly discussed in the tradition, "How can the Absolute somehow be understood as personal?" instead of "How can the eminently personal One be appropriately conceived in his absoluteness?"[103] By the same criterion, however, the new theism proposed here seems immeasurably more adequate. For it, just as for Scripture, the first (and last!) thing to be said about God is that he is the supreme Self or Thou, whose absolute relativity or all-embracing love is the beginning and end of man and, indeed, of the whole creation (cf. Romans 8). Is it really too much to say, then, that this form of theism is the expression in abstract philosophical concepts of the same understanding of God represented more concretely in the mythologoumena of Holy Scripture? Is one unreasonable in claiming that it is the "theory" for which the scriptural myths provide the "model"—and that theory and model together effect *one* disclosure of the encompassing mystery of our existence?[104]

The only way to answer these questions, so far as they can be

---

[103] Cf., e.g., Anselm's question in *Proslogium*, VIII: "But how art thou compassionate, and, at the same time, passionless? For if thou art passionless, thou dost not feel sympathy; and if thou dost not feel sympathy, thy heart is not wretched from sympathy for the wretched; but this it is to be compassionate. . . . How, then, art thou compassionate and not compassionte, O Lord, unless because [and this, incredibly enough, is Anselm's answer to his question] thou art compassionate in terms of our experience, and not compassionate in terms of thy being" (*St. Anselm: Proslogium; Monologium; etc.*, trans. S. N. Deane, La Salle, Ill.: Open Court Publishing Co., 1903, p. 13).

[104] See Ian T. Ramsey, *Models and Mystery*, London: Oxford University Press, 1964; also Frederick Ferré, "Mapping the Logic of Models in Science and Theology," *Christian Scholar*, Spring, 1963, pp. 9–39.

answered at all, is to make use of the new conceptuality in the actual hermeneutical process, continually testing it against the designations of God in the texts of Scripture.[105] But, if the answer should prove to be the one I am implying, it would be hard to exaggerate the importance of the new theism to Protestant theology. The whole task of this theology, finally, is to provide a critical, constructive interpretation of the understanding of faith in God to which witness is borne in Holy Scripture. To accomplish this task, however, requires a fully developed conceptuality which is understandable in the present situation *and* appropriate to the essential claims of the scriptural witness. My suggestion is that the new theism is adequate by the second criterion as well as the first—or at least is sufficiently superior by this standard to the other available options to deserve the most serious testing.

This suggestion is further supported when one considers the new theism in relation to the response to the scriptural witness historically represented by Protestant Christianity. As often noted, Protestantism's most distinctive claims all share a certain paradoxical or dialectical character. Beginning with its central doctrine of justification by grace and faith alone, all its main teachings seem either to affirm or to imply what Kierkegaard spoke of as "the infinite qualitative difference" between God and the world. On the one hand, God

[105] Thus one should even ask, for example, whether the new theism enables us so to conceive God that we may meaningfully pray to him as Scripture plainly enjoins us to do. Of course, those who regard this as *the* test question often betray an understanding of prayer that is not only superstitious from the standpoint of secularity, but also sub-Christian by the criterion of faith itself. Where man's prayers have been subjected to the "permanent revolution" effected by the Christian witness, they are invariably defined by two characteristics: first, they are always addressed to the One whom Jesus calls Father (in accordance with the old maxim, *oratio semper dirigatur ad Patrem*); and, second, they are for that reason always offered "through" or "in the name of" Jesus Christ our Lord. But this means that, whatever else Christian prayers are, they can never be a matter either of informing God as to what he otherwise would not know or of importuning him to do what, but for our prayers, he is unwilling to do. If we are Christians, we pray, as Luther suggests, not to instruct God, but to instruct ourselves. Our "praying teaches us to recognize who we are and who God is, and to learn what we need and where we are to look for it and find it" (*Luther's Works,* Vol. XXI, ed. Jaroslav Pelikan. St. Louis: Concordia Publishing House, 1956, p. 145; cf. pp. 143 f.). But, even on this understanding, prayer has no sense, unless God himself is genuinely affected by all that we say and do. The minimal condition of our praying, as of our life generally, is that it have an ultimate significance, that it be "heard" by God. This condition the new theism clearly seems able to meet in a way that the old view, in principle, never could.

is said to be "wholly other" than the world, and the world by itself utterly secular or profane; on the other hand, the very otherness of God is understood as his being for the world, not against it, so that the world in itself is affirmed to be of ultimate significance. This genuinely dialectical vision of God's relation to the world has always been the despair of Catholic interpreters of our common Christian heritage; and it is evident that even Protestant theologians have only seldom caught a glimpse of its full implications. Too often, it has seemed to combine, as it were, the worst of both worlds, what with an extreme otherworldliness, which is alleged to destroy nature instead of perfecting it, and an extreme this-worldliness, which its critics claim dulls man's sense for his final supernatural end. Yet it is clear, I think, that, if anything is to be called "the spirit of Protestantism," it is just this dialectical vision of God and the world and the total style of Christian life to which it gives rise. And equally clear is the reason why Protestants tend to share this vision almost as if by instinct: from the beginning, their chief inspiration has not been the spirit which informs the rich culture of classical antiquity, but the quite different Spirit who moves over the pages of Holy Scripture, witnessing simply that "God is love." It is precisely and only eminent love, in the distinctively scriptural sense of pure personal relationship, that could relate God to his world by such a profound dialectic of difference and identity. But the question the Protestant theologian must ask is how this eminent love is to be clarified *conceptually,* if not by means of something like the new theism. Is it not evident, in fact, that this dipolar theism is an analysis in the general terms of philosophy of just that love and its dialectic?

Throughout its history, Protestant theology has rarely succeeded in bringing together fidelity to the scriptural witness, to the word of God's "pure unbounded love," and constructive formulations of undoubted conceptual power. When it has been most systematic, its concepts have usually been determined in one way or another by classical metaphysics and so have tended to obscure its evangelical inspiration. In other cases, when it has remained truest to that inspiration, its conceptual structure has often been unclear and uncertain, thus making it seem outside of, or even opposed to, the rest of our reflective life. But, with the resources provided by the new theism and, more generally, by a neoclassical metaphysics, there is every reason why this fateful divorce should no longer be necessary. Now, at last, we can develop a comprehensive philosophical outlook for which the words "God is love" are no longer foolishness, but the very sum of wisdom. In its terms, therefore, it should prove possible to bear witness not only through preaching and worship, but through theological formulations as well, to the peculiar paradox of Protestant Christianity—that God is radically other than the world and never to be confused with it, but that, *just for this reason,* the world itself has an unconditioned worth and significance.

It may appear strange and even suspicious that a form of theism which seems genuinely possible for secular man should turn out to be thus conformable to Christian faith. But such strangeness should be dispelled as soon as it is recalled that neither secularity itself nor the new metaphysics in which it is most completely expressed is without a history. The evidence is clear that both phenomena trace their origin to the distinctively Christian understanding of existence, especially in its Protestant form. Thus, as many others have pointed out, even the ethos of modern science must be understood against the background of the Christian doctrine of creation, with its claim that the world is utterly secular and therefore open to the most probing inquiry, and yet is also sufficiently significant to be worthy of our most careful attention.[106] And so, too, with our modern moral attitude, our insistence, in the words of a contemporary philosopher, that "Morality is made for man, not man for morality."[107] As is clear even from the allusion of this statement, our secular emphasis on man's full autonomy as moral agent and on the surpassing importance of his present decisions is a principal part of our Christian inheritance.

Consequently, there is nothing strange, much less contradictory, about the notion of a "secular Christianity." Rightly understood, Christianity has always been secular, because in its essence, in the presence in our human history of Jesus Christ, it is simply the representation to man and the world of their ultimate significance within the encompassing mystery of God's love.[108] But it is also only to be expected that neoclassical theism should prove peculiarly transparent to Christian claims. As with the secularity of which it is the integral expression, its roots reach down deep within the soil of Christianity, and it is not to be explained historically except as "secularized" Christian theology.

[106] See, e.g., H. Richard Niebuhr, *op. cit.,* especially pp. 78–89, 127–41.

[107] William K. Frankena, *Ethics,* Englewood Cliffs, N.J.: Prentice-Hall, Inc., 1963, p. 98.

[108] Cf. the parallel development and defense of this judgment in Ronald Gregor Smith, *Secular Christianity,* New York: Harper & Row, 1966, which I have been privileged to read in proof only after these pages were in the press.

Yet, strange or not, the fact seems to be that here is a form of theism that not only is understandable to secular men, but is also appropriate to Christian faith. One can only hope, therefore, that the significance of this fact will not be lost on the Protestant theology of our time. By making resolute use of this "system of thought," theology today should be able, in considerable measure, to accomplish its proper task: to bear witness in the most adequate conceptual form now possible to the reality of God which is re-presented to us all in Jesus Christ.

II

Y

Theology and Objectivity

A problem at the center of recent theological discussion is "The Problem of Nonobjectifying Thinking and Speaking in Contemporary Theology."[1] Although this formulation as such might suggest that the interest behind it is essentially historical, it is evident that the main concern of the discussion quite transcends any merely descriptive treatment of the problem. The real focus of interest is on the systematic or normative issue which this formulation expresses; and the purpose of the present essay is to help to clarify and perhaps even to resolve this issue.

This being so, it will hardly do to remain wholly within the frame of reference in which the issue as thus formulated arises. Questions are to a considerable extent already answers;[2] and when one's controlling purpose is to arrive at a normative judgment on an issue, his first order of business is always to take pains with how the question itself is to be formulated. Recognition of this seems to me nowhere more important than with respect to the assertion that theological thinking and speaking are, or (since the assertion is really normative) ought to be, nonobjectifying. If the previous discussion of this assertion has proved anything, it is that one must first of all unpack the word "nonobjectifying" to see just what kinds of goods it contains, what kinds of questions it is capable of expressing and, therefore, what kinds of answers it also partially determines.

I do not suppose this essay can provide all such clarification as

[1] This was the theme of the Second Consultation on Hermeneutics convened by the Graduate School of Drew University, Madison, New Jersey, April 9–11, 1964. The present essay was originally offered as a contribution to that consultation.

[2] See Felix Cohen, "What Is A Question?" *The Monist,* July, 1929, pp. 350–64 (cited by Susanne K. Langer, *Philosophy in a New Key: A Study in the Symbolism of Reason, Rite, and Art,* New York: Penguin Books, 1948, p. 2).

may be necessary. Yet it can at least make a beginning; and I ask that what follows be considered primarily as an attempt to heighten our self-consciousness about the real issue under discussion. I shall analyze four related yet distinct meanings which the term "nonobjectifying" has disclosed itself to have and in this way try to illumine some of the main alternatives for approaching and answering the principal question. At each stage, I will also seek to enter into discussion with these alternatives, pointing up some of the difficulties they entail and suggesting which of them, if any, indicate the direction in which an adequate answer is most likely to be found. Thus, although the burden of the essay will be analytic and, I hope, clarifying, I will also attempt to develop at least the outlines of a possible constructive position with respect to the underlying issue. To do less than this would seem to me to disappoint the expectation aroused by my title—even if to do more is impossible, given the present status of the discussion and the limitations of a single essay.

Before turning to the analysis, however, I must offer a provisional clarification of the phrase "theological thinking and speaking." Since it is just what is to be understood by this phrase that is the real underlying issue expressed by the original formulation, my own position on this issue can be made clear only by the whole of the subsequent argument. Yet this argument can hardly be either developed or understood unless we have a general idea of the question it is directed toward clarifying and, to some extent, answering. Accordingly, I propose the following preliminary definition of how "thinking" and "speaking" are to be taken when used in connection with the undertaking properly designated "theology." I assume, naturally, that the sense of the word "theology" appropriate here is not the generic sense with which we might properly use it in other contexts, but the specific sense explicitly conveyed by the words "Christian theology."

On this assumption, *theological thinking and speaking are a more or less distinguishable type or level of thinking and speaking about God as apprehended through the witness of faith of Jesus Christ*. It will be noted that this definition leaves open exactly how one is to understand the relation of theology to other possible types or levels of thought and speech about God as known through Christ. This is done deliberately, since one of the purposes of the later discussion will be to clarify this relation. The thing to recognize now is simply that all theological thought and speech are thought and speech having the God of Jesus Christ as their object or referent, although it is not possible, on the view to be developed here, to convert this proposition.

But even this, it may be thought, is a "persuasive definition" that already begs too many of the questions needing clarification. Surely one must recognize that the Christian theologian properly thinks and speaks about all sorts of things other than God and that, if the language he uses is any indication, much of what he thinks and says, when considered out of its total context, is not strictly "about" anything whatever. The point of this objection is well taken, although it does not, I believe, affect the validity of the provisional definition. Even if one grants that Christian theologians do properly think and speak about matters other than God and that assertion of some kind is not the only use to which they put their language, it does not follow that these things account for their being theologians or that they could be such at all apart from the specific difference set forth in the definition. That God is somehow the object of all theological thinking and speaking need not mean—nay, perhaps, cannot mean—that he is the only such object; and one may hold that theological language, when taken in its total context, always functions somehow to assert something without claiming that this is the only function it serves. But far from obvious to me is that one could properly speak of "theology" at all without assuming the minimal meaning suggested by the word as used historically and also re-expressed in the proposed definition—namely, a thinking whose primary object is God as disclosed through the witness of Christian faith and a speaking which, whatever its other uses, intends to assert something meaningful about that same divine object.

This does not mean that some particular concept of God or its corresponding vocable is an essential element in theological thinking and speaking. According to the definition, thought and speech are determined as theological by their actual intentional object or referent, God himself, not by any concept of God or the term expressing it. Therefore, unlike certain verbally similar definitions, the tentative definition of theology given above is not persuasive or tendentious in the sense of covertly assuming some particular conception of God and arbitrarily restricting what may be counted as theological speech. Whether the term be "God" or "the transcendent" or "the unconditioned" or "being-itself," or any number of other terms that readily come to mind, it can very well function as an instance of theological speaking in the sense of the definition. And the same is true, *mutatis mutandis,* of the various conceptualities of which all such terms are the linguistic expressions. If any conceptuality serves in a certain way or at a certain level to conceive God as understood by Christian faith, then it is, on my terms, a theological conceptuality, and the thinking it makes possible is theological thinking.

There are no doubt many other questions that the provisional definition raises. But perhaps enough has been said to provide the essential preliminary clarification, and, in any event, it is necessary now to go on to the analysis itself. Some of the remaining questions will be answered as we proceed, and one definition should come to seem less arbitrary than it may now appear.

1

It may be assumed, I think, that the word "nonobjectifying," which appears in the original formulation of the problem, is the literal English equivalent of a German word formed from the infinitive *objektivieren.* This, then, should be sufficient indication of the general frame of reference presupposed by the formulation. Broadly speaking, one may say that the standpoint thereby revealed is that of the existentialist philosophy and theology which have been such determinative influences on the thought of our century and whose principal exponents are all more or less well known.

One of the hallmarks of such philosophy and theology is the claim that our cognitive encounter with reality is disclosed by careful analysis to have a basic twofold form.[3] On the one hand, there is our original internal awareness of our own existence in relation to the manifold reality encountering us, which awareness in some modification is the most distinctive feature of our being as men, as selves or persons. On the other hand, there is the quite different kind of perception somehow grounded in this original existential awareness. This is our derived external perception of reality distinct from our selves as the object of our ordinary sense experience. I cannot pause here to show how this characteristically existentialist analysis of our knowledge as both "existential" and "objectifying" is directly connected with the Kantian and neo-Kantian analyses that preceded it. But I believe it will be granted that just this analysis, in its context in a certain strand of post-Kantian philosophy, is the natural home of the word *objektivieren,* its various cognates, and their English equivalents. If so, then one may say that the notion of nonobjectifying thinking and speaking is to be understood, first of all, in relation to

[3] A classically simple statement of this claim is Rudolf Bultmann's in "On the Problem of Demythologizing," *Journal of Religion,* April, 1962, pp. 96–102.

this account of our knowledge as, in one of its basic forms, an objectifying knowledge. Accordingly, the first form of the principal question is whether, given the understanding of nonobjectifying thinking and speaking suggested by this account, theology as provisionally defined is nonobjectifying.

So formulated, the question is not difficult to answer, and there is likely to be considerable agreement in answering it. It is widely recognized by contemporary Protestant theologians that theological thinking and speaking are, or ought to be, "nonobjectifying" in this first meaning of the word. This is certainly the case with those whom I have broadly spoken of as existentialist theologians; whether one thinks of Rudolf Bultmann or Paul Tillich or any of several others whose positions are essentially similar, the claim that theology is in this sense nonobjectifying is self-evident. But the same is true of a large number of other theologians whom one would hardly speak of as existentialist in their basic standpoints.

Thus, wherever theologians argue—as perhaps most Protestant theologians today do argue—that there is a difference in principle between the thinking and speaking of science and the thinking and speaking proper to theology, this same claim is, in effect, advanced. This becomes evident as soon as one recognizes that science generally, and the so-called "special sciences" individually, are but developments at a certain level of the objectifying knowledge that is one of the basic forms of our cognitive encounter with ourselves and the things around us. What the scientist thinks and speaks about is reality insofar as it can be made the object of particular external perceptions. Hence, to hold that the theologian's thinking and speaking differ in principle from those of the scientist is to hold in fact, if not in so many words, that theology is in this sense nonobjectifying. A common way of maintaining this in terms made current by the analytic philosophers of our English-speaking tradition is to deny that the meaning of theological assertions is of the same logical type as that of scientific statements. Whereas the test of the meaningfulness of a scientific hypothesis is that it should be capable, in principle, of falsification by external perception, the same test cannot be applied to the distinctive statements of theology, since they are logically different from scientific hypotheses and so incapable of this kind of falsification.

There are theologians, to be sure, who are unwilling to concede that theological thought and speech are nonobjectifying even in this first meaning of the word. Fearing lest this concession imply that theological language asserts nothing at all and thus has some wholly noncognitive use and meaning, they reject any sharp distinction between theology and science and hold that theological statements are, after all, in principle falsifiable. The serious difficulties of this position, however—especially of the device of "eschatological verification" by which some seek to defend it—are notorious, and I myself regard it as untenable.[4] The decisive objection to it is its implication that theological assertions about the being and nature of God are somehow about an actual or potential object of our ordinary sense perception. If such assertions are even "eschatologically" verifiable in the manner of scientific hypotheses, it is not clear to me why they should be considered properly theological assertions at all. Here I would recall Bultmann's insistence that the chief objection to a "mythological" representation of God is not that it comes into conflict with the essential procedure and claims of modern science, but that it seriously misrepresents God's transcendence as apprehended by Christian faith. By objectifying God in the sense of thinking and speaking of him under the same conditions as apply to the objects of our external perception, myth in effect denies God's qualitative difference from all things other than himself and thus fails to express its own intention in an appropriate way. The same would be true, Bultmann argues, of any representation of God in the terms and categories of modern science. Like myth, science can think and speak about reality only as the object of our sense perceptions, and so could represent God only by similarly misrepresenting the uniqueness of his reality as God. Consequently, the main reason for demythologizing and for seeking a theological conceptuality alternative to that of science as well as to myth is, as Bultmann says, "faith itself"—by which he means not only faith's character as a mode of existential self-understanding, but also faith's distinctive apprehension, precisely as such self-understanding, of the transcendent reality of God.[5]

Reference to demythologizing also enables me to introduce a certain refinement in the answer to the first form of the question. If, as I have argued, theological thinking and speaking ought by all

[4] For a summary discussion of these difficulties, see William T. Blackstone, *The Problem of Religious Knowledge,* Englewood Cliffs, N.J.: Prentice-Hall, Inc., 1963, pp. 108–24.

[5] H. W. Bartsch (ed.), *Kerygma und Mythos,* Vol. II, Hamburg: Herbert Reich-Evangelischer Verlag, 1952, p. 207 (English translation by R. H. Fuller in H. W. Bartsch [ed.], *Kerygma and Myth,* New York: Harper & Row, 2d ed., 1961, p. 210).

means to be nonobjectifying in the first meaning of the word, this implies neither that all that has usually been regarded as such thinking and speaking conforms to this norm nor that failure to conform to it *eo ipso* disqualifies thought and speech from any theological relevance. Obviously much of what has been traditionally accepted as theology, to say nothing of the far larger corpus of the church's pretheological witness, is not nonobjectifying even in this first sense. True, if we consider the actual uses of traditional theological language, it becomes clear that, far more often than not, it served, and continues to serve, a rather different primary purpose from that of the language of modern science and of the ordinary objectifying thinking of which such science is the development. Even so, the view that theology should, at least to this extent, be nonobjectifying requires one to say that much which has hitherto passed for theology can no longer be so considered, except as an essentially inadequate approximation to the norm thereby expressed.

On the other hand, one need not conclude that such "theology" is without real theological significance, although one does have to give a revised account of what its significance is. So-called "theological" thinking and speaking that are in this first sense objectifying are related to theology proper not as thought and speech about God of the same type or at the same level, but as part of the pretheological thinking and speaking that I comprehend by the word "witness" and take to be the primary datum of the critical interpretation in which theology properly consists. This is also the view expressed by Bultmann when he stresses that the task of demythologizing is not to *eliminate* mythology, but to make the genuinely hermeneutical effort to *understand* it. In this view, objectifying thinking and speaking about God definitely have a place and, at their own level, maybe even an indispensable place. Yet this place is not that of an essential element in theology itself, but that of a certain level or stratum in the historically given witness to God, which it is the business of theology to understand and critically interpret.[6]

---

[6] In Bultmann's terms, myth has the place of "symbol," "figure" (*Bild*), or "cipher." See, e.g., his *Jesus Christ and Mythology,* New York: Charles Scribner's Sons, 1958, pp. 67–70. Significantly, an almost identical view is expressed by Charles Hartshorne, who holds that religious "symbols" must be interpreted in terms of theological "analogies," which belong to a different "stratum" of "religious discourse" (*The Logic of Perfection and Other Essays in Neoclassical Metaphysics,* La Salle, Ill.: Open Court Publishing Co., 1962, pp. 133–47).

2

We move to the next stage of the analysis by observing that even some of the existentialist philosophers and theologians themselves hold the basic twofold account of our knowledge as either existential or objectifying (in the sense previously explained) to be inexhaustive. They recognize that, in addition to the awareness of ourselves and others through our self-understanding and the perception of reality as the object of our sense experience, there is a third form of knowledge that discloses itself in our being able to distinguish between the other two forms. The type of knowledge illustrated by a phenomenological analysis of our existence and of the basic types of cognition it makes possible is neither existential nor objectifying (again, in the sense previously clarified), but is a distinct type related to, yet different from, these other types. Thus Martin Heidegger, in *Sein und Zeit,* distinguishes between the "existential" (*existenziell*) understanding uniquely present in each individual existence as his own personal encounter with reality and the "existentialist" (*existenzial*) understanding exemplified in a descriptive analysis of the phenomenon of existence in general, such as constitutes the first step toward what he there calls "ontology."[7]

Interestingly, just this distinction opens the way to giving a second meaning to the word "objectifying." The introduction of this ambiguity is perhaps most obvious in Bultmann's use of the word; for him, objectifying thinking and speaking come to include not only modern science and the more basic level of thought and speech of which such science is the methodical development, but also the existentialist analysis that Heidegger takes to be the fundamental task of philosophy.[8] If one asks how this extension of meaning is possible, the most likely answer seems to be that, from the beginning, the objectify-

[7] *Sein und Zeit,* Halle: Max Niemeyer Verlag, 1927, p. 12.

[8] See *Kerygma und Mythos,* Vol. II, pp. 187, 189, where Bultmann refers to existentialist analysis as a "science that speaks of existence without objectifying it to worldly being" and as "a science that is nothing more than the clear and methodical explication of the understanding of existence given with existence itself." On the face of it, Bultmann here seems to deny that existentialist analysis is objectifying. Elsewhere, however, in his discussion with Karl Jaspers (see below), it becomes clear that this is not his intention; and the apparent contradiction is in fact resolvable if one gives due heed to the words "worldly being." What Bultmann here denies is not that existentialist analysis is objectifying, but that it is objectifying in the same sense as modern science.

ing thinking and speaking which have become fully developed in modern science are different from their existential counterparts not simply in one respect but in two. In the first place, they have to do not with our own existence, but with reality as distinct from ourselves. This, one may say, is their difference with respect to the object to which they are directed. But they also differ from existential thinking and speaking in being derived rather than original, peripheral rather than central, with respect to the real origin or center of human existence. Whereas existential thinking and speaking have to do quite directly with the gain or loss of our authentic existence as selves, our thought and speech about the objects of our external perception are only indirectly related to this paramount concern. Hence another familiar way of expressing this second difference between existential and objectifying knowledge is to represent the former as "concerned" or "involved," the latter as "disinterested" or "detached."[9]

However the second difference is expressed, it has to do not with the object of our knowledge, whether ourselves or reality as other than ourselves, but with what one may call the subjective form of our knowledge. In this respect, there is obviously something common between our external perception of objects, particularly in its developed form as science, and the kind of knowledge illustrated by an existentialist analysis such as Heidegger presents in *Sein und Zeit*. As contrasted with our existential self-understanding, such analysis is a reflective matter which has to do only indirectly with realizing our authentic existence and so is (relatively) disinterested instead of concerned, detached instead of involved.

Whatever the reason, Bultmann holds that existentialist understanding is also scientific with respect to its subjective form and must therefore be regarded as objectifying in character. But with this, the words "scientific" and "objectifying" take on new and slightly different meanings, which require a second and correspondingly different formulation of the question as to the character of theological thinking and speaking.

Other existentialists, to be sure, have denied that a scientific analysis of human existence is possible and have refused to accept this more extended meaning of the term "objectifying." Karl Jaspers,

[9] See, e.g., Paul Tillich, *Systematic Theology*, Vol. II, Chicago: The University of Chicago Press, 1957, p. 26.

notably, has held that "the philosophy of existence would at once be lost were it again to believe that it knows [*wissen*] what man is,"[10] and he has insisted on the difference between Heidegger's existentialist analysis and his own "clarification of existence" (*Existenzerhellung*).[11] But, as I have argued elsewhere,[12] Bultmann's reply to Jaspers at this point seems conclusive. Whatever Jaspers' intention, he "cannot help explicating what he calls 'clarification of existence' in such a way that it becomes universally understandable, i.e., he must objectify it as doctrine."[13] Bultmann concludes, significantly, that so long as we recognize this to be true of Jaspers' clarification, it is a merely verbal issue whether we call it "existentialist analysis" or speak of it as "scientific." I should hope the preceding analysis has made clear the sense in which this issue is verbal and has also shown how it is to be resolved.

Much more significant for my main purpose, however, is Bultmann's contention in the same context that theology, too, is objectifying in this second sense.[14] If, with him, one includes under "objectifying" all thinking and speaking sharing in a reflective subjective form essentially like that of modern science, the claim that theology ought to be nonobjectifying may well appear more problematic than it did at the first stage of the analysis. Indeed, this claim proves to be sufficiently problematic that the contrary position taken by Bultmann presents itself as a more adequate way of answering the principal question when posed in this second form. Since I have developed the reasons for this judgment rather fully in another essay,[15] I confine myself here to a brief summary of the essential points.

Even if one grants with Heinrich Ott that theology is "a movement

---

[10] *Die geistige Situation der Zeit,* Berlin: Walter De Gruyter & Co., 1931, p. 146. In places, Jaspers indicates a willingness to speak of philosophy as in some sense "science" (*Wissenschaft*); see, e.g., *Über Bedingungen und Möglichkeiten eines neuen Humanismus,* Stuttgart: Philipp Reclam Jun., 1962, p. 14.

[11] See H. W. Bartsch (ed.), *Kerygma und Mythos,* Vol. III, Hamburg: Herbert Reich-Evangelischer Verlag, 1954, pp. 14 ff. (English translation in Karl Jaspers and Rudolf Bultmann, *Myth and Christianity,* New York: The Noonday Press, 1958, pp. 7–11).

[12] See James M. Robinson and John B. Cobb, Jr. (eds.), *The Later Heidegger and Theology,* New York: Harper & Row, 1963, p. 165.

[13] *Kerygma und Mythos,* Vol. III, p. 54 (Eng. trans., pp. 64 f.). Here I correct my earlier translation by a more literal rendering of the original (see James M. Robinson and John B. Cobb, Jr. [eds.], *op. cit.,* p. 165).

[14] *Kerygma und Mythos,* Vol. III, p. 58 (Eng. trans. p. 70).

[15] See James M. Robinson and John B. Cobb, Jr. (eds.), *op. cit.,* pp. 159–73.

of faith itself" and that there is, in consequence, a continuity between the existential understanding of faith and the more reflective levels of thinking and speaking represented by witness and theology,[16] still it is imperative that one be able to distinguish clearly between each of these different levels. Only so, as Ott himself recognizes,[17] can one escape the untenable consequences that the man of faith alone can either witness to faith or understand it theologically and that the witness or theologian is to be regarded *ipso facto* as a faithful man. Yet how is one to distinguish between faith, witness, and theology, except by seeing them as points along the continuum defined by the two poles of existential self-understanding and objectifying knowledge, in the second sense I have tried to clarify?

Faith as such is obviously the extreme contrast to objectifying knowledge in this meaning of the term, and this is true, even though, as itself a type of understanding, faith is quite distinct from immediate feeling and somehow identical with the other points lying closer to the opposite end of the continuum. Insofar as it is conscious—and it is doubtful whether one can really speak of an "unconscious faith"— it is already explicit as some form of belief, although such belief represents the maximum of personal concern and involvement. As for witness, its character is well suggested by Alfred North Whitehead in a remarkable description of the sayings of Jesus in the Sermon on the Mount and the parables.

The reported sayings of Christ are not formularized thought. They are descriptions of direct insight. The ideas are in his mind as immediate pictures, and not as analyzed in terms of abstract concepts. He sees intuitively the relations between good men and bad men; his expressions are not cast into the form of an analysis of the goodness and badness of man. His sayings are actions and not adjustments of concepts. He speaks in the lowest abstractions that language is capable of, if it is to be language at all and not the fact itself.[18]

What Whitehead says here about Jesus' witness seems to me applicable, *mutatis mutandis,* to all witness whatever, which is to say, to spontaneous confession and preaching, prayer, and the more non-reflective forms of the church's teaching. In all these, too, speaking is ideally more a matter of action than of adjusting concepts, and the

---

[16] *Ibid.,* pp. 77–111; see also Ott's *Denken und Sein, Der Weg Martin Heideggers und der Weg der Theologie,* Zollikon-Zürich: Evangelischer Verlag, 1959, pp. 171–75, especially p. 174.

[17] See James M. Robinson and John B. Cobb, Jr. (eds.), *op. cit.,* p. 92.

[18] *Religion in the Making,* New York: The Macmillan Co., 1926, pp. 56 f.

language naturally used tends to be only slightly less concrete than the reality to which it refers. There are, to be sure, differences between the various things I am comprehending under the word "witness." But common to them all is what I spoke of earlier as their pretheological character. They represent a type of thinking and speaking distinct from the more original existential understanding of faith, on the one hand, and the more derived reflection of theology proper, on the other. The latter's distinctive character, as Whitehead also suggests, is precisely its higher degree of generality as betrayed by its use of universal concepts and the greater abstractness of its language. Just when theology is true to its hermeneutical task of critically interpreting the church's witness in an appropriate and understandable conceptuality, it cannot but involve a more reflective and so more objectifying type of thinking and speaking than is represented either by the various forms of witness or by the still more existential phenomenon of faith itself.

Such, at any rate, is the conclusion I draw in the absence of any equally clear and convincing explanation of the distinctions one must make between faith itself and the witness and theology through which it is differently expressed. Although I fully concur in Ott's insistence that these distinctions are not absolute and that we must think of faith and theology as different levels of understanding somehow continuous with one another, I do not see how the difference between the levels can be adequately accounted for except by regarding theological thinking and speaking as objectifying in the sense he wishes to deny.

Before passing to the next stage of the analysis, I must consider another objection to the position that theology is necessarily objectifying in the second sense that has been distinguished. There are those who would take this position, or one rather like it, but only on condition that the object of theological thinking and speaking be understood differently from the understanding of it in my provisional definition. While faith, they argue, may indeed be made the object of the scientific or objectifying reflection which is theology, the same can hardly be said of God himself. God is always Subject and never object, and so theology can be held to have a scientific character only by restricting it to the critical interpretation of Christian faith or witness and denying that it is in any sense an objectifying thinking and speaking about the God to whom faith is directed.[19]

[19] See, e.g., Gustaf Aulén, *The Faith of the Christian Church,* trans. E. H. Wahlstrom, Philadelphia: Muhlenberg Press, 2d ed., 1960, p. 3.

Some such view is widely enough represented on the contemporary theological scene that it might seem to require either that one radically revise the definition of theology with which we began or else reconsider the position at which we have now arrived, that theological thinking and speaking are in this second sense objectifying. I hold, however, that it is this conventional view itself which must be reconsidered and revised, since it is open to at least two decisive objections.

In the first place, it involves an obvious self-contradiction. The assertion that one may not think and speak about God in an objectifying way is itself an instance of such thinking and speaking— or, at any rate, can be defended as more than an empty assertion only by appealing to such. It is one thing to acknowledge God existentially as eminent Subject or Thou, but it is quite another to lay down the general principle that only by thus acknowledging him can one know him concretely as God. Clearly, such a principle or the general assertions about God from which it alone can be deduced cannot be anything but objectifying thinking and speaking directly about God himself. But, in the second place, this view begs the very question to which only objectifying thinking about God can provide the answer. As Charles Hartshorne has convincingly demonstrated, the hidden premise of the view is the ancient dogma of classical natural theology that God is so essentially "simple" that one cannot distinguish diverse aspects of his being, but must think of him either as wholly subject or as wholly object.[20] Since, however, this particular objectifying conception of God is only slightly more problematic with respect to its understandability than with respect to its appropriateness as a conception of the God of Jesus Christ, it provides an odd basis on which a Christian theologian should argue his case.

I conclude, therefore, notwithstanding the conventional wisdom on the issue, that theology may very well be objectifying in this second sense, even when thought of in terms of the provisional definition. If one understands the issue properly, there is as much reason for God to be the object of the objectifying thinking and speaking of theology as for him to be the eminent Subject whom I can know as *my* God here and now only in my own existential understanding of faith.[21]

[20] See Charles Hartshorne, *op. cit.*, pp. 3 f.

[21] See my essay in William L. Reese and Eugene Freeman (eds.), *Process and Divinity: The Hartshorne Festschrift*, La Salle, Ill.: Open Court Publishing Co., 1964, pp. 493–513.

3

The definition of theology we set out with is certain to seem questionable from still another standpoint, which is closely connected with a third meaning that the word "nonobjectifying" is sometimes taken to have. There are several philosophers of religion and theologians oriented to modern analytic philosophy who hold that any thinking or speaking that is nonobjectifying in the first sense of the word I distinguished is not only "nonscientific" (again, in the first sense of the word), but also "noncognitive."

The assumption these thinkers make is that the form of knowledge represented by modern science—or, more broadly, by the ordinary external perception of which science is the methodical refinement—is the only form of knowledge there is. True, they also allow for the purely analytic knowledge constituted by the tautological statements of mathematics and formal logic. But these statements, they claim, involve no knowledge in the sense of reference to "how things are," the possibility of such reference being restricted solely to the assertions of the various sciences and other assertions open in principle to the same kind of falsification. From this standpoint, to affirm, as I did earlier, that theological assertions are not subject to this kind of falsification is to concede that they are not really (i.e., logically) assertions at all, but linguistic expressions having some other noncognitive meaning or use. Since those who occupy this standpoint would also affirm this, they can only conclude that a definition of theological thinking and speaking such as I began by proposing is utterly problematic. Theological utterances, they argue, cannot really be "about" anything, much less about some divine object called "God." Rather, they can only have some function other than that of making assertions, and the values "true" and "false" simply have no application to them.

This general view has been worked out in different ways by a number of analytic philosophers making what has been called "the left-wing response" to the positivist challenge that all meaningful assertions must be falsifiable by external perception.[22] The familiar proposal of R. M. Hare that religious and theological utterances be taken as expressions of a *"blik"* or basic attitude toward the world has usually been understood as a particular development of such a

22 See William T. Blackstone, *op. cit.*, pp. 73–107.

view.[23] This is certainly how one must understand the equally well-known lecture of R. B. Braithwaite, *An Empiricist's View of the Nature of Religious Belief,*[24] which is perhaps the classic formulation of this viewpoint from the strictly philosophical side.

More recently, this view has been given forcible theological expression by Paul M. van Buren in his book, *The Secular Meaning of the Gospel.*[25] Following closely the interpretation of religious utterances set forth by Braithwaite and Hare, van Buren argues that the statements of the Christian gospel are in no sense to be taken cognitively as assertions about a divine reality, but are to be interpreted as expressions of a certain human stance or attitude which he calls a "historical perspective."[26] He recognizes, of course, that such a view entails a radical "reduction" of what have traditionally counted as theological statements.[27] But this by itself, as we have seen, in no way distinguishes his proposal from the position fairly widely shared by contemporary Protestant theologians. Once one grants that theological thinking and speaking cannot be objectifying in the sense for which modern science provides the paradigm, the extent of what can pass for theological statements is bound to be reduced—mythological statements, for instance, no longer qualifying as properly theological.

What *is* distinctive about van Buren's proposal, however, is that this necessary reduction of what can be counted as genuinely theological statements is, in its terms, also the delimiting of such statements to wholly noncognitive and, in that sense, nonobjective utterances. Putative assertions about the being or nature of the Christian God (to which van Buren does not wish to deny a place in the church's witness) must be critically interpreted by theology as really expressions of the attitude or perspective of the Christian man.[28] As such, they are indirectly related to certain meaningful assertions. Although in themselves they assert nothing at all, the statement that a certain person has the perspective they express is open to empirical falsification. Hence, insofar as theological utterances may be considered even indirectly to assert something, they assert nothing whatever about God, merely something about man and

[23] See Anthony Flew and Alasdair Macintyre (eds.), *New Essays in Philosophical Theology,* London: SCM Press Ltd., 1955, pp. 99–103.
[24] Cambridge: Cambridge University Press, 1955.
[25] New York: The Macmillan Co., 1963.
[26] *Ibid.,* pp. 97, 135–45.
[27] *Ibid.,* pp. 197 ff.
[28] *Ibid.,* pp. 156, 157–92.

his conative perspective or posture. Indeed, van Buren argues, the relation between the church's traditional witness, with its statements about a transcendent God, and a properly critical theology is analogous to the relation between astrology and scientific astronomy or alchemy and modern chemistry.[29] This does not mean, to be sure, that the congruence between such a theology and our "empirical attitudes" as modern secular men is the only reason for demanding it. While van Buren insists that this congruence must indeed characterize any adequate contemporary theology, he also claims a far deeper justification for his apparently radical redefinition of theological thinking and speaking. The gospel itself, he holds, makes both possible and legitimate this reduction of theology to a merely "secular" content.[30]

The merit of van Buren's argument, as I see it, is to have brought to the point of genuine decision a central issue that has too long been left ambiguous and undecided in much recent Protestant theology. If his view is accepted, then, as I suggested above, the more traditional definition of theology with which this analysis began can only be abandoned. If, on the other hand, some such definition is still to be maintained, this can be done only by showing that it remains the most tenable alternative open to us even after the objections of van Buren and those who share his general view. Since I am confident this can be shown, and that, of the two alternatives, the revisionist position involves by far the greater difficulties, I must now try, in the remainder of the essay, to lay down the lines of an effective counterargument.

I consider, first, van Buren's claim that his wholly nonobjective interpretation of the church's gospel is justified as both possible and legitimate by the character of that gospel itself. I submit that this claim is starkly paradoxical, in the sense that the primary use of language evident in Christian witness is, on this interpretation, explained away instead of theologically accounted for. Whatever else Christians have usually supposed themselves to be doing in witnessing to their faith, whether through personal confession, prayer, preaching, or teaching, they have most surely believed they were somehow responding cognitively to a divine reality radically different from themselves, in whose gracious initiative and approach alone their witness has its basis and object. They have also known that their response through these various forms was an expression of the

29 *Ibid.*, pp. 197 f.
30 *Ibid.*, pp. 199 f.

existential understanding of faith and that the various assertions they supposed themselves to be making about this divine reality were all bracketed, as it were, by the words "I believe," which so characteristically open their creeds. Even when, in the ages of "orthodoxy," the content of their witness has been most consistently misunderstood as "right doctrine," there has remained at least some recognition of its double reference to an existential decision that each individual believer alone is required to make. But what Christians have hardly ever recognized, I believe, is that their witness is *nothing but* this human decision, that it can be appropriately interpreted as making no reference whatever to the objective reality of God, and that it asserts, if anything, merely something about themselves and their own subjective attitude toward life.

My point, in brief, is that van Buren's interpretation of the Christian witness has but a one-sided relation to the actual uses of language evident in that witness and utterly fails to account for the most truly distinctive of these uses. Hence it seems to me that one can accept his proposal not as a literal account of the meaning of Christian witness, but only as (in a phrase I borrow from another analytic philosopher, Stephen Toulmin) a "disguised comparison."[31] I hope we would all agree that the language in which faith comes to expression is in important respects *like* the language in which we otherwise express our attitudes or seek to get others to share them. Yet, when this perfectly acceptable comparative judgment is made as it is by van Buren, only under the disguise that the language of witness simply *is* such expressive or imperative language, then we have no choice, I believe, but to reject it. We may fully agree with him that the witness of faith evinces no use of language literally identical with the use distinctive of modern science. But we can hardly join him in inferring from this that Christian witness is wholly noncognitive in meaning, making no assertions whatever. Even logically this conclusion can be made to follow only by assuming a further premise; and, if we respect all the uses of language the witness of faith evinces, we will not find it easy to make this assumption. The most we can say is that, while the language of witness is indeed not

---

[31] *An Examination of the Place of Reason in Ethics*, Cambridge: Cambridge University Press, 1950, pp. 190–93. Much the same idea is also expressed by P. H. Nowell-Smith's "Janus-principle," according to which "a given word cannot only do two or more jobs at once, but also is often, in the absence of counter-evidence or express withdrawal, presumed to be doing two or more jobs at once" (*Ethics*, Harmondsworth: Penguin Books Ltd., 1954, p. 100).

literally the same as that of science, it is in important respects sufficiently *like* the language of science that to deny it any assertive meaning whatever is seriously to misunderstand it.

The reason van Buren can conclude more than this is that he makes this further assumption. And here I would consider the second line of argument by which he seeks to justify his proposal. He claims, as has been noted, that no theology can be fully congruent with the empirical commitments of the modern secular man unless it concedes that (apart from mathematics and formal logic) the scope of thinking and speaking as involving cognition is strictly coextensive with the thinking and speaking fully developed in modern science.[32] But this claim, too, in my judgment, involves one rather obvious but nevertheless serious difficulty. It is simply a fact that nothing which can claim to represent a "consensus" in contemporary philosophy—even in contemporary analytic philosophy!—can be fairly made to include the demand for such a concession.[33] A generation and more ago, no doubt, the situation did appear rather more as van Buren represents it. But, in recent years, this characteristic demand of the earlier logical positivists has been increasingly subjected to critical scrutiny, so that even among philosophers who are the sons of the positivists it has lost much of its erstwhile plausibility.

Thus an ordinary language philosopher like Toulmin, for instance, has presented a most impressive case against the philosopher who has "too narrow a view of the uses of reasoning" because "he assumes too readily that a mathematical or logical proof or a scientific verification can be the only kind of 'good reason' for any statement."[34]

[32] At points, van Buren seems to want to qualify this claim by appealing to a "loose" meaning of "empirical" (*op. cit.*, p. 106) and to "a modified verification principle" (*ibid.*, p. 15). This is because he is forced to recognize that "words such as 'free,' 'love,' and 'discernment' are not empirically grounded in the same way as are 'undiluted,' 'gravitational attraction,' and 'sense data'" (*ibid.*, p. 171). Yet, so far as I can see, this in no way leads him to extend the scope of cognition beyond the limits allowed for by ordinary empirical falsification. If statements having to do with the field of the "personal" or the "ethical" have any meaning, then this is the meaning determinable, however indirectly, solely through the tests of external perception (see, e.g., what is said concerning the verification of "sense-content statements" generally and Peter's Easter confession in particular, *ibid.*, pp. 129 f.).

[33] In general, van Buren's attempt to support his position by referring to "a rough consensus among contemporary analysts of the language of faith" (*ibid.*, p. 96) must be taken *cum grano salis*. I regard it as highly questionable, for example, whether Ian Ramsey can be made a *Bundesgenossen* of Hare and Braithwaite in the way van Buren seeks to do.

[34] Stephen Toulmin, *op. cit.*, p. 46.

The words "I know" as we ordinarily use them, Toulmin argues, have an exceedingly broad scope, being properly used (although not with literally the same meaning in each case) in fields as different as science, ethics, aesthetics, and theology.[35] If some such view as Toulmin's has come to be more frequently expressed even by linguistic analysts, to recall the great number of modern philosophers who have never accepted the positivistic restriction of cognition is to have ample reason to question van Buren's reading of the contemporary philosophical consensus. It is one thing to claim that sentences having the logical form of scientific assertions must prove their cognitive status by reference to the principle of verification as conventionally interpreted. It is quite another thing to claim with the positivists that this principle determines the only kind of cognitive status there is. I hold that Bultmann is completely justified in regarding the former claim as something no responsible contemporary theology can fail to accept. But I also hold that van Buren's attempt to regard the latter claim in the same way is lacking in anything like the same justification. Modern man cannot so easily be made a positivist in his understanding of the scope of cognition.

My conclusion is that van Buren fails to show that his proposal to interpret theological thinking and speaking as wholly nonobjective is either possible or necessary and that one still has ample reason to stand by my original definition in spite of van Buren's counsel to abandon it. One may admit that an adequate contemporary defense of the understanding of theology which this definition formulates requires far more than many who subscribe to it have been either able or willing to offer. Of this I shall have more to say in the fourth section of the essay. But when this admission is set over against the difficulties entailed by van Buren's own proposal, its problems seem to me by far the less serious—although I realize that my confidence in the defensibility of the more traditional view is largely based on a different understanding of the present situation in philosophy from that shared by van Buren and many of my other theological colleagues.

It is significant, I think, that Bultmann, for all his insistence on the need for thoroughgoing existentialist interpretation, has stoutly resisted the kind of theological reduction that van Buren and others hold to be required. In replying to the charge of his critics that consistent demythologizing makes any direct objective reference to

[35] *Ibid.*, pp. 67–85, and especially *The Uses of Argument*, Cambridge: Cambridge University Press, 1958, *passim*.

God and his action impossible, Bultmann has clarified his intention in the following terms: "If speaking about God's act is to be meaningful, *it must indeed be not simply a figurative or 'symbolic' kind of speaking* [i.e., simply a way of designating man's own subjective self-understanding], but must rather intend a divine act in the fully real and 'objective' sense."[36] That Bultmann sets the word "objective" here in quotation marks may prove that he has not yet found a fully adequate conceptuality in which to state his position—or even that he himself is finally reluctant to accept all that an adequate defense of this position demands. But I submit that the direction he here points is far closer to the direction in which a tenable answer to the question can be found than that pointed by the other main alternative. From him one may receive at least token support for the view that theology neither can nor must be nonobjectifying, if that means wholly non-cognitive, and so lacking in all direct objective references to God and his gracious action.[37]

4

Much more than this, however, I do not believe Bultmann is in a position to provide. True, he has attempted to show how his intention could be more adequately realized by sketching out a theory of analogy that complements or, as I should prefer to think, more fully explicates, his hermeneutical method of existentialist interpretation.[38] Yet this theory of analogy, while profoundly suggestive, and even essentially correct, is too fragmentary and undeveloped to secure Bultmann's intention against misunderstanding and to enable

[36] *Kerygma und Mythos,* Vol. II, p. 196 (Eng. trans., p. 196).

[37] Such support is also provided by John A. T. Robinson, who graciously but firmly rejects van Buren's attempt (*op. cit.,* p. 200, n. 5) to represent their two views as essentially the same (John A. T. Robinson and David L. Edwards [eds.], *The Honest to God Debate,* London: SCM Press Ltd., 1963, pp. 249–56). Robinson holds that theological statements "are not objective propositions about 'things in themselves'; but neither are they simply affirmations of my outlook or perspective on life. They are statements about the reality in which my life is grounded as I respond to that reality at the level of 'ultimate concern' (as opposed to proximate concern—the level at which scientific statements, etc., are true)" (*ibid.,* pp. 252 f.). Robinson's view is thus essentially the same as Bultmann's, though like Bultmann, he has not yet developed it with the necessary adequacy (see my essay, "Beyond Supernaturalism," *Religion in Life,* Winter, 1963–64, pp. 7–18).

[38] See *Kerygma und Mythos,* Vol. II, pp. 196 f. (Eng. trans., pp. 196 f.); also *Jesus Christ and Mythology,* pp. 67–70.

one who shares it to make a carefully reasoned defense of his case.[39]

Moreover, Bultmann so largely shares yet another characteristic assumption of his existentialist colleagues that it is doubtful whether he is even open to all one must take upon himself if he is to make such a defense. This is the assumption that, if theological thinking and speaking are nonobjectifying in the first sense I clarified, they must also be exempt from any kind of rational assessment or justification. Although, as we have seen, Bultmann resists the view that the statements of Christian witness and theology are wholly noncognitive, he also seems to reject the demand that these statements make good their claim to cognitive status by reference to some clearly specified criterion of meaning and truth.[40] Thus it is evident there is yet a fourth meaning that the notion of a nonobjectifying thinking and speaking may have. With Bultmann, one may also understand this notion to imply that, although theological utterances do somehow have a genuine cognitive meaning or use, they nevertheless cannot be referred to any generally applicable principle of verification, so that the issue of their truth or falsity cannot be rationally adjudicated. In consequence, still another form of the principal question is whether theological thinking and speaking are or should be "nonobjectifying" in this fourth (and, for this essay, final) meaning of the word.

[39] See my *Christ Without Myth: A Study Based on the Theology of Rudolf Bultmann*, New York: Harper & Row, 1961, pp. 90 ff., 147; see also the essay referred to above in n. 21.

[40] I say "seems" here because there are places that perhaps point to another interpretation. Bultmann has consistently opposed any merely authoritarian understanding of the decision of faith and, in this context, has been willing to speak of a "criterion for the truth" of Christian witness and theology (see *Glauben und Verstehen*, Vol. I, Tübingen: J. C. B. Mohr, 2d ed., 1954, p. 284; also *Kerygma und Mythos*, Vol. III, pp. 57 f. [Eng. trans., pp. 69 f.]). Furthermore, he at one point forthrightly rejects the relativistic conclusion of Dilthey and others by maintaining that the question of the true or legitimate *Weltanschauung* can and should be answered by reference to the "historicity of the human being" invoked as a criterion (*The Presence of Eternity: History and Eschatology*, New York: Harper & Brothers, 1957, pp. 148 f.). On the other hand, his most characteristic statements evidently entail a blanket denial that theological assertions are subject to rational justification (on this, see the evidence brought forward by Ronald W. Hepburn in Anthony Flew and Alasdair Macintyre [eds.], *op. cit.*, pp. 227–42). Thus, while it is tempting to argue, rather as I did above in n. 8, that Bultmann's intention in such statements is to exempt theological assertions, not from all rational tests, but only from those of the special sciences and history, the bulk of the evidence supports the contrary interpretation. Nevertheless, one may hold that at this point Bultmann is at cross-purposes with himself and fails fully to follow through with certain of his other basic intentions.

It is already evident that the only answer I am able to give to this form of the question, too, is negative. This is because I fully accept the argument, not only of van Buren, but of virtually all contemporary analytic philosophers, that cognitive status may be claimed for statements only if one is prepared to support the claim by clearly specifying the principle in accordance with which the truth of the statements can be rationally determined. If we neither can nor need deny that theological statements intend to assert something true about the objective reality and action of God, then we neither can nor need deny that these statements are somehow susceptible of rational justification.

This answer is frequently taken to be problematic, I believe, because of certain conventional assumptions and confusions. Thus Bultmann himself, for instance, characteristically denies that theological assertions can in any way be rationally verified, because he tacitly assumes that the only meaning of verification is that illustrated by the deductive proofs of mathematics and logic or the inductive procedures of the special sciences and history. But this assumption clearly belongs to the narrow, positivistic view of the scope of cognition which we considered earlier and saw Bultmann rightly refusing to accept. If the class of meaningful assertions cannot be restricted solely to those of mathematics and the empirical sciences, then why should we suppose that the only kinds of rational argument are those employed in these particular disciplines? I conclude there is no good reason and that the temptation of all of us in our age to succumb to scientism and positivism is nowhere more clearly confirmed than in the case of theologians who assume otherwise. As Toulmin and other analytic philosophers have been trying to remind us, "the uses of argument" are actually many, and acceptance of the challenge that theological assertions also must be argued for does not require one to hold that the relevant kind of argument is that either of mathematics or of the special sciences.

Yet perhaps an even greater obstacle to such acceptance is the common confusion that faith itself must then be held to be directly verifiable or demonstrable. From standpoints for which the distinction between faith and theology is either denied or obscured, such confusion may be all one has the right to expect. But when this distinction is clearly made in some such way as I suggested earlier, it is hard to see why this issue need be confused. In any case, I should agree immediately that there is something profoundly mistaken in supposing that faith itself either must or could be directly verified. If faith is taken *stricto sensu* as existential self-understanding, then one may indeed speak of a justification *by* faith, but certainly not of a justification *of* faith. To speak of the latter is clearly a μετάβασις εἰς ἄλλο γένος, since the level of our actual existence, which is the level of faith as such, is simply not the level at which the question of rational justification arises. Where it does properly arise is at the level of thought and speech through which the existential understanding of faith is theologically explicated—provided, of course, that such thought and speech are held to have some genuine cognitive import. If theological statements not only express faith, but also assert something about the divine reality in which faith understands itself to be based, the question of how they are to be rationally justified is an altogether appropriate question. To object to this on the ground that faith as such cannot be verified, which in itself is true enough, is to confuse an issue about which a theology oriented to the Reformation has little excuse to be unclear.

But such confusions and assumptions are hardly the only or the most important reasons why the position I am proposing is so rarely held today by Protestant theologians. A more basic reason is what can only be described as a profound skepticism about metaphysics, which both reinforces and is reinforced by a highly selective reading of philosophical developments in the modern period. If, as I have argued, the primary (although not the only) use of theological statements is to make what are in some sense meaningful assertions, the only kind of assertions they can logically make is metaphysical assertions. That is, they express assertions which at once have objective reference to "how things are" and yet are not empirically falsifiable as are the hypotheses of the special sciences. Such assertions cannot be thus falsifiable because their specific use or function is to represent not the variable details of our experience of reality, but its constant structure—that which *all* states of experience, regardless of their empirical contents, necessarily have in common. Thus, if a theological or metaphysical assertion is false, this is not because it fails in predicting what is disclosed by our particular external perceptions, but because it misrepresents the common structure of all of our experiences, of which we are originally aware internally, and thus is falsified by *any one* of them we choose to consider. Please notice, however, that I have not said theological assertions simply *are* metaphysical assertions. On the definition of theology given here, this could not be said, since theological statements have a necessary relation to specifically *Christian* faith in God that would not obtain in the case of metaphysics. My point, rather, is that the class to which theological statements, insofar as they express assertions, logically belong is the general class of metaphysical assertions and that, therefore, the kind of rational justification to which they are open is the kind generically appropriate to all assertions of this logical class.

Yet it is the deep doubt whether there either can or should be any such metaphysical justification that is one of the chief underlying conditions of much recent Protestant theology. It is widely held that the intensive critical work of Spinoza, Hume, and Kant, as well as others, has rendered untenable the *philosophia perennis* or "Christian philosophy" of the classical metaphysical tradition. Equally evident to most theologians is that the great idealistic systems of the nineteenth century are scarcely less problematic than the classical metaphysics their builders intended them to replace. The dominant movements in the philosophy of our own century, whether on the Continent or in the English-speaking countries, have been un- or even anti-metaphysical, and it is from them that most Protestant theologians have taken their orientation. Thus to "overcome metaphysics," either in Heidegger's way or in some other, has come to be one of the most frequently expressed goals of the Protestant theology of our time.

All but completely ignored by most theologians, however, is that metaphysics itself has recently passed through one of the decisive transformations in its long history and is now showing every sign of having a future as well as a past. I cannot detail this important development here, beyond suggesting that as good a characterization of it as any is Hartshorne's, when he says that "Leibniz was its Newton," and "Whitehead is its Einstein."[41] In Whitehead's thought especially, all the main themes of the metaphysical tradition are given a neoclassical expression, which seeks to incorporate the contributions of modern philosophy, while also showing how its criticisms of classical metaphysics might possibly be met and overcome.[42] Through Hartshorne and others, then, these same neoclassical insights have been extensively developed and applied to the traditional problems of "natural" or philosophical theology. Thus Hartshorne, for instance, has given considerable attention to the logic of metaphysical statements and has issued a clear challenge to the positivistic

[41] *Reality as Social Process: Studies in Metaphysics and Religion,* Glencoe, Ill.: The Free Press, 1953, p. 31.

[42] See especially Ivor Leclerc, *Whitehead's Metaphysics: An Introductory Exposition,* London: George Allen & Unwin Ltd., 1958.

dogma that no assertion can both have objective reference and not be empirically falsifiable.[43] More important, he has also worked out in detail the neoclassical theory of analogy to which Bultmann's remarks on the subject are at best a pointer, and he has made plain to all who have eyes to see that the whole question of the theistic proofs has far more than a merely historical interest.[44]

All this, of course, is strictly of a piece with a method of approach and conception of God, as of being generally, that are in important respects radically different from the method and conception of classical metaphysics. But just this points up the limitation of the wholesale denunciations of metaphysics that are the stock in trade in certain theological quarters. The conventional view that one's only choices are either to accept some traditional metaphysics or else reject metaphysics altogether is the result of selective perception and is utterly misleading as to the philosophical options which are presently available. I have not the slightest question that the metaphysics of Whitehead and Hartshorne may one day be superseded, and I would dispute the claim that it is even now the only place to which one needs to look for philosophical resources significant for the theological task. Yet I have equal confidence that no contemporary

---

[43] See his "Metaphysical Statements as Nonrestrictive and Existential," *Review of Metaphysics,* September, 1958, pp. 35–47; *The Logic of Perfection,* pp. 280–97; and his contribution to Ivor Leclerc (ed.), *The Relevance of Whitehead,* London: George Allen & Unwin Ltd., 1961, pp. 107–21. In the latter essay, Hartshorne formulates the criterion of metaphysical necessity or truth as "the absence of any positive meaning for the denial of a statement or—the same thing—the failure of the statement to exclude any positive state of affairs" (p. 111). Subsequently he explains that "although a statement which denies no contingent possibility also affirms no contingent possibility, yet it does not follow that it affirms nothing at all, and 'says nothing about the world.' The necessary is indeed compatible with any affirmation you please, but not with any negation you please. Rather it is exclusively positive. It affirms that about the world which would be real no matter what possibilities were actualized, and which therefore cannot be denied except by impossible formulae. If 'information' means a description of what distinguishes one state of affairs from other conceivable states, then necessary statements are not informative; but if 'information' includes reference to the factor which all possible positive states of existence have in common, then necessary statements are informative" (*ibid.,* pp. 112 f.). In terms of some such criterion, I suggest, one can also take responsibility for the proper assertions of Christian theology.

[44] See *The Logic of Perfection,* pp. 28–117, 133–47; *Man's Vision of God and the Logic of Theism,* New York: Harper & Brothers, 1941, pp. 174–205, 251–341; and "The Idea of God—Literal or Analogical?" *Christian Scholar,* June, 1956, pp. 131–36.

philosophy is nearly so well qualified to integrate the cumulative insights of the whole Western philosophical tradition, so as to do justice to the legitimate motives both of classical metaphysics and of the various forms of modern, critical philosophy. Unlike existentialism and linguistic analysis, process philosophy is not simply a philosophical fragment that purchases a greater depth of phenomenological insight or a higher degree of conceptual precision at the price of abandoning philosophy's ancient quest for an integral secular wisdom. To the contrary, it offers itself as a comprehensive philosophical outlook, which has something of the same dimensions as the "Christian philosophy" of our intellectual tradition and whose possible hermeneutical significance for theology would seem to be at least correspondingly great.

Students of recent ecumenical developments have commented more than once on the challenge put to us as Protestants by Roman Catholic theology at just this point. As Jaroslav Pelikan formulates the question, "Can Protestantism provide its adherents with a world view which is as comprehensive and yet as Christian as the Thomistic? Or must Protestant thought choose between comprehensiveness and evangelical loyalty?"[45] To agree with Pelikan that Protestantism by its nature will always have room for a plurality of world views is neither to deny the need for a comprehensive philosophy nor to be willing to settle for fragmentary alternatives whose hermeneutical significance, however genuine, is nevertheless partial. But if an integral metaphysics in some form is a theological necessity—the only possible basis of a fully adequate hermeneutical principle and procedure—then, I ask, what metaphysics has more claim on one's attention as a Protestant theologian today than that represented by Whitehead and Hartshorne? It is simple to show—in fact, it has already been largely shown[46]—that the points at which these thinkers have revised classical metaphysics are the very points at which an evangelical understanding of Christian faith has found such metaphysics most seriously lacking. I am prepared to argue, therefore, that if any contemporary philosophy can be regarded historically as a "secularized" Protestant theology, it is far less likely to be the philosophy of Heidegger or existentialism generally than the philosophy of process in its most mature and fully developed forms.

[45] *The Riddle of Roman Catholicism,* Nashville: Abingdon Press, 1959, p. 227.
[46] See especially Hartshorne's discussion of "the two strands in historical theology" in *Man's Vision of God,* pp. 85–141.

In any case, I am quite certain that, apart from the resources that some such philosophy is in a position to provide, the claim of theological statements to cognitive status cannot be responsibly made or supported. If theological thinking and speaking have to do properly and primarily with the God who discloses himself in Jesus Christ, then they involve claims to truth that can be conceptually stated and justified solely in terms of an adequate metaphysics and philosophical theology. I wholly agree, therefore, that the challenge laid down by van Buren and others can be effectively met only by a theology that is frankly and fully metaphysical and thus is prepared to take responsibility for the meaning and truth of its assertions.

That I have not even tried to develop such a theology here is consistent with the critical, analytical emphasis of this whole undertaking. Yet I have at least sought to show how it might be developed by pointing to the philosophical resources that seem to me adequate to the task. I would be less content with this than I am if the resources to which I have pointed had been critically appropriated in the theological discussion or if this kind of a theology itself had already been seriously tried and found wanting. But, as it is, the resources have for the most part not even been discovered, much less discussed, and the theological approach I have proposed is so far from having been tested that there is time enough to see whether it cannot be worked out as a serious contemporary alternative.[47]

[47] Here I may refer to the criticisms directed to some of my earlier statements in the second part of Robert C. Coburn's article, "A Budget of Theological Puzzles," *Journal of Religion*, April, 1963, pp. 83–92. Coburn is no doubt justified, given his primary interests, in finding many of my statements about "the thing called 'God'" in *Christ Without Myth* "puzzling." And I quite agree that the constructive alternative I tried to outline there is peculiarly vulnerable at just the logical or philosophical points to which he gives attention. Nevertheless, I cannot regard his criticisms as a serious test of that alternative, since they proceed on the unexamined assumption that the only criterion of meaningful assertions is that which is relevant to scientific statements, thus failing to consider the one possibility that would, I think, make sense of what is said about God in that book, as well as explain its several clear indications of the philosophical ground on which I should want to stand. Coburn does seem to see that I should be content with none of the four replies he imagines my possibly making to his Flew-like demand that all assertions be falsifiable by external perception. But whence his confidence that these are the only possible replies? I can only think that Coburn, like van Buren and many others, is so under the spell of a certain logical dogma that he has still to discover the challenge put to it by analytic philosophers like Toulmin, as well as contemporary metaphysicians such as Hartshorne. On the other hand, I acknowledge that each of us must take responsibility for his own assertions and that I as a theologian cannot

I have comprehended the argument of this essay under the title, "Theology and Objectivity," and I trust by now the reason for this will have become obvious. Although I agree, and even insist, that theological thinking and speaking are different in principle from what goes on in modern science, this point also seems to me to exhaust the claim that they ought properly to be nonobjectifying. For the rest, the important points are the old ones, long since made by the church's Fathers, Doctors, and Reformers: that theology is in its own way scientific; that its statements in their most proper part are assertions about God and his action; and that the justification of these assertions, so far as they are rationally justifiable at all, can only be a metaphysical justification. As I see it, the problem of nonobjectifying thinking and speaking in contemporary theology is that this threefold objectivity, which is of the very essence of the theological enterprise, will be obscured rather than clarified, abandoned rather than forthrightly affirmed.

---

evade this responsibility by appealing to Hartshorne or Toulmin or any other philosopher. The value of Coburn's criticisms has been to underline the job that must be done, and I can only hope the present essay, as well as this volume as a whole, gives indication that I am at work on it.

III

Y

Myth and Truth

One of the forms in which the general question of myth and modern man commonly arises is the special question of myth and truth. For most men today whose outlook has been shaped by the dominant forces in modern Western culture, the relation between myth and truth is at least problematic. There are many who recognize no positive relation between the two concepts at all because they have long since come to associate the word "myth" exclusively with what is fictitious, illusional, or false.

Of course, this association is nothing distinctively modern. From as early as the classical Greek enlightenment, *mythos* was sharply distinguished from *logos* as the false from the true. This sense of "myth" subsequently became fixed in our usage when Jewish and Christian theologians availed themselves of it in their polemic with paganism—as witness the uses of the word in the later New Testament writings (I Tim. 1:4; Titus 1:14; II Pet. 1:16). The dangers in this theological disparagement of myth finally became clear in the nineteenth century with the collapse of the conventional distinction between "natural" and "supernatural" knowledge of the divine. Once the Jewish and Christian Scriptures were exposed to the same historical-critical scrutiny as other religious traditions, they, too, fell subject to description as in large part mythical, and the arrogance of traditional theology was avenged. At the same time, the growing acceptance of empirical science as the only means to reliable knowledge provided a new basis for the customary reference of "myth" to what is untrue. The result is that many educated men today who have inherited this nineteenth-century attitude are disposed to see only a negative relation between myth and truth. Like their less sophisticated contemporaries, whose sense of the word "myth" is the pejorative sense fixed by centuries of theological tradition, they instinctively think of myth as cognate with falsehood.

Nor is the case of most other modern men very different. It is true that among serious students of myth the attitude toward it now tends to be rather different from that which prevailed at the turn of the century. The contemporary ethnologist or historian of religion is much less likely than his nineteenth-century predecessor to evaluate myth primarily from the standpoint of his own presuppositions as a modern Western man. He is apt to view it more in its context in the total sociocultural life of which it is originally a part and thus is appreciative of its actual functions in enabling and enhancing that life. Yet it would be wrong to assume that this more sympathetic and genuinely scientific attitude toward myth entails the conviction that myth can be true. Anyone who acquaints himself with the literature on the subject can confirm at once that scholars may very well evaluate myth positively, while leaving the question of its truth unsettled. In fact, there are certain positivistically-minded theorists who recognize quite clearly myth's important function as, say, an instrument of social control and yet frankly deny that it is capable of truth. But even where such a denial is notably absent, the question of myth's truth is often enough left open and largely unclarified.[1] Consequently, even among contemporary men whose attitude toward myth is not simply that of the nineteenth century, but is informed by a more mature science of mythology, the claim that myth can be true will hardly be easily made or received. At best, they will regard it as a problematic claim which is in need of clarification and support.

There are good reasons, then, for reconsidering the claim. And this becomes all the clearer when one takes into account the current state of scholarship in Protestant theology. In this discipline, too, recent decades have seen the emergence of a new, more positive evaluation of myth, which has relativized much of the theological controversy between orthodoxy and liberalism of the preceding century. But, more than this, most Protestant theologians at present hold that the claim of myth to be true in some sense is integral to the case which they as theologians are charged with representing. There are differ-

[1] See, e.g., the sensitive writings of Bronislaw Malinowski, especially *Magic, Science and Religion and Other Essays,* Garden City, N.Y.: Doubleday & Co., Inc., 1954, pp. 17–92; 93–148. In places, Malinowski seems to think of myth, like religion, as having "an immense biological value" and thus as revealing "truth in the wider, pragmatic sense of the word" (pp. 89 f.; cf. pp. 84, 143 ff.). Elsewhere, he dismisses the question of religious truth as "a problem of theology or metaphysics": "The anthropologist has done enough when he has shown the value of a certain phenomenon for social integrity and for the continuity of culture" (p. 62).

ences, naturally, in the ways they understand this claim; and, as shall be seen later, these differences can only too easily obscure the substantial amount of agreement between the various theological approaches to myth. Yet the claim itself is very near the center of the present consensus in Protestant theology. Hence, to share in this consensus and to be concerned with developing and refining it can only mean, for the reasons given, that one must join in the attempt to clarify and defend the claim that myth is somehow capable of truth.

It might be held that this is hardly a pressing task today, since it has already been largely accomplished by the Protestant theologians of the last generation. But there is reason to believe that, while the contributions of these theologians are indeed impressive, no one of them presents as adequate a treatment of the question of myth and truth as the resources of the present situation give us the right to demand, and that fresh approaches to it are still very much in place. Needless to say, the thoughts to be developed here can do no more than outline what is possibly one such approach. And this is so for reasons more basic than the restricted scope of a single essay. The question itself is extremely subtle and complex, and my own thinking about it is still far from having come to rest in certain conclusions. Therefore, the most I can hope is to contribute somewhat to an ongoing discussion, of whose importance I have not the slightest doubt, but whose outcome I do not pretend to foresee.

No sooner does one begin to reflect on the question of myth and truth than he is faced with an apparently insurmountable obstacle to ever adequately answering it: the lack of any generally accepted definition of just what the word "myth" should be taken to mean. Even if one confines his attention, as I shall do here, to the attempts at defining the word in Protestant theology, his first impression is likely to agree with the recent verdict of two Roman Catholic theologians, that myth is "one of the most obscure concepts of the history of religion."[2] It seems as though every theologian who presumes to talk about myth brings with him his own peculiar proposal as to how the word should be understood. Thus nothing so characterizes theological discussion of this theme as that "talking past one another" which has its basis in an equivocal use of fundamental terms.

Proof of this is abundantly provided by the so-called "demytholo-

[2] Karl Rahner and Herbert Vorgrimler, *Kleines theologisches Wörterbuch*, Freiburg: Herder Verlag, 1961, p. 252.

gizing debate," which has been the main event in Protestant theology since World War II. As is well known, the demand of Rudolf Bultmann that the proclamation of the New Testament be demythologized is still stoutly resisted by many theologians even after almost a generation of extensive discussion. That this should be the response from certain quarters is only natural, since there is no question that Bultmann's demand spells the end of any uncritical biblicism, which would exclude or restrict the theological employment of genuinely historical methods. But what many an observer doubtless finds puzzling is that there should be resistance to demythologizing even from theologians like, say, Reinhold Niebuhr and Paul Tillich, who otherwise seem quite close to Bultmann's general position. The puzzle vanishes, however, once one recognizes the equivocation in using the term "myth" and its cognates that has muddled this whole debate. When Tillich says, for example, that "complete demythologization is not possible when speaking about the divine,"[3] he is not so much disagreeing with Bultmann as, like many another, making a different proposal as to how the word "myth" should be used.

One must reckon, then, with certain obvious differences in the treatment of myth by Protestant theologians. Verbally, at least, there is no one definition of "myth" that has currency among them, and this fact confronts one with his first problem in dealing with the question of this essay.

Yet it is important not to overstate the problem. Variety of opinion about myth there certainly is, and a good deal of semantic confusion about it as well. But this does not mean either that there is not also a rather substantial amount of actual agreement about it—enough, in fact, that one may consider such agreement part of the present theological consensus—or that none of the proposed definitions of myth is worthy of general acceptance. Indeed, I believe the demythologizing debate has made clear both that the definition of myth proposed by Bultmann is essentially adequate and that acceptance of this definition enables one to share quite fully in such consensus as now exists in Protestant theology. In any case, this is the definition I shall follow here; and, as I hope to make clear, my doing so is not nearly as arbitrary as it may seem at first glance.

I noted above that most Protestant theologians today not only evaluate myth positively, but also agree that it is in some sense capable of being true. Whereas for many moderns, as for certain representatives of the earlier liberal theology, myth is *eo ipso* false

[3] *Systematic Theology*, Vol. II, Chicago: The University of Chicago Press, 1957, p. 29.

because it cannot be verified by the criteria of empirical science, only a few contemporary theologians would subscribe to such a position. The far more common view is that the meaning of "truth" is sufficiently complex that an identification of the true with what can be scientifically verified is an intolerable oversimplification. At the same time, theologians now rather generally concede that myth is incapable of scientific truth and argue that any attempt to claim otherwise, whether by old orthodoxy or by new, betrays theology into an impossible situation. As I see it, these two convictions—that myth can be true, but that such truth as it can have is not that of empirical science—are so widely represented in contemporary Protestant theology that one is justified in regarding them as part of the current consensus in that discipline. There are numbers of theologians, of course, who do not share these convictions; and, as I have indicated, there is a variety of ways in which they can be understood and developed even if one accepts them. Still, if there is any consensus at all in Protestant theology today, it surely includes the view most succinctly expressed in the now-classic dictum of Reinhold Niebuhr, that myth must always be taken "seriously but not literally."[4]

Nevertheless, assuming this to be true may seem only to disclose more clearly that the approach to the question of myth and truth to be outlined here is arbitrary. The reason for this is the prevalent belief that Bultmann's demand for demythologizing, together with the definition of myth from which it logically follows, is basically incompatible with the view expressed in Niebuhr's famous dictum.[5] If this belief is correct, then to assume that Niebuhr's view is not merely his

[4] *The Nature and Destiny of Man,* Vol. II, New York: Charles Scribner's Sons, 1943, p. 50. It is interesting to note that this dictum has at least inexact parallels in the nontheological literature on the subject of myth. Joseph Campbell, for example, lays down "as a basic principle of [his] natural history of the gods and heroes, that whenever a myth has been taken literally, its sense has been perverted; but also, reciprocally, that whenever it has been dismissed as a mere priestly fraud or sign of inferior intelligence, truth has slipped out the other door" (*The Masks of God: Primitive Mythology,* New York: The Viking Press, 1959, p. 27). As it stands, Campbell's "principle" is compatible with a denial that myth can in any sense be true, whereas, for Niebuhr, to take myth seriously means somehow to accept its claim to truth. See Niebuhr's important essay in E. G. Bewkes (ed.), *The Nature of Religious Experience,* New York: Harper & Brothers, 1937, pp. 117–35.

[5] For an exposition of this belief, see Hans Hofmann, *The Theology of Reinhold Niebuhr,* trans. L. P. Smith, New York: Charles Scribner's Sons, 1956, pp. 75–84. But see also the sharp criticisms of Hofmann in the far more sensitive comparison of Bultmann and Niebuhr by Dietz Lange, *Christlicher Glaube und soziale Probleme, Eine Darstelling der Theologie Reinhold Niebuhrs,* Gütersloh: Gütersloher Verlagshaus Gerd Mohn, 1964, p. 61, n. 45.

alone, but is expressive of a substantial amount of theological agreement, would be in effect to deny to Bultmann's position or one like it any support from the representative thinking of Protestant theologians.

The belief, however, cannot bear examination, despite its prevalence and despite certain factors that may make it plausible. That there are differences between Niebuhr and Bultmann in their treatments of myth is not in dispute. Yet it would be easy to show that these differences all fall within, rather than outside of, the general agreement about myth which exists in Protestant theology and of which Niebuhr's dictum is a classic summary. Even so, my concern in this essay is not to engage in detailed historical comparisons, but to clarify and try to answer an important systematic question. Hence the essential tasks at this stage of my argument are two: (1) to offer a definition of "myth" which is intentionally close to that previously worked out by Bultmann; and (2) to indicate why this definition not only is compatible with the theological consensus, but also provides a singularly apt means for expressing it.

1. "Myth" may be defined by means of three closely related statements. First, "myth" refers to a certain language or form of speaking which, like other languages, functions to represent (to *re-present*, to present *again*) some field of human experience in a particular way. Second, the field of experience that the language of myth represents is our original internal awareness of our selves and the world as included in the circumambient reality within which all things come to be, are what they are, and pass away. Third, the particular way in which the language of myth represents this awareness is in terms and categories based in our derived external perception of reality as the object of our ordinary sense experience.

There are doubtless other characteristics of myth (for example, its typical narrative form) that would need to be included in a more explicit definition. But, so far as I can see, the characteristics covered by these three statements are the really essential ones, in which any others are more or less evidently implied. I wish now briefly to comment on the three statements.

Basic to this definition of myth is the assumption that human experience has different fields and that this is reflected in our (logically) different languages and in the different functions which even (grammatically) the same terms and categories may perform.[6] The

[6] See H. A. Hodges, *Languages, Standpoints and Attitudes,* London: Oxford University Press, 1953. I recognize that to speak of a "field of experience" may seem odd. Yet I have ventured to do so not only better to express the

definition further assumes that two such fields of experience in particular need to be focused and distinguished if the phenomenon of myth is to be understood. In the technical terminology of existentialist philosophy, these two fields are identified respectively by the terms "existential" and "objective." Properly understood, these terms convey quite accurately the distinction that I, too, am concerned to make. Nevertheless, I have decided against relying on them here, not only to avoid unnecessary technical jargon, but also to express the conviction that the distinction itself is in no way the property of a particular philosophical school. It seems clear to me that no careful analysis of our experience can fail to confirm the difference between our inner nonsensuous perception of our selves and the world as parts of an encompassing whole and the outer perceptions through our senses whereby we discriminate the behavior of all the different beings of which we are originally aware. One of the reasons for believing this is that precisely this difference has also been given technical expression in other important philosophical systems.[7] But, be this as it may, the definition of myth I am proposing assumes the reality of this difference and all it imports with respect both to our experience itself and to the representation of our experience in language.

It is at the level of language that myth as thus defined is first encountered. And, according to the definition, the main thing to note is that myth's very nature involves what may be called, in the helpful phrase of the philosopher, Gilbert Ryle, a "category mistake." As Ryle uses this phrase, such a mistake is committed whenever there is "the presentation of facts belonging to one category in the idioms appropriate to another."[8] Thus, for example, we might represent

---

connections between the main stages of my argument, but also because we commonly say something like this in our phrase, "field of view," meaning a particular area to which observation is limited. My point, at any rate, should be clear: experience itself, as the sum total of our observings, encounterings, and undergoings, has at least as many different areas as there are logically distinct languages in which we represent it.

[7] See, e.g., Alfred North Whitehead's distinction between the two perceptual modes of "causal efficacy" and "presentational immediacy" in *Symbolism: Its Meaning and Effect,* New York: The Macmillan Co., 1927.

[8] *The Concept of Mind,* London: Hutchinson & Co. Ltd., 1949, p. 8. Significantly, this clarification of "category mistake" has its context in the following sentences: "A myth is, of course, not a fairy story. It is the presentation of facts belonging to one category in the idioms appropriate to another. To explode a myth is accordingly not to deny the facts but to reallocate them." I may add that it is in exactly *this* sense that what Bultmann means by "demythologizing" may be said to "explode" myth.

Oxford University as though it were something that could be visited in addition to the several colleges. As the statements of the definition seek to make clear, just such a misrepresentation is the chief characteristic of myth. Although the "facts" myth presents are our selves and the world as fragments of the totality of being, the "idioms" in which it speaks are those appropriate to the world itself as disclosed to us through the particular perceptions of our senses. Myth functions, in other words, to represent one fundamental field of our experience and of reality as thus apprehended; and yet it does so only by making use of terms and categories whose proper function is to represent a very different field of our experience of the real.

This is well illustrated by myth's typical misrepresentation of the divine transcendence as though it involved an immense spatial distance. In speaking of God (or the gods) as located somewhere "out there," myth really intends to express our inner awareness of our selves and the world as related to the encompassing reality from which we come and to which we return. But this, its true intention, is in fact obscured by the linguistic terms in which it speaks; for the category of space that its terms presuppose is based not in this inner awareness of our existence in relation to totality, but in the very different perception through our senses whereby we objectify the world external to us. The point of the proposed definition is that this obscuring of its real function or intention is the distinctive trait of mythical language. Whatever its concrete contents, any form of speaking may be properly regarded as mythical that exemplifies an inappropriate use of categories of this particular type.

One must be clear, however, about the exact type of "category mistake" that myth involves. Contrary to the opinion of many theologians, what identifies a language as myth is not simply that it speaks of the divine in terms and categories that may also be applied to the nondivine. Rather, on the definition offered here, a form of speaking is mythical only insofar as it represents a certain field of our human experience in linguistic terms whose proper use is to represent one of our experience's other and very different fields. In a word, "myth," as I have defined it, has a far more restricted reference than is allowed on many other theological definitions of the term. It does not refer to every logically possible form of analogical discourse in which we may speak of the ultimate whole of which we experience our selves and the world to be parts. It refers, instead, solely to that one form of such speaking in which this field of our experience is in principle misrepresented—that is, is expressed in terms that properly represent the quite different field of our sense perceptions.

2. Just this gain in precision of reference seems to me to mark the superiority of the present definition. By construing "myth" in a relatively narrow sense, it enables one not only to take account of the agreement about myth current among Protestant theologians, but also to do this with a refinement and discrimination that many other definitions exclude.

That the definition is compatible with the current consensus is, I trust, evident from the preceding comments. Although myth, as understood here, can never be taken literally, because its use of its terms and categories is not their proper use, it nevertheless must always be taken seriously, because it functions to express one basic dimension of our encounter with the real. In what sense myth thereby lays claim to truth is, of course, still to be considered. But even now it should be clear that the question left unsettled by the proposed definition is not whether myth entails such a claim, but only how that claim is to be understood.

As to the second point, that this definition is more adequate than certain others, I wish to hold simply that, by using the word "myth" in this strict sense, one can respect certain distinctions that are otherwise obscured and thereby avoid some typical difficulties. In many definitions, "myth" is construed so broadly that it covers any language in which we could possibly represent our religious experience. This is the case, for instance, with the definition of "myth" implied by Tillich in the statement previously quoted, that "complete demythologization is not possible when speaking about the divine." When "myth" is used this loosely, its scope of reference is the same as the phrase "religious language" or "religious symbolism," and some obvious distinctions are lost to view. Thus it becomes just as mythical to say with Luther that God is "nothing but love" (*eitel Liebe*) as to say with Isaiah that the Lord is "an everlasting rock" (Isa. 26:4)—despite the evident difference between the two fields of experience in which the terms of the respective statements have their bases. I conclude, therefore, that in comparison with such a crude use of "myth" as equivalent to "religious symbol," the careful distinctions made by the scholastic theologians between the different species of "analogy" (of metaphor, of attribution, of proportionality, etc.) provide the preferable model. The word "myth" obviously has an important job to do in any adequate analysis of religious language.

But it can perform its job the more effectively if it leaves at least certain tasks to such other fellow workers as "analogy" and "symbol."

One evidence of this is a typical difficulty to which the looser use of the term unavoidably leads. Reflection discloses that one can proceed in accordance with the current agreement about myth only if he is prepared to meet certain conditions. Thus, as I shall be arguing below, to claim that a given mythical assertion is true, although not literally so, is to commit oneself to state the meaning of the assertion at some point in other, nonmythical terms. And yet, if "myth" is defined so broadly that it covers *all* language in which the reality that myth represents can be spoken of, it is plainly impossible to make good on this commitment. True, there are cases—I think especially of Reinhold Niebuhr—where casual inspection may confirm a contrary impression. But, as more careful analysis makes clear, this impression is deceptive. In spite of their claim that "the transcendent source of the meaning of life . . . can be revealed and expressed only in mythical terms,"[9] such theologians continually offer nonmythical (or demythologized) interpretations of their mythical language. So Niebuhr, for example, tells us that when "the idea of the divine creation of the world" is "taken profoundly," it "describes the limits of the world's rationality and the inadequacy of any 'natural' cause as a sufficient explanation for the irrational givenness of things."[10] One may question, perhaps, whether Niebuhr's interpretation of the creation myth is adequate; but it is hard to see why anyone should call it "mythical." At any rate, to speak of it so is to expose his theology to an unanswerable criticism. If what he wishes to maintain is that the myth of creation is true, although not literally so, this he can do only by sooner or later expressing the meaning of the myth in other than mythical terms. That Niebuhr himself recognizes this, or, at least, proceeds as though he did, is what makes his actual handling of mythical language so instructive. But how his practice in this respect can be reconciled with the claim of his theory that "myth" covers the whole field of religious language is, for me, an unanswered question.

There are other reasons for holding that the more restricted definition of "myth" offered here is to be preferred to certain of its

---

[9] See E. G. Bewkes (ed.), *op. cit.*, p. 135.

[10] *Faith and History,* New York: Charles Scribner's Sons, 1949, p. 33. For a demythologized statement of virtually all the essential themes in Niebuhr's theology, see his important essay in *Religion and the Modern World,* University of Pennsylvania Bicentennial Conference, Philadelphia: University of Pennsylvania Press, 1941, pp. 89–108.

well-known competitors. But I hope enough has been said to bring us to the next stage of the argument: to enable us henceforth to understand the term "myth" in a sense which is far from arbitrary, but which requires that we now consider the meaning of the claim that myth can be true.

Reference was made earlier to the view now common among Protestant theologians that the general issue of the meaning of "truth" is not simple but complex. If, for many a modern man, the true and the scientifically verified are apt to be thought of as one and the same, the position typical of the theologian today is to deny this identification. True, there are those at both theological extremes for whom the identification remains a fundamental presupposition. Thus, on the far "right," the resurrection of Jesus Christ is still asserted to be a "historical fact," and attempts are made from time to time to verify it by what pretend to be scientific procedures. Other conservatives of considerably more sophistication also maintain that theological assertions are thus verifiable, but feel forced to resort to some such expedient as "eschatological verification" to eke out their case. On the far "left," by contrast, there are those who, while unquestioningly making the same identification, deny that theological utterances are even capable of being true. Such utterances, they claim, are not really assertions at all, but serve to express a decision to behave in a certain way or a "historical perspective," which has a wholly "noncognitive" character. Still, for the most part, theologians have broken with positions which hold that man in his need for truth must live by the bread of science alone. Like certain of their secular contemporaries, they have resisted the pretensions of a narrow positivism, in the conviction that "true" and "false," as we actually use the words, have legitimate applications beyond the limits prescribed by any conventional "verification principle."

The problem has been to give an acceptable rationale for this conviction; and, while some of the attempts by theologians to do this are certainly instructive, it may be questioned whether any one of them provides an adequate solution. In any case, each theologian must stand on his own philosophical feet, and this means he must essay an independent treatment of the common problem. Such an attempt is more likely to succeed if it takes into account the philosophical resources now available in our situation. Especially important, I believe, is the work of some of the so-called analytic philosophers, who are devoting themselves to the painstaking analysis of our various languages. The evidence continues to mount that the writings of these philosophers often have a profound theological relevance and that this is particularly so with respect to problems like the general one of the meaning of "truth." Accordingly, in the summary discussion of this problem that follows, I shall draw quite heavily on certain insights with which analytic philosophers are providing us. The analyst from whom I have learned the most is the ordinary language philosopher, Stephen Toulmin, whose efforts to establish what he calls "the versatility of reason" have a very direct bearing on the issue now to be considered.[11]

It is characteristic of philosophical treatments of the problem of truth that they focus on two different questions, which they nevertheless frequently fail to distinguish. The first question has to do with the meaning of the word "true"; the second, with the criterion or criteria whereby one can adjudicate the truth or falsity of putative assertions. Time and again, philosophers have proposed answers to one of these questions as though they were answering the other, thereby confusing their solutions to the general problem. Among the consequences of such confusion is that they have typically found themselves forced to choose between two equally mistaken conclusions. Some, recognizing that we use the word "true" over a wide range of fields of experience that hardly allow for common criteria of truth, conclude that the word simply has no common meaning, but functions quite differently from field to field. Others, however, are quick to deny such pluralism, insisting that "truth," after all, does have a single meaning. At the same time, having confused the question of meaning with that of criteria, they commit the even more serious mistake of making some one criterion of truth the only one.

A classic instance of this mistake is the position of logical positivism, for which the meaning of the word "true" is fully exhausted by the criteria of formal self-consistency and falsifiability by ordinary sense perception. Against this position, one may obviously urge the most formidable objections. It is simply a fact that most of us would never think of limiting "true" and "false" and other such terms of logical assessment to the uses permitted by these particular criteria. In the usage characteristic of our ordinary life, we habitually employ

---

11 See Stephen Toulmin, *An Examination of the Place of Reason in Ethics,* Cambridge: Cambridge University Press, 1950, especially pp. 67–117; and most important, *The Uses of Argument,* Cambridge: Cambridge University Press, 1958.

these terms in connection with a whole variety of fields of experience, from our sense of beauty and our awareness of moral obligation to our perception of the world by means of our senses. In consequence, the positivist's proposal to restrict truth to the tautologies of logic and mathematics and the findings of the sciences is bound to seem, in the bad sense, "paradoxical." It strikes us as the solution of a revisionist who drastically oversimplifies the real complexity of the problem.

This is not to say that the positivist is wholly wrong in insisting that the word "true" does somehow have a single meaning. It is hardly accidental that one and the same word has valid uses in relation to all these different fields of our experience. Nevertheless, this fact can be properly appreciated only when one frees himself from that confusion of different questions which keeps the positivist, along with many others, from arriving at clear and defensible answers. To ask about the *meaning* of "truth" is one thing; to ask for the *criteria* of truth, something else. To be sure, the repeated confusion of the two questions is sufficient indication that they are also in some way closely related. But their relationship can be rightly understood only if one first takes pains clearly to distinguish them.

What, then, would be an adequate solution to the problem? The clue to it, I believe, is to recognize that the word "true" as we actually use it is "the most general adjective of commendation" pertaining to matters of belief.[12] Regardless of the field of experience implied or referred to, to call an assertion "true" is to commend it as worthy of being believed or accepted. In this way, "true" functions in our usage similarly to such other familiar terms of assessment as "good" or "beautiful." Like them, it is what Toulmin calls a "gerundive"; it does not merely express a subjective preference, but has the force of claiming objective worth—specifically, of assessing a given assertion as in itself deserving of credence.[13] This means that "true" is properly used only where it is possible to specify a criterion or criteria of credibility. Because when we say that an assertion is "true," we do not mean simply that someone happens to believe it, but that it is *worthy* of our belief, we commit ourselves in using the word to stating the criteria that govern its use.

This is the reason, indeed, that the question of the meaning of "truth" is so often confused with the question of criteria. Yet, clearly, to state that the use of the word "true" demands that there be

[12] Stephen Toulmin, *The Uses of Argument*, p. 32.
[13] *An Examination of the Place of Reason in Ethics*, pp. 70 ff.

specifiable criteria for using it is something different from actually specifying such criteria. And this difference becomes significant if one remembers the wide variety of types of assertions that most of us insist on speaking of as somehow "true" or "false." If our usage gives any indication, the criteria of truth are not one but many, reflecting the quite different fields of experience that our assertions variously represent. We have to recognize, in other words, that, while the meaning of the word "true" is *constant,* the standards determining its proper use are *variable*—or, as Toulmin puts it, while the *"force"* of the word is "field-invariant," the *"criteria"* implied in using it are "field-dependent."[14]

The importance of this distinction is that it enables us to ask the right questions as we pursue the necessary task of assessing claims to truth. To advance such a claim is to commend a certain assertion as worthy of belief or assent. In this respect, as regards what Toulmin calls its "force," each such claim is exactly on a par with every other. But, in testing the merits of a claim, we must always take pains to determine the specific "criteria" whereby the credibility of the relevant assertion can be judged. Thus, we should never ask whether the assertion conforms to canons for assessing judgments of some other logical type, but only whether it meets *its own* appropriate standards of achievement. To ask, for example, whether a moral judgment is true by inquiring whether it is formally analytic or empirically falsifiable is simply to put the wrong kind of question to that particular judgment.

In a similar way, the distinction between the constant force of "true" and the varying criteria for using it enables us to reformulate our questions concerning the truth of logically different *types* of assertions. Sometimes, as in the present essay, what we wish to know is not whether some particular judgment is true, but whether any utterance of a distinguishable logical type is capable of truth or falsity. To determine this, it is never enough to ask whether such utterances meet the standards by which some other type of assertion is properly assessed. We must inquire, instead, whether there are any canons whatever whereby this kind of utterance can be established as worthy of credence. To condemn a child for not being a man is an act of injustice that even a child can understand. Yet just such injustice is perpetrated every time we reject assertions of one type because they prove unacceptable by standards appropriate solely to another.

14 *The Uses of Argument,* p. 38.

Rightly understood, the question whether a certain kind of utterance can be verified is always the question whether there are any criteria and procedures that can be commonly agreed on for testing the claim of such utterances on our attention and belief. If such criteria and procedures can be specified, then, whatever the kind of utterance or however different its standards from those pertaining to other types of assertion, the word "true" unquestionably has a proper use.

But how does one set about specifying such standards? In representing our experience, assertions always function, even if not explicitly, as answers to questions; and the questions, in turn, always have certain presuppositions, insofar as asking them at all already assumes that something is true.[15] If I ask a friend, for instance, "What's the best way down to the South Side?" I assume, among other things, that one of the ways of getting to that part of Chicago is more expedient than all the others. Hence, to answer my question, my friend must make the same assumption and also be prepared to show that the route he recommends is, in fact, the most expedient. What is thus the case with particular assertions also holds good, *mutatis mutandis,* for different logical *types* of assertions. Indeed, what enables us to classify utterances as assertions of a certain logical type is that they so function in representing our experience as to give answers to a distinct type of question. If, then, each type of question also has certain presuppositions, it should be easy to see how one can specify the criteria of truth for a given type of assertion. To determine such criteria, one must first establish the kind of question to which assertions of that type are possible answers and then make explicit what this kind of question presupposes. By thus stating the presuppositions of the kind of question, one automatically discovers the relevant standards of credibility for assessing any assertion that purports to answer it.

Inadequate as it is, this brief discussion of the general problem of truth should be sufficient for my present purpose. If the solution it outlines is correct, I have established two conclusions that are important for this specific inquiry. First, the question of the sense in which myth can be true must be formulated as the question of the criteria and procedures whereby the claim of mythical utterances to be believed can be tested. Then, second, this question can be answered by determining the presumably quite different question to which mythical utterances themselves are possible answers and focus-

[15] See R. G. Collingwood, *An Essay on Metaphysics,* Oxford: Oxford University Press, 1940, pp. 21 ff.

ing the presuppositions of that question. My task now must be to indicate how this might be done.

I begin by recalling the definition of myth previously presented. According to that definition, myth is characterized, first of all, as a way of representing linguistically a basic field of human experience—namely, that field in which each of us is aware of himself and the world as parts of an encompassing whole. From this it would seem to follow that the question to which mythical assertions are possible answers must somehow arise within *that* field of experience. But if this is the case, one must obviously ask just what question this is.

My answer is that it is the religious question or the question of faith, where "faith" is understood to mean the confidence or assurance that life as such is worth living. Presupposed by this answer are certain judgments about the human self or person, which can be supported only by a philosophical analysis of just that field of experience in which the question of faith itself arises. Among these judgments, the most important is that even to exist as a self is possible only on the basis of "faith" in this sense of the word. Because to be a self is not merely to exist, but to understand that one exists, human existence and action are never the relatively simple processes that we observe in the case of other beings. Rather, man lives and acts, finally, only according to certain principles of truth, beauty, and goodness, which he understands to be normative for his existence. Invariably implied in this understanding is the confidence or assurance that these norms have an unconditional validity and that a life lived in accordance with them is truly worth living. In this sense, our experience of our selves and the world in relation to totality is always essentially religious or an experience grounded in faith. We are selves at all only because of our inalienable trust that our own existence and existence generally are somehow justified and made meaningful by the whole to which we know ourselves to belong.[16]

This is not to say that such trust is wholly unproblematic. To the contrary, we so experience our selves and the world that our understanding of the faith by which we live is continually called in question. This is so in part because existence as we know it is always existence in such "boundary situations" as are constituted by death, chance, conflict, suffering, and guilt. Any of these ever-present limits to our existence can lead us to ask the "limiting question" of how our

[16] See above, pp. 32–43.

inescapable confidence in life is to be understood.[17] But, beyond this, being selves who can exist only in and through our own self-understandings, we are, as Jean-Paul Sartre has said, "condemned to be free."[18] We must continually choose in responsible freedom some understanding of our existence and of the ground of confidence it necessarily presupposes. Therefore, our lives can never be made wholly secure, both because of the fixed limits of our finitude, which can always challenge our present self-understanding, and because we ourselves must constantly decide anew how we are to understand and lead our lives.

To this extent, there is a parallel between our experience in this field and that constituted by our sense perceptions. It has often been pointed out how the whole human activity that results finally in what we know today as scientific explanation has its basis in a problematic situation of everyday life. This is the familiar situation in which our sense perceptions suddenly surprise us by disclosing phenomena our previous experience had not led us to expect. We can be thus surprised only because of our all but instinctive trust that the world is sufficiently ordered and intelligible that we may anticipate its future behavior from our experiences in the present and past. Repeatedly, however, this trust is put to the test by some wholly unexpected perception, and we are faced with the problem of how we may reaffirm it. This gives rise, then, to something like the modern scientist's well-known task of "saving appearances," of so revising our understanding of the world that the unexpected once again becomes the expected. In a similar way, the shocks administered by such facts as our own death or guilt to our general confidence that life is worth living also confront us with an urgent question. It is not the question *whether* there is a ground for such confidence—any more than the question being answered by the scientist is *whether* the world has order and intelligibility. The fact of the matter is that the boundary situations of life are problematic for us only because we already have a confidence in life's meaning which first permits them to become problems. Hence, the kind of problem they pose for us is to make sense somehow of this confidence we inevitably have. They confront us with the limiting question of how to understand the whole

---

[17] See Stephen Toulmin, *An Examination of the Place of Reason in Ethics,* pp. 202–211.

[18] *L'existentialisme est un humanisme,* Paris: Editions Nagel, 1962, p. 37 (English translation by Philip Mairet in Walter Kaufmann [ed.], *Existentialism from Dostoevsky to Sartre,* New York: Meridian Books, Inc., 1957, p. 295).

to which we belong so that, even when such unalterable conditions as death and guilt are taken into account, our assurance that life is worth while may still be affirmed.

This is the question I call "religious" or "the question of faith." To speak of it so seems to me justified because it is in fact the question to which all the so-called "religions" or "faiths" of mankind are so many efforts to provide an answer. I recognize, naturally, that religion as one cultural expression alongside of others is not the only means whereby this question is raised and answered. Because it is a limiting question, all forms of culture from art to politics indirectly imply it and may be correctly interpreted as representing some possible answer to it. Moreover, history offers several examples of attempted philosophical substitutes for religion in which the question of faith has been answered in "nonreligious" terms. Nevertheless, it is in religion as we commonly think of it that this question is most directly formulated and spoken to. Thus religious language, for example, functions quite explicitly to provide reassurance, to enable us so to understand ourselves in our ultimate environment that our confidence in the meaning of life will seem to be justified.[19]

But, whatever one chooses to call it, this question of how we are to understand our actual confidence in life's meaning clearly seems to me the question to which mythical utterances are possible answers. Consequently, if we focus what is presupposed by this question, it should be possible to discern the criterion for assessing the truth of such utterances.

According to the preceding analysis, the question entails at least two presuppositions: first, that life as we live it is somehow of ultimate worth; and, second, that it is possible to understand ourselves and the world in their relation to totality so that this assurance of life's worth may be reasonably affirmed. Therefore, the criterion for assessing the truth of myths may be formulated as follows: *mythical assertions are true insofar as they so explicate our unforfeitable assurance that life is worth while that the understanding of faith they represent cannot be falsified by the essential conditions of life itself.*

As thus formulated, the criterion is obviously an analogue to the conventional principle of verification whereby we assess the credibility of assertions based on our external perceptions. It, too, specifies that no understanding is worthy of credence which is falsified by the

[19] See Stephen Toulmin, *An Examination of the Place of Reason in Ethics,* pp. 202–21; also above, pp. 30 ff.

facts of our experience. The difference, however—and it is a fundamental difference—is that the "facts" in this case are not the variable details of our experience, but its constant structure. The reality with which mythical assertions must come to terms is not the ever-changing world disclosed by our senses, but our own existence as selves, as those who, whatever their external perceptions, always experience themselves and the world as finite-free parts of an infinite whole. It is for this reason that mythical assertions, when true, express an understanding of faith which not only *is* not falsified by our experience, but also *can* not be so falsified. To object that this disqualifies mythical utterances from even being true at all is simply to invoke a criterion of truth that has no jurisdiction over this kind of utterance. The truth of mythical assertions, like that of religious assertions generally, is *sui generis;* and it must be assessed, if at all, solely in terms of its appropriate criterion.[20]

Having specified this criterion, however, I would now recall the other characteristic of myth as previously defined. Also distinctive of mythical language, I argued, is that it speaks of the reality of our existence as selves in relation to totality only by making use of terms and categories that in principle misrepresent that reality. Because this is so, the process of actually verifying mythical assertions always presents a peculiar problem. If a mythical utterance is taken literally, and thus is judged by the criterion of truth naturally suggested by its terms and categories, it must sooner or later be rejected as false. If, on the other hand, one tries to judge it in terms of the quite different criterion I have just specified, he has no choice but to take it as a symbol, whose meaning must first be translated into other, non-mythical terms before its truth can be assessed. In other words, one can actually verify mythical assertions only by following the twofold hermeneutical procedure that Bultmann has called "demythologizing." Such assertions can never be verified directly but must always be handled like other assertions involving a "category mistake"; they must be taken not literally but symbolically and so interpreted as, in Ryle's words, to reallocate the "facts" of which they speak to another more appropriate "idiom." This means, specifically, that mythical utterances must be interpreted so as to disclose the answer they give

---

[20] A similar formulation of the criterion for judging religious assertions is offered by Toulmin, *ibid.*, pp. 212 ff. See also Bultmann's statement that a " 'Weltanschauung' . . . is the more legitimated the more it expresses the historicity of the human being" (*The Presence of Eternity: History and Eschatology,* New York: Harper & Brothers, 1957, p. 149).

to the question of faith and that this answer must then be restated in terms in which such answers can be literally and properly given. Only after both of these steps have been taken can one actually determine whether a mythical assertion is true. For the truth of such an assertion is like that of a metaphor: it is really the truth of the understanding of faith of which the assertion itself is but an inadequate symbol.

This assumes that it is possible somehow to restate the meaning of mythical assertions in nonmythical language.[21] Yet just this assumption is the most generally disputed point in the whole procedure of demythologizing. Time and again, critics of this theological approach have contended that mythical language can be thus translated only at the price of sacrificing its essential meaning. In support of this contention, they have sometimes pointed to the classical theological tradition, where, without a doubt, the mythical utterances of Holy Scripture have been badly mishandled by being restated in the terms of a so-called "Christian philosophy." The personal God clearly witnessed to by the scriptural myths has been utterly misrepresented in this tradition as the impersonal Absolute of the Greek metaphysics of being. In a similar way, critics of Bultmann's use of Martin Heidegger's existentialist philosophy have quite properly questioned whether even it provides a wholly adequate conceptuality for translating the meaning of mythical assertions. But to establish the inadequacy of some attempts at demythologizing is not to prove that every such attempt is bound to fail; and this must seem all the clearer once one recognizes that the attempts usually criticized by no means exhaust the alternatives actually open to us. The point, in any event, is that the claim of a mythical utterance to be true is simply unsupportable unless one has some conceptuality in which its meaning can be literally and properly stated. It is all well and good to insist that there is a truth in myths and that they therefore must always be taken seriously. But this insistence alone does little more than point

[21] To avoid any misunderstanding, I should no doubt stress that I am here speaking solely of mythical *assertions*. I not only grant but insist that mythical utterances, like religious and theological utterances generally, have other uses than the specifically cognitive use of asserting something to be true. Moreover, I consider it likely that, with respect to these other noncognitive uses (to express, to evoke, to enjoin, etc.), mythical utterances may be translatable only with a more or less serious loss of their meaning. But further consideration of this matter lies outside the scope of the present essay, which is concerned solely with the question of myth's use to make meaningful assertions. With respect to *this* use, the assumption that demythologization is possible seems to me, for the reasons stated above, quite unavoidable.

the direction to an adequate treatment of mythical assertions. If one is actually to take responsibility for such assertions, he must be able to make use of terms and categories in which, unlike those of myth itself, our understanding of our selves and our faith may be appropriately represented. Thus, to make good the claim that myth can be true requires a prodigious philosophical undertaking. One must provide nothing less than that "right" philosophy which is the essential prerequisite of any adequate theological construction.[22]

Yet, if a concern for truth makes definite demands on the treatment of myth, a concern to do justice to myth also has its effect on the understanding of truth. However mistaken the view that mythical language is indispensable, it at least attests one important point: such language does have a valid use, and a use, moreover, that makes the question of its truth entirely fitting. At his best, modern man has been distinguished by a peculiar passion in pressing just this question. But, often enough, he has also delimited the true too narrowly by treating the criterion of truth appropriate to empirical science as though it were the only such criterion there is. Against this narrowness, the very existence of myth is a standing protest. Like our moral or aesthetic language, it is a constant reminder that the scope of truth is wide and is never to be circumscribed by a single criterion.

All this, the proponent of demythologizing has every reason to affirm. For the whole point of his approach is to meet not one concern but two: to insist not only that the question of myth's truth must be answered, but, quite as important, that we must exercise the greatest caution in formulating it.

[22] See my essay in William L. Reese and Eugene Freeman (eds.), *Process and Divinity: The Hartshorne Festschrift*, La Salle, Ill.: Open Court Publishing Co., 1964, pp. 493–513.

IV

Y

The Strange Witness of Unbelief

The safest generalization about Protestant theology since World War II is that it has evidenced a growing concern with its inescapable apologetic task. After a generation whose preoccupation was dogmatic and some of whose spokesmen even proclaimed the radical *diastasis* of Christian faith and modern culture, theologians today seem more and more to be resuming the line of march begun in the nineteenth century. There is, to be sure, widespread agreement that the corrections of the intervening years constitute a gain which the present and future must at all costs consolidate. We now see more clearly that Protestant theology is nothing if not the appropriate interpretation in a given situation of the witness of Holy Scripture to the God of Jesus Christ. Yet equally clear to many of us is that no theology today can be adequate which restricts itself to this dogmatic task alone. It is simply not enough to proclaim God's "mighty act in Christ" in a situation whose most characteristic question is whether the word "God" even has any reference. Beyond his duty to speak appropriately to the scriptural witness, the theologian must speak understandably to his contemporary hearers by taking full responsibility for the meaning and truth of his assertions.

Of course, anyone who assumes this responsibility exposes himself to a certain danger. The word "apologetic" has not come to be used so often pejoratively without good reason. Few would want to deny, indeed, that the apologetic efforts of the nineteenth century, however well-intentioned, tended toward a definite compromising of theology's total concern. In trying to show that their claims were meaningful and true, the liberal theologians frequently proceeded uncritically, accepting the then current expressions of secular experience and reason as definitive norms. Hence, if they succeeded in speaking understandably (and even that must be questioned), this was too often at the price of failing at their dogmatic task of speaking appropriately to the witness of Scripture. That we today, with our growing apologetic concern, are in danger of a similar failure is evident enough. But it is important to be clear about just where the danger really lies. It lies, I believe, not simply in accepting the apologetic task (although that certainly exposes one to it), but in proceeding uncritically in carrying out that task.

Properly understood, the responsibility of the theologian to speak understandably allows for offensive as well as defensive moves in his discussion with those who do not share his first duty to secure an appropriate interpretation of Scripture. What is required of him is not that he conform his claims to the secular thought of his situation, but that he establish their validity in terms of the same general standards of experience and reason to which that thought itself is subject. I hold that this requirement is more or less clearly implied by the very nature of the scriptural witness. In confessing that Jesus is the Christ, and, indeed, the very *Logos* of reality (John 1), Scripture implies that the truth he decisively re-presents is somehow of a piece with whatever truth men know anywhere. This does not mean, however, that men's claims to truth ever have to be accepted at face value. On the contrary, whether these claims themselves are really valid is always a question; and the theologian has both the right and the responsibility to press this question in his dialogue with the exponents of secular experience and reason. It is always possible that a traditional claim of theology is more genuinely understandable than the claim, say, of a secular philosophy with which it proves to conflict. In that case, the only satisfactory way to resolve the conflict is for philosophy to abandon or revise its disputed claim—not, however, because philosophy is nothing but the handmaid of theology, but because it must otherwise fail in its own proper service to mankind's search for an integral secular wisdom.

Take, for example, the issue so central in current discussions of the reality of God. So far as most theologians have been concerned, the only conception of God appropriate to Scripture entails the affirmation of his necessary existence. Many philosophers today, on the other hand, find the whole idea of necessary existence absurd, since they assume without question that the relation of essence and existence must in all cases be contingent. My view is that a theologian would proceed uncritically were he simply to take for granted that either party to this dispute is correct. He should at least consider whether the traditional assertion of God's necessary existence really is the only way in which the God of Holy Scripture can be appropriately represented. After all, there have been several cases where assertions traditionally regarded as essential to theology have proved on reconsideration to be inessential; and abandoning them has enabled theologians to speak more appropriately to Scripture, not less. If, however, one concludes, as I believe one must, that this assertion in some form *is* theologically essential, then it is incumbent upon him to make clear that the prevailing assumption of contemporary philosophers does not have the backing of experience and reason to which it pretends. To decline *this* obligation would indeed be to concede that theology's claims to truth are not to be taken seriously. On the other hand, to accept this obligation hardly requires one to conform these claims to the norms currently recognized by secular thought.

One thing, at any rate, seems clear: no theology can possibly be adequate unless, within the limits of a given situation, it is an appropriate interpretation of the scriptural witness. This witness plainly has its own integrity, which any theology worthy of the name is bound to respect. Hence to exclude from one's theological constructions any element that this witness includes as essential would be to forfeit one's claim to offer an adequate interpretation; and this is true however great our concern that the assertions we make as theologians also be genuinely understandable.

The basic assumption of this essay is that no theology can lay claim to adequacy which proposes to treat all assertions about the being and nature of God as inessential. I am not concerned here to argue for this assumption, mainly because I do not think it necessary, but also because my present purpose requires a different kind of argument. It is important, however, that the reason for the assumption be clearly stated.

A theology *post mortem dei* is impossible simply because theology's *cura prior* is to interpret a given witness for which the reality of God is necessary. And this is so in two somewhat different senses of the word "necessary." God is necessary, first, in the sense that the witness of Scripture would be entirely different than it is without the affirmation of his reality. If, as some have claimed, the whole idea of God is an absurdity, far more obviously absurd is the notion of a scriptural faith without God. But, second, God is necessary for Scripture in the sense that he is there understood to be the ultimate source and end of all that either is or could ever be. By this I do not mean that the God affirmed in Scripture is the wholly necessary being of the classical metaphysical tradition. I hold, on the contrary, that the scriptural witness to God can be appropriately interpreted only if his nature is conceived neoclassically as having a contingent as well as a necessary aspect. Nevertheless, *that* God is, as the "pure unbounded love" whom Jesus re-presents, is for the faith of Scripture no mere contingency but the strictest necessity. It follows that for an adequate theology, also, the reality of God is necessary in both of these senses. Theology's most essential assertion must always be the affirmation of that reality, which it cannot conceive at all except as somehow necessary existence.

If this is correct, the only theologically important question is whether the reality of God is also thus necessary for the experience or faith of men generally; and whether, therefore, a wholly secular account of this experience, such as philosophy has the task of providing, also becomes absurd if it tries to deny all assertions of God's reality. The crucial question, in other words, is not whether theology's witness to God is appropriate, but whether it is understandable. My purpose here is to clarify this question and to indicate some of the reasons why I believe it may be answered affirmatively. I contend that among the most important of such reasons is the evident untenability of positions that attempt to answer it negatively. In what follows, therefore, I want, first of all, to offer support for this contention and in that way to contribute toward answering the question. Then, with this as background, I want to speak to the question more directly by defending an argument whereby the assertion of God's reality may be made understandable in the general terms of reason and experience. Through all of this, I hope it may also become clear that an apologetic theology need not be the merely defensive operation it is always in danger of becoming. This, at any rate, is one of my motives in seeking to show that the theologian has questions to ask as well as to answer in his dialogue with contemporary unbelief.

Before entering that dialogue, we must remind ourselves of certain implications of the scriptural affirmation of God's reality. If that affirmation is true, then any secular or philosophical account of our experience which tries wholly to deny God cannot be entirely consistent and free of absurdity. The reason for this, as was noted above, is that God is understood by Scripture to be the necessarily existent. This is not to say that Scripture anywhere refers to God by the abstraction *ens necessarium*. For the most part, the scriptural writers speak of God's reality in the concrete and imaginative terms of myth, representing him as a supreme Person who freely creates the world and redeems it. Just in so doing, however, they clearly intend to affirm that God is both Alpha and Omega, the ultimate source and end of whatever is or could ever be. He is not simply one being among others, the mere actualization of some among the infinite wealth of possibilities. Rather, as sovereign Creator and Redeemer of all things, he is universally immanent in both actuality and possibility, and so is in the strictest sense necessary.

Thus it is with evident fidelity to Scripture that theologians have traditionally maintained, in the words of Pseudo-Dionysius, that God is not only "his own being," but also "the being of all." In our time, Paul Tillich has sought to renew this tradition by insisting that God is not *a* being, but rather "being-itself" or "the ground of being." By so formulating the matter, Tillich destroys the balance of traditional formulations, which never simply deny that God is *a* being. Even so, he at least makes clear that the reality of God is not one contingent factor alongside of others, but is the necessary ground of any and all beings, whether actual or merely possible. In any case, the more serious weakness in Tillich's view, as in classical theism itself, is that God is finally conceived to be *nothing but* necessary and thus as lacking in all real internal relations to the contingent beings of which he is the ground. Yet, even if one is concerned to overcome this weakness, he can scarcely claim to interpret Holy Scripture if he simply abandons its affirmation of God's necessary existence. The neoclassical theist, also, must clearly recognize that "the import of the word 'God' is no mere special meaning in our language, but the soul of significance in general, for it refers to the Life in and for which all things live."[1]

This means that the reality of God is essential to, or constitutive of, not only the special faith attested in Scripture, but also the common faith or experience of all men simply as such. If God is the necessarily existent, to experience anything at all, even as merely possible, is to experience it together with God as its ultimate ground. To this extent, the witness of Scripture implies by its very nature that no man can be wholly without faith in the God decisively represented in Jesus Christ. It is possible, naturally, for this common faith of mankind to be realized only in the deficient or distorted mode which Scripture designates as idolatry. Instead of trusting in God *alone* as the ultimate ground of being and meaning, men may always divide their basic confidence by directing it in part to some thing or

[1] Charles Hartshorne, *The Logic of Perfection and Other Essays in Neoclassical Metaphysics*, La Salle, Ill.: Open Court Publishing Co., 1962, p. 297.

things besides God. Even then, however, the reality of God remains constitutive of their experience, both of themselves and of the environing world of fellow beings. Because apart from God there could be nothing at all, not even as barely possible, all our experience must be the experience of his reality, if only in the mode of an idolatrous or inauthentic faith.

Here, too, classical theologians have been more or less of one mind in their interpretation of the scriptural witness. The position of so-called Augustinian thinkers is no doubt the most forthright, although even Thomas Aquinas is remembered for his statement that "all cognitive beings know God implicitly in any object of knowledge."[2] This statement is but echoed, then, by neoclassical thinkers who tell us that the reality of God is "inherent in all basic secular conceptions and only intellectual inhibitions can keep it from being formulated."[3]

And this brings us to the further implication that no reflective account of even our common experience simply as men can be in the least degree adequate which does not somehow bear witness to the reality of God. If that reality is constitutive of the experience, as of the being, of anything whatever, then it must be expressed or implied by every assertion which is so much as even meaningful. In the last analysis, our assertions have meaning at all only through our actual human experience, broadly and fairly construed. But, given the essential affirmation of Scripture, this can only mean that all our assertions which have any sense have God himself as their direct or indirect referent. Of course, nothing guarantees that this reference will be direct or made explicit, as is abundantly clear from the different kinds of nontheistic philosophy. Furthermore, the existence of various atheistic philosophies shows that it is at least verbally possible for the reality of God to be denied. Still, both types of philosophy, nontheistic and atheistic alike, must prove on analysis to be unstable, if the faith attested in Scripture is true. Nontheistic philosophies cannot but be essentially incomplete, in the sense that they imply any number of assertions as to the being and nature of God which they themselves decline to make explicit. Atheistic accounts of our experience, on the other hand, must exhibit the even more radical instability of outright inconsistency. By denying the reality of God altogether, they contradict the necessary implication of all their other assertions about man and the world. Or, as one may

[2] *Truth,* Vol. III, trans. R. W. Schmidt, Chicago: Henry Regnery Co., 1954, p. 42 (22, 2 *ad* 1).

[3] Charles Hartshorne, "Abstract and Concrete Approaches to Deity," *Union Seminary Quarterly Review,* March, 1965, p. 268.

also say, precisely in making these other assertions, they bear implicit witness to God's reality, which, strangely enough, they at the same time explicitly deny.

As far as my own experience goes, atheistic philosophies have uniformly turned out to be inconsistent in just this way. I have found that those who call themselves atheists typically fail to establish any clear distinction between their own obviously real confidence in the ultimate meaning of human life and the faith in God they claim to deny. Their main difference from those who share in the Christian witness has seemed to me invariably to lie in a basic confusion or lack of clarity in attesting what they themselves also most surely believe. This has been so, at any rate, insofar as their unbelief pretends to be total, and thus more than a rejection of some particular theistic scheme, like classical theism, which we may well hesitate to regard as the only such scheme. The point I wish to emphasize, however, is that just this would *have* to be the case with atheistic philosophies if the scriptural witness to God is in fact true. Were it possible to give an account of our experience which would not bear even a strange witness to God, that by itself would be the falsification of the essential claim of Christian faith. This follows, as I have suggested, from the very meaning of the word "God" as Christians must understand it if they are to remain faithful to Holy Scripture. Unless every man somehow has faith in the reality to which this word refers and in some way attests this in giving account of his experience, no man has such faith except verbally, and Scripture's affirmation of God must be put down as having neither truth nor consistent meaning.

Whether theology's witness to God is understandable, then, depends on some witness to him being discernible even in philosophies where his reality is expressly denied. I would now like to show that in one notable case unbelief can be discerned to bear such witness—and that most surely.

Few would question that one of the classic expressions of post-modern atheism is Jean-Paul Sartre's lecture of 1946, *L'existentialisme est un humanisme*.[4] Intended by Sartre as a popular state-

[4] Paris: Editions Nagel, 1962 (English translation by Philip Mariet in Walter Kaufmann [ed.], *Existentialism from Dostoevsky to Sartre,* New York: Meridian Books, Inc., 1957, pp. 287–311). Except where otherwise noted, quotations in the text are from this edition of Mairet's translation, to which the page references in the notes refer.

ment and defense of his philosophical intentions, this lecture has been widely received as a contemporary atheist manifesto. For this, Sartre himself is largely responsible, since he explicitly states that the existentialism he wishes to defend is "nothing else but an attempt to draw the full conclusions from a consistently atheistic position."[5] Yet, as I shall argue, Sartre's position in this lecture is so far from being "consistently atheistic" as to provide both the reasoning and the premises of one rather good argument for the reality of God. His ostensible statement of thoroughgoing atheism is really an almost perfect instance of what I have called the strange witness of unbelief. Whether the same could be said of his philosophy as a whole is, of course, another question, which I shall not consider in this essay. But, if the following criticism of this one lecture is valid, one would clearly have some reason to expect an affirmative answer to it as well.

It is important for understanding Sartre's lecture to note its explicitly apologetic motive. "My purpose here," he states in the opening sentence, "is to offer a defense of existentialism against several reproaches that have been laid against it."[6] The reproaches Sartre has in mind are those which have been made mainly by Christian and Communist critics—thus, for example, that existentialism undercuts social action by encouraging a "quietism of despair"; that it induces pessimism by over-emphasizing the dark side of human life; that it so isolates the individual as to make human solidarity impossible; and that its denial of any absolute norms of value entails all the consequences of complete moral relativism. Taken together, such objections amount to the charge that existentialism is an anti-humanistic doctrine. But it is just this charge that Sartre is concerned to answer, which explains, he tells us, why he has entitled his lecture, "Existentialism Is A Humanism." His claim is that "existentialism, in our sense of the word, is a doctrine that does render human life possible"; and, turning the tables on his critics, he proceeds to argue that "what is annoying them is not so much our pessimism, but, much more likely, our optimism."[7] As we shall see, it

---

[5] *Ibid.*, p. 310; cf. also pp. 289 and 290, where he describes himself as a representative of "atheistic existentialism."

[6] *Ibid.*, p. 287.

[7] *Ibid.*, pp. 288 f.; cf. p. 301, where it is stated that "what people reproach us with is not, after all, our pessimism, but the sternness of our optimism"; and p. 311, where the concluding sentence of the essay declares that "existentialism is an optimism, a doctrine of action, and it is only by bad faith, by confusing their own despair with ours, that Christians can speak of us as without hope" (my translation; cf. French text, p. 95).

is precisely the defense of his philosophy as a genuine humanism which betrays Sartre's position as untenable. To the extent that this defense succeeds, it raises the profoundest question about the atheistic premise on which his whole philosophy is alleged to rest.

First, however, we must understand the conclusions that Sartre regards as following from this premise. Significantly, the argument of his lecture is not *for* atheism, but *from* it. He states, in fact, that "Existentialism is not atheist in the sense that it would exhaust itself in demonstrations of the nonexistence of God. It declares, rather, that even if God existed that would make no difference from its point of view."[8] By this Sartre means that, whether God exists or not, man can be rightly understood only as radically free and responsible, so that the chief tenet of existentialism remains valid: "Existence comes before essence."[9] Thus he can even say (in apparent contradiction to the statement just quoted) that "there are two kinds of existentialists," Christian and atheistic, because this tenet is held in common by representatives of both kinds of position.[10] At the same time, his conviction is that atheism, once granted, makes existentialism's chief claim inescapable: "If God does not exist there is at least one being whose existence comes before its essence, a being which exists before it can be defined by any conception of it. That being is man."[11] In other words, whether or not existentialism is atheistic, atheism must definitely be existentialist. This, indeed, is Sartre's whole point when he says that his existentialism is "nothing else but an attempt to draw the full conclusions from a consistently atheistic position."

Sartre's reasoning here requires closer analysis. In basic logical structure, his argument is a mixed hypothetical syllogism. Its minor premise is the claim of atheism, which, as we have just seen, he does not argue for, but simply assumes. The major premise also is not original with Sartre, but, in one formulation, is directly taken over from Dostoevsky: "Everything is . . . permitted if God does not exist."[12] In another place, Sartre reasons, "Thus, there is no human nature because there is no God to have a conception of it;"[13] and, in yet another, "There can no longer be any good *a priori,* since there is no infinite and perfect consciousness to think it."[14] Combining these

8 *Ibid.,* p. 311.
9 *Ibid.,* p. 289.
10 *Ibid.*
11 *Ibid.,* p. 290.
12 *Ibid.,* p. 295.
13 *Ibid.,* pp. 290 f.
14 *Ibid.,* p. 294.

different formulations, we may express the major premise of Sartre's reasoning as follows: If God does not exist, or if there is no infinite and perfect consciousness to have a conception of human nature and so to think a good *a priori,* everything is permitted, or there is no human nature and so also no *a priori* good. Assuming, then, the truth of atheism's claim that "God does not exist," one may infer by *modus ponens* that "Everything is permitted" is also true; and this, for Sartre, is equivalent with establishing the main tenet of existentialism, "Existence precedes essence."

Against this background we can understand Sartre's polemic in the lecture against what he speaks of indifferently as "radicalism," "secular moralism," or "the philosophic atheism of the eighteenth century."[15] If atheism implies that existence comes before essence, any claim that essence is prior to existence logically commits one to theism. This is the contrapositive of Sartre's own major premise; it makes explicit the warrant for the inference by *modus tollens,* whereby, in denying the consequent of that premise, one may also deny the antecedent. But it also makes clear, Sartre thinks, that much modern atheism has really been inconsistent. Because many atheists have sought "to suppress God at the least possible expense" and have continued to hold to notions of a universal human nature and an *a priori* good, they have affirmed the priority of essence to existence and so have been theists, as it were, in spite of themselves. "The existentialist, on the contrary, finds it extremely embarrassing that God does not exist, for there disappears with Him all possibility of finding values in an intelligible heaven."[16] Therefore, on Sartre's own showing, theism, or the affirmation of "an infinite and perfect consciousness," is the necessary implication of any talk of a universal human nature or *a priori* moral values. Hence, if one's atheism is to be consistent, he must go beyond much that has passed for "atheism" and leave all such talk behind him.

The question is whether Sartre himself succeeds in meeting this condition. On the face of it, there is no doubt much to indicate an affirmative answer. He tells us explicitly that "Man is nothing else but that which he makes of himself" and that a possibility of choice "has value only because it is chosen" by man.[17] Likewise, there is the whole discussion summarized in his famous dictum that "man is condemned to be free"—which means that "every man, without any

15 *Ibid.,* pp. 294, 290.
16 *Ibid.,* p. 294.
17 *Ibid.,* pp. 291, 294.

support or help whatever, is condemned at every instant to invent man."[18] But, as becomes evident from even a moment's reflection on just such statements, the meaning of Sartre's position may not be as obvious as it seems. If man is *condemned* to be free, then there is one thing, at least, with respect to which he has no freedom whatever: his own distinctively human capacity for free and responsible action. It is not man who invents man the man-inventor; and man's power to make himself is not itself a man-made power. Thus one is led to wonder whether the tenet "Existence comes before essence" is not at best elliptical and, in consequence, misleading if taken as an adequate summary of Sartre's position.

That this is in fact so is placed beyond doubt by the whole last part of the lecture. Here, in replying to the objections of his critics, Sartre states explicitly that, "although it is impossible to find in each and every man a universal essence that can be called human nature, there is nevertheless a human universality of *condition*."[19] By the word "condition," he says, we are to understand "all the *limitations* which *a priori* define man's fundamental situation in the universe. His historical situations are variable. . . . But what never vary are the necessities of being in the world, of having to labor and to die there."[20] ". . . diverse though man's purposes may be, at least none of them is wholly foreign to me, since every human purpose presents itself as an attempt either to surpass these limitations, or to widen them, or else to deny or to accommodate oneself to them. . . . In every purpose there is universality, in this sense that every purpose is comprehensible to every man. Not that this or that purpose defines man for ever, but that it may be entertained again and again."[21] Elsewhere, Sartre defines "the *situation* of man as one of free choice, without excuse and without help" and further holds that "man is always the same, in face of a situation which changes, and choice always remains a choice in a situation."[22]

From all this it becomes clear that Sartre is by no means the radical nominalist as regards man that he may at first sight appear to be. If, on his view, "Existence precedes essence," he also argues, by implication, that "Condition (or situation) precedes existence." Contrary to his statement quoted earlier, a man is not simply what exists

18 *Ibid.*, p. 295.
19 *Ibid.*, p. 303.
20 *Ibid.*
21 *Ibid.*, pp. 303 f.
22 *Ibid.*, pp. 307, 306 (my translation; cf. French text, p. 79).

after the fact of his own free decisions, but is also defined by "limitations" which Sartre himself speaks of as *a priori* and which serve to bind each man, whatever his decisions, into solidarity with every other. Because this is so, it is far from obvious that Sartre turns his back on *all* talk of a universal human nature. The phrase "human nature," as he uses it, does not refer to anything strictly universal; but it is quite otherwise with "human condition," which has just such universal reference. Thus one might well interpret Sartre's analysis of "human existence" by saying that "human nature" is really an abstract variable of which "human condition" is the abstract constant —somewhat as, in an analysis of "change," "difference" and "sameness" are alike abstractions, although the latter is a constant which the former as a variable necessarily implies. The fact that Sartre himself, as we shall see, elsewhere introduces the distinction between "variable content" and "universal form" with respect to morality makes this interpretation all the more plausible.

Even more revealing is Sartre's reply to the objection that his philosophy is completely relativistic, and so excludes the possibility of passing any absolute judgments. To the contrary, he maintains, we *can* make such judgments, and that in both the logical and the moral senses of the word "judgment." "One can judge, first, . . . that certain choices are founded upon error, others upon the truth. One can judge a man by saying that he is a man of bad faith."[23] By "bad faith" Sartre means an understanding of one's existence in which one seeks to escape from his "condition" (or "situation") as a human being. As we have seen, Sartre holds that every man *qua* man shares in the universal human condition of radical freedom and responsibility for himself and his fellow men. But one denies the reality of this condition whenever he seeks to excuse his decisions by appealing, say, to his passions or to some scheme of values alleged to be incumbent upon him. Therefore, Sartre concludes, "one cannot avoid pronouncing a judgment of truth." "If anyone says to me, 'And what if I want to be a man of bad faith?' I answer, 'There is no reason why you should not be, but I declare that you are and that the attitude of strict consistency is the attitude of good faith.' "[24]

This, however, is not all Sartre claims the right to declare.

Furthermore, I can pass a moral judgment. For I declare that freedom in and through each concrete circumstance can have no other end but to will

[23] *Ibid.*, p. 307 (my translation; cf. French text, p. 80).
[24] *Ibid.* (my translation; cf. French text, pp. 81 f.).

itself; and if a man has once recognized that it is he who posits values in the state of abandonment, he can will only one thing, and that is freedom as the foundation of all values. This does not mean that he wills freedom in the abstract; it is to say simply that the acts of men of good faith have the quest for freedom as such as their ultimate significance. . . . Thus in the name of that will to freedom implied by freedom itself, I can form judgments on those who seek to hide from themselves the utter gratuitousness of their existence and its complete freedom. The ones who hide their complete freedom by a spirit of seriousness or by deterministic excuses I shall call cowards; the others who attempt to show that their existence was necessary, when it is just the contingency of the appearance of man on earth, I shall call scum. . . . Thus, although the content of morality is variable, a certain form of this morality is universal.[25]

Whereas from the first part of Sartre's argument one gets the distinct impression that morality *as such* is variable, that impression is here subjected to an important correction. It turns out that there is an aspect of morality which is not variable but constant; and this explains why there can be a judgment of a man's decisions which is not posited by them but is prior to them—again in contradiction to Sartre's earlier statement that a possibility of choice has value only because man chooses it. As a matter of fact, Sartre now even goes so far as to concede the partial validity of the Kantian categorical imperative, for which earlier in the lecture he has nothing but criticism.[26] "Kant states that freedom wills itself and the freedom of others. Granted. But he thinks that the formal and the universal suffice to constitute a morality. We think, on the contrary, that principles that are too abstract break down in defining action. . . . The content [*sc.* of morality] is always concrete, and therefore unforeseeable; there is always invention. The one thing that counts is to know whether the invention which is made is made in the name of freedom."[27]

It should be evident by now that there is more than sufficient reason to question the consistency of Sartre's self-styled atheism. Far from holding simply that man is nothing but what he makes of himself and that there is no *a priori* good, he actually asserts a universal human condition and appeals to freedom as an absolute standard of moral judgment. In other words, in his view, too, "Everything is permitted" is false, if taken strictly or without qualification. "One can choose anything," he states, *"but only if it is upon the*

25 *Ibid.*, pp. 307 f. (my translation; cf. French text, pp. 82, 84 f.).
26 See *ibid.*, especially p. 296.
27 *Ibid.*, p. 308 (my translation; cf. French text, pp. 85 f.).

plane of free commitment"[28]—which is to say that *not* everything is permitted after all.

I cannot go into the question whether the position Sartre seems to express in this statement (as well as elsewhere in the lecture) is fully tenable. On my view, the logic of his ethic is drastically oversimplified, since it is impossible for the content of morality in a concrete situation to be as independent of its fundamental form as he holds it to be. But this question could not so much as arise unless Sartre himself plainly denied the consequent of his initial major premise. And yet, because he does deny its consequent, we are permitted by *modus tollens* to deny its antecedent as well, with the result that "God exists" is shown not to be false but true.

In a word, the very reasoning Sartre uses against earlier forms of atheism makes clear that he, too, is a theist *malgré lui*. Strange as his witness to God's reality certainly is, there cannot be the least question that he bears one.

This is not to say that the God whom Sartre attests is the wholly necessary being of classical theism. As far as his own reasoning goes, the most that can be said is that, since there is, after all, the *a priori* good of freedom, there also has to be an "infinite and perfect consciousness" to think it. It is by no means obvious, however, that such a consciousness must—or even could—be a reality which is in every respect necessary. "Consciousness" by its very meaning seems to entail that any conscious subject be related to the objects of its awareness by real internal relations. Supposing, then, that its objects are contingent, as must surely be the case with the ideal of *human* freedom, one can hardly deny that even a perfect consciousness would have a contingent or nonnecessary aspect. Furthermore, if human freedom is at all the reality Sartre claims, how could the God of classical theism be anything but an illusion? A God whose knowledge of the world would have to be strictly identical with his wholly necessary essence could be said to know the world only if the world itself were wholly necessary. Yet it is just such a necessary world that the fact of human freedom, if it is a fact, belies. Therefore, Sartre is fully justified in implying that "Man is the future of man" can be affirmed only if classical theism as such is denied. If one understands this statement "to mean that the future is inscribed in heaven and beheld by God, it is false, because the future would then no longer even be a future."[29]

28 *Ibid.*, p. 309; my italics.
29 *Ibid.*, p. 295 (my translation; cf. French text, pp. 38 f.).

Thus the claim that Sartre's argument is implicitly theistic does not mean that it requires, or even that it is compatible with, traditional supernaturalistic theism. On the contrary, the whole implication of his central emphasis on man's freedom is that this form of theism must definitely be rejected. In this sense, his position is undoubtedly "atheistic," and nothing would be gained by claiming otherwise. But the striking thing, as I have tried to show, is that the very freedom which implies *this* kind of atheism is also implicitly "theistic," given the broader sense of that word assumed by Sartre's major premise. One can only conclude, therefore, that the scope of his so-called "atheism" is considerably more restricted than it has been alleged to be, whether by himself or by others. Insofar as his position in this lecture is more than merely verbally atheistic, it is the rejection not of the reality of God as such, but of a particular theistic scheme for conceiving that reality.

And this leads to a summary comment on Sartre's argument. If the premise of his implied theism is his insistence on the absolute value of human freedom, at stake in that insistence is the whole defense of his philosophy against the charge that it is anti-humanistic. "Existentialism *is* a humanism!"—that, as we have seen, is the verdict Sartre struggles to secure against the reproaches of his critics. Yet his efforts to that end owe whatever success they achieve to his unqualified affirmation of the fact and value of man's freedom. It is solely because he acknowledges that men universally are and ought to be free prior to their own decisions that his philosophy is not simply an expression of quietism and despair and neither denies the fact of human solidarity nor gives way to unmitigated relativism. In the light of the foregoing criticism, however, this has an important implication. It follows by the logic of Sartre's own reasoning that he succeeds in meeting his critics' objections only by implying the falsity of his apparently thoroughgoing atheism. He makes good the claim that his existentialism is genuinely humanistic only because his witness to man is, strangely but surely, a witness to God.

The obvious reaction to this criticism of Sartre's atheism is that it exploits a particular—and, perhaps, unfortunate—statement of his case in one lecture. Granted that the criticism as such is valid, that Sartre's own reasoning implies a theistic rather than an atheistic conclusion, one may still question the truth of that reasoning. Maybe all that has been shown is that an extremely dubious conclusion can be made to follow formally from premises that are themselves unacceptable.

I want to speak briefly to this reaction. My purpose is in no sense to develop a fully adequate counterargument, but simply to indicate why I find the reaction ill-founded. If I am right, Sartre's unintended argument for God's reality is not only formally valid, but also rests on premises that have a fair claim to be materially true.

We may begin by considering the argument's minor premise, that not everything is morally permissible after all. For Sartre, as we have seen, there is an impassable limit to man's freedom of choice, which is set by the absolute value of freedom itself. Together with Kant, he holds that the will to freedom both for oneself and for others is a categorical imperative. But even if one were to reject the view that freedom (or freedom alone) is the *summum bonum,* he might still grant that something, at least, provides the firm "foundation of all values." In fact, it would seem that no one, except, perhaps, the complete moral relativist or skeptic, could fail to affirm all that the minor premise of the argument really requires. To claim that any value, whether freedom or some other, is prior to our decisions and an absolute standard for judging them is to deny with Sartre that "Everything is permitted" is true. Therefore, the question of the truth of the argument's minor premise reduces to the question of the truth of complete moral skepticism; and once this is recognized, the answer is not, I believe, difficult to determine.

One must ask, first of all, whether the idea of a moral skepticism at once complete and true even makes any sense. If the force of the word "true," as I should argue, is properly analyzed as "worthy of being believed,"[30] in making any claim to truth whatever, one at least tacitly presupposes that we should always believe only those assertions that are worthy of credence, however their worth may be specifically determined. But then how could one make the claim that "Everything is permitted" is true? Evidently the one thing any claim to truth excludes as *not* permissible is disbelief in the presupposition apart from which that claim itself would have no meaning.

Then, too, there is the fact that our ordinary experience and language preclude the possibility of such complete skepticism. At issue in our everyday moral disputes is never *whether* there is a standard of value by which our particular choices can be judged, but

[30] See above, pp. 111 ff.

only *what* that standard requires of us as we make our decisions between concrete courses of action. True, a few philosophers have from time to time tried to maintain that our moral disputes are really only pseudo disputes, since they are in principle beyond any possibility of rational adjudication. But not the least achievement of certain recent practitioners of linguistic analysis is to have demonstrated that such a view can derive no support from our actual moral experience as attested by ordinary speech. In matters of morals, as in those of our everyday knowledge of the world, our all but instinctive assumption is that true judgments are somehow to be had, and it is on this basis that we carry on all our inquiry and discussion.[31] This is the reason, needless to say, why, at the more reflective level also, the vast majority of men have been anything but ethical skeptics. The philosophical accounts of our experience do indeed express something less than a *consensus gentium moralis*. But on one point their convergence is unmistakable: like the experience on which they are the critical reflection, they confidently affirm the possibility of moral truth and thus exclude complete skepticism as a serious alternative.

For all these reasons, I think we may proceed with the confidence that the minor premise of Sartre's implied argument is materially sound. Short of being thoroughly skeptical of any absolute standard of moral judgment, one cannot affirm that everything is permissible, and so cannot deny that the premise is true. In this connection, we may also recall the comment made earlier about the logical dependence of Sartre's defense of his philosophy as humanistic on his rejection of any thoroughgoing moral skepticism. The point of this comment may be generalized to remind us that other would-be humanists as well have a particular reason to avoid the skeptical extreme. If their affirmations of human values are to be serious and more than claims which are as arbitrary as their denials, they clearly require a firmer foundation than complete skepticism is able to provide.

The more difficult question is whether they require the *theistic* foundation which the major premise of Sartre's reasoning alleges to be necessary. Does the mere acknowledgment of some nonrelative standard of moral judgment entail the conclusion that *God* exists? Is there really no alternative between thoroughgoing moral skepticism

[31] See especially Stephen Toulmin, *An Examination of the Place of Reason in Ethics,* Cambridge: Cambridge University Press, 1950; also above, pp. 29, 33.

and express affirmation of the reality of an "infinite and perfect consciousness"?

Obviously, the answer to these questions is not to be discovered by consulting some given consensus of experience and reason. If there are those, like Sartre, who have answered them affirmatively, there are also others who have challenged such answers—if not explicitly, at least by implication. In the modern period in particular, nothing has been more common among philosophers than attempts to account for our moral experience without making any explicit theistic commitments. Sometimes these attempts have been frankly atheistic, asserting the validity of absolute values, while denying the reality of God as in any sense the necessarily existent. More often modern philosophers have developed ethical positions best described simply as nontheistic, since they have restricted themselves to our moral confidence as such, leaving the foundation of this confidence wholly out of account. In both cases, however, the possibility, or at least the necessity, of any moral argument for the reality of God has been questioned. Consequently, if one is to hold that some such argument is a path to truth, he must be aware that the major premise of the argument has been and is disputed and so is nowise self-evident.

Still, utter falsehood is not the only alternative to immediate self-evidence. The relevant question is not whether this premise is indisputable—for what philosophical premise is?—but whether there are good reasons that can be adduced to support it. My conviction is that there are such reasons and that we can give an adequate account of our all but instinctive rejection of moral skepticism only by developing an explicitly theistic position. For the present, however, I must confine myself to simply outlining the argument for this conviction in its essential steps.[32]

[32] An argument similar to the following is developed by William James in *The Will to Believe and Other Essays in Popular Philosophy*, New York: Longmans, Green & Co., 1897, pp. 184–215. James holds that "the stable and systematic moral universe for which the ethical philosopher asks is fully possible only in a world where there is a divine thinker with all-enveloping demands" (*ibid.*, pp. 213 f.). He supports this conclusion by showing, first, that "nothing can be good or right except so far as some consciousness feels it to be good or thinks it to be right" (*ibid.*, pp. 192 f.); from which it follows that "an overarching system of moral relations, true 'in themselves,' . . . must be treated as a merely provisional abstraction from that real Thinker in whose actual demand upon us to think as he does our obligation must be ultimately based" (*ibid.*, p. 194). In this reasoning, James is in essential agreement with Sartre's contention that only an "infinite and perfect consciousness" can make possible absolute moral judgments. But James also argues that the idea of God

The first step is to show that the minor premise of Sartre's implied reasoning—not everything is permitted—begs a question logically distinct from the one it directly answers. The latter question is the one sharply pressed on Sartre by his critics, of whether, if "Existence precedes essence," one possibility of choice is not morally as good or as bad as every other. His reply, as we have seen, is finally negative, and he defends this reply by appealing to freedom as "the foundation of all values." Given this one absolute standard, he is able to reject the charge of complete skepticism by showing that true moral judgments are in fact possible. To be sure, as was suggested above, the logic of his ethic is grossly oversimplified, since it covers solely the form of our moral action, which it treats as completely independent of all content. Even so, Sartre shows that he can at least judge the *how* of our action, if not its *what,* and that he is therefore able to give some reply to questions having to do with decision between concrete possibilities of choice.

Questions of this kind, however, are not the only questions to which our experience of moral choice gives rise. There is also the kind of question which is accurately described as a "limiting question," since it arises not within our moral experience but at its limits.[33] Thus someone might ask Sartre, "But why ought I to realize freedom anyway?" Assuming that this question is intended as many other similar questions are, Sartre could not satisfactorily answer it simply by pointing out that freedom is the *summum bonum* and thus by definition is always to be chosen in preference to its opposite. The reason this answer will not do is because it misses the point of the question. What the questioner wishes to know (although the language of his question is admittedly somewhat misleading) is not why he should act to realize freedom rather than some other end, but why he

---

is the only way to explicate what he calls the "strenuous mood" with respect to our moral obligations. "The capacity of the strenuous mood lies so deep down among our natural human possibilities that even if there were no metaphysical or traditional grounds for believing in a God, men would postulate one simply as a pretext for living hard, and getting out of the game of existence its keenest possibilities of zest" (*ibid.,* p. 213). It is this second kind of argument that is also developed below, with the notion of "basic confidence in the worth of life" playing a somewhat similar role to James' "strenuous mood." The important difference is that what I mean by "basic confidence" is, in Heideggerian terms, the "existential" (*Existenzial*) of which James' "strenuous" and "easy-going" moods are respectively "authentic" and "inauthentic" modifications.

33 See Stephen Toulmin, *op. cit.,* pp. 202–11; also above, pp. 30 f.

should act to any end at all. He is not asking the properly *moral question* of why *some* course of action is better than another, but the *limiting question* of why *any* course of action is ultimately meaningful or worth while. That our actions are thus worth while he of course takes for granted even to ask his limiting question. But the same is true of anyone who denies that everything is permitted and appeals to some supreme good as "the foundation of all values." To assert that freedom or any other value is the absolute standard of moral choice is to beg the question of the ultimate meaningfulness of our actions in accordance with that standard.

That this is so may become clearer if we look at the logic of the limiting question a bit more closely. Such a question, I have said, presupposes the basic confidence that our actions are somehow meaningful or worth while and is asked for the purpose of understanding more clearly how or why this is so. But what prompts us to seek such clearer understanding in the first place? The answer, it seems, is that our original understanding of this basic confidence is for one reason or another called in question. Thus, for example, reflection on the "boundary situation" of death may completely shatter any quasi-animal-like assurance that life is worth living.

Then I said to myself, "What befalls the fool will befall me also; why then have I been so very wise?" And I said to myself that this also is vanity. For of the wise man as of the fool there is no enduring remembrance, seeing that in the days to come all will have been long forgotten. How the wise man dies just like the fool! So I hated life, because what is done under the sun was grievous to me; for all is vanity and a striving after wind. (Eccles. 2:15 ff.)

If the one fate of death comes to all of us indifferently and there is no "enduring remembrance," then, indeed, all is vanity and empty striving. As a matter of fact, on these terms, even the hatred of life is without point and the pronouncement of life's vanity as meaningless as everything else. Albert Camus writes:

From the moment one says that all is nonsense, one expresses something which has sense. Refusing all meaning to the world amounts to abolishing all value judgments. But to live, and, for instance, to take food, is in itself a value judgment. We choose to continue existing from the moment we do not let ourselves die, and thus we recognize a value, at least a relative one, in life. Anyway, what is the meaning of a literature of despair? Despair is silent. After all, silence itself has sense if the eyes speak. True despair is agony, tomb, or abyss. If it speaks, analyzes, especially if it writes, immediately a brother stretches forth his hand to us, the tree is justified, love is born. A literature of despair is a contradiction in terms.[34]

In the nature of the case, our judgment of the foundational value of freedom or anything else rests on the assurance that the world is finally meaningful and that our striving to realize values is not simply vain. We may indeed inquire as to the reasons for this assurance; and our limiting questions in fact arise because the boundary situations of life may lead us to press beyond superficial understandings of it. But necessarily implied by any claim to moral truth whatever is the unconditioned meaningfulness of our life as subject to that claim.

This being granted, the second step in the argument is fairly easy. It consists in showing that, if the assertion of a moral standard presupposes the unconditioned worth of our choices, the central claim of theism offers the best answer that can be given to our limiting questions as to the nature of that worth. The argument concludes, in other words, that the idea of God alone explicates and makes fully intelligible the presupposed ground of our confidence that life is ultimately meaningful. In this way, "If not everything is permitted, God exists" is shown to be a true assertion.

There is, to be sure, one major difficulty in establishing this conclusion: it must be admitted that the idea of God of classical theism is far from offering the best answer to our limiting questions. There are several reasons for this. For one thing, a number of critics have shown that the classical idea of God fails to meet the minimal demand for the answer to any question, that its terms have a self-consistent meaning. Combining as it does the conceptions of God both of classical metaphysics and of Holy Scripture, traditional theism has proved to be a veritable nest of contradictions. On the one hand, it has held that God is a reality wholly necessary and absolute, and so without real internal relations to the contingent beings of which he is the ground. On the other hand, it has predicated of God the personalistic perfections found in Scripture, all of which entail that he enjoy just such real relations. There have been repeated attempts, naturally, to compose the resulting contradictions. But— and this is a second failure of classical theism—these attempts have been successful only because they have reduced the perfections

---

[34] "The Riddle," *Atlantic Monthly,* June, 1963, p. 85.

attributed to God by Scripture to empty symbols. God is said to "know" or to "love" the world only as the wholly necessary being whose sole relation to his creatures is the purely external one of their relation to him. This means that the idea of God as classically conceived sheds no clear light at all on the ground of our confidence in life's meaning. The very idea that something is meaningful or worth while assumes that the ground of its worth is bound to it by genuine ties of real internal relationship. Yet this is just what the traditional conception of God makes it impossible to assume, except at the price of radical inconsistency. Therefore, if there is to be a moral argument for theism along the general lines Sartre suggests, the "theism" in question must be something quite different from what has most commonly gone by that name.

It is simply a fact, however, that classical theism can no longer pretend to be the only, or even the most adequate, formulation of a genuinely theistic position. As suggested earlier, another form of theism has been developed which is properly described as neoclassical, since it seems to achieve the very goal to which the classical view is but a first and, by comparison, rough approximation. The defining characteristic of this new theism is that, in conformity with quite untraditional metaphysical premises, it conceives the reality of God as in principle dipolar. Thus, while God is indeed understood to exist necessarily, his nature is also conceived to have a genuinely contingent pole or aspect by reason of his real internal relations to his wholly nonnecessary creatures. Then, because he enjoys such real relations, God is also thought of as utterly different from the mere Absolute of traditional metaphysics. Although his relativity to others is itself wholly nonrelative, and so quite literally absolute, God himself is the supremely relative One, for whom nothing whatever is merely indifferent or lacking in interest.

I submit that, when the idea of God is conceived in this neoclassical way, the moral argument for God's reality implied by Sartre is immeasurably strengthened—to the point, in fact, of being genuinely convincing. Because the nature of God is now understood to have aspects that are necessary *and* contingent, absolute *and* relative, *both* the conditions can be met for making the notion of a ground of ultimate confidence fully intelligible. Thus this ground may now be conceived as itself ultimate, so as to account for our assurance that the meaning of our life is unconditioned. Because, as the new view holds, the sheer existence of God is in the most literal sense necessary and absolute, this first condition is amply satisfied. At the beginning and end of all our ways is One in whose steadfast will and purpose there is indeed no shadow of turning and in whom all our confidences have their unshakable foundation. This same God, however, is infinitely other and more than the *deus philosophorum,* the mere metaphysical Absolute. In his inmost actuality he is "pure unbounded love," pure personal relation to others, who has no other cause than the ever more abundant life of the creatures of his love. Far from being something to which even the greatest of our accomplishments is worth nothing at all, he is the One who makes even the least of things to be of infinite worth by giving it to share in his own infinite and all-encompassing life. He is, in fact, just that "enduring remembrance," except for which our perishing lives as creatures would indeed be vanity and a striving after wind. But this makes clear that the new theism can also satisfy the second condition for any answer that would explicate our assurance of life's meaning. Because it conceives God as the eminently relative One, to whom each of our choices makes an enduring difference, it enables us at last really to understand our confidence that the whole of our life is unconditionally worth while.

If this argument is correct, Sartre's strange witness to faith in God is due to something more than an unfortunate assumption of faulty premises. It is due, finally, to the inescapable logic of our common human experience, which forbids a consistent denial of such faith as a violation of its own rationality. Because, in whatever we say or do to witness to the cause of man, we must beg the question of the ultimate meaningfulness of human life, there is a profound sense in which the phrase "atheistic humanism" must always seem self-contradictory, even as its opposite "theistic humanism" must always sound redundant. This does not mean that every humanist is forthwith to be called a "theist," and much less does it mean that he may be said already to bear the name "Christian." But it does mean, as Karl Rahner puts it,[35] that the humanist is in a sense "anonymously" both theist and Christian, and that theologians, above all, must be quick to realize this. Only then can they do their part toward the one end of all Christian witness: so to bring each man to the full consciousness of his actual faith that he is confronted anew with the free claim of God

[35] See Karl Rahner, *Schriften zur Theologie,* Vol. V, Einsiedeln: Benziger Verlag, 1962, pp. 155, 379–410; also "Philosophy and Theology," *Theology Digest.* Summer, 1964, pp. 118–22.

on his life and, in answering freedom, may choose to bear the name of Christ as his own. For to bear that name is simply to participate in a witness to God in which all elements of strangeness are overcome. It is to share in the one ministry among men in which "the whole fulness of deity dwells bodily" (Col. 2:9).

V

The Temporality of God

It is generally acknowledged that the philosophy of Martin Heidegger has been one of the most important influences on much of the significant theological thinking of our time. Less commonly recognized is that the converse of this proposition is equally true—that, at decisive points, Heidegger's work as a philosopher has been stimulated and even determined by influences emanating from contemporary theology.

One of the many merits of the recent study by Otto Pöggeler, *Der Denkweg Martin Heideggers*,[1] is to have made clear both the fact and the nature of this reciprocal influence. Speaking of the marked shift in Heidegger's thinking during the years immediately after the First World War, Pöggeler comments: "Heidegger began his pilgrimage in proximity to a theology which had become ever more firmly convinced that now, after centuries and even millennia of obscuring primitive Christian faith by philosophy as well as theology, it was necessary to experience this faith anew in its primal meaning. Witnesses of faith like Luther and Kierkegaard supported this view, and it was just they who became important to the young Heidegger. From the outset, Heidegger's relation to the modern thinking about history, which with Dilthey became philosophically self-conscious, was eclipsed by a relation to another more primal historical thinking: prior to the modern form of thinking about history was the experience of history as manifested by primitive Christian faith."[2]

According to Pöggeler, it was by reflecting on primitive Christian religiousness as the model of an experience of life as "factual" or "historical" that Heidegger acquired the guiding concepts by means of which he subsequently undertook in *Sein und Zeit* to explicate the

[1] Pfullingen: Günther Neske Verlag, 1963.
[2] *Ibid.*, pp. 35 f.

144

ontological structure of human existence. At the same time, Heidegger increasingly recognized that a clear focusing of this primal experience could lead to nothing less than a "dismantling" (*Destruktion*) of the whole metaphysical-theological tradition originating in classical Greece. His studies of Augustine, for example, convinced him of the irreconcilable opposition between the conceptuality of this metaphysical tradition and the understanding of existence Augustine and others had sought to explicate theologically by means of it. He saw that, given this traditional conceptuality, one could do justice neither to "the actualization of factual existence" (or the historicity of man) nor to "the godness of God" as Christian faith understands them.[3] On the other hand, he realized that an ontological analysis which would look to this understanding of faith for its guiding concepts could only result in the most radical reorientation of traditional metaphysical thinking. Thus, in Pöggeler's view, the author of *Sein und Zeit* was a thinker whose mediated encounter with the New Testament and with theologians like Augustine, Luther, and Kierkegaard had aroused "the suspicion that the God of philosophy is not the living God of faith and that metaphysical theology is not the final answer to the questions of thinking."[4]

The importance of Pöggeler's view for my concern here is that it may help better to understand a passage from *Sein und Zeit* that I propose to consider in this essay. In a footnote to the section of this work in which Heidegger discusses the genesis of "the vulgar concept of time," there occur the following remarkable sentences: "It requires no extensive discussion to show that the traditional concept of eternity, in the sense of the 'stationary now' (*nunc stans*), is drawn from the vulgar understanding of time and is limited by an orientation to the idea of 'constant' presence-on-hand. If the eternity of God would admit of being 'construed' philosophically, it could be understood only as a more primal and 'infinite' temporality. Whether the *via negationis et eminentiae* could offer a possible way to this goal would remain uncertain."[5]

I have called these sentences remarkable for four closely related reasons. First, they constitute one among only a very few explicit references to God or to theology in a work whose central purpose and

[3] *Ibid.*, p. 45.
[4] *Ibid.*, p. 46.
[5] *Sein und Zeit,* Halle: Max Niemeyer Verlag, 1927, p. 427, n. 1 (English translation by John Macquarrie and Edward Robinson in Martin Heidegger, *Being and Time,* New York: Harper & Row, 1962, p. 499, n. xiii).

theme are quite different from those that properly determine the task of the theologian. Second, this passage is the only place in the book where Heidegger at all makes explicit what his attempt to reorient metaphysical thinking would mean for a philosophical doctrine of God. In his other directly theological references, his purpose is invariably historical or critical: either to point to the antecedents of certain ideas in the theological tradition or else to distinguish his own "ontological" use of concepts from their "ontic" meaning as generally used by theologians. Here, however, in this one footnote, his purpose is primarily constructive: to make clear at least the bare outlines of the philosophical "construction" of God suggested by his new analysis of the basis of metaphysical reflection. Third, the philosophical theology Heidegger here presents, as it were, *in nuce* involves a radical departure from the classical philosophical-theological tradition. Judged from the standpoint of this tradition, his proposal that the eternity of God be construed as his " 'infinite' temporality" represents the abandonment of just those premises from which alone an adequate doctrine of God can be developed.

If, however, Pöggeler's view of the theological background of *Sein und Zeit* is correct, there is also a fourth and more important reason why these sentences are worthy of consideration. Even as, on this view, Heidegger's phenomenological analysis of human existence represents the translation into formal ontological terms of the understanding of man set forth in the New Testament, so his proposal for a philosophical construction of God's eternity as infinite temporality would seem to represent a similar "ontologizing" of the primitive Christian understanding of God.

Admittedly, Heidegger himself does not seem to have interpreted his remarks in this passage anywhere in the way Pöggeler suggests. On the face of it, the footnote does nothing more than propose a philosophical interpretation of God that is coherent with Heidegger's analysis of human existence and that, like this analysis, thoroughly revolutionizes the conventional metaphysical wisdom. Nevertheless, I am persuaded we are not far from the truth if we regard his proposal as stimulated and perhaps even determined by the same theological influences that were otherwise so decisive for this phase of his work. I regard it as highly probable that here, as in *Sein und Zeit* generally, the historical background of Heidegger's statements is the understanding of man and of God with which his encounter with Christian theology served to acquaint him.

But, be this as it may, my main concern in this essay is less with the historical antecedents of Heidegger's proposal than with the meaning and relevance of the proposal itself. To my knowledge, this passage in *Sein und Zeit* has rarely if ever been carefully considered by other students of Heidegger's thought; and, on this ground alone, there would seem ample room for the kind of consideration of it to be attempted here. At the very least, an interpretation of Heidegger's footnote may itself provide something like a footnote to the extensive interpretation of his philosophy that continues to preoccupy so many learned and capable minds. And yet, if I am right, this is not the most that can be claimed for an effort to interpret this passage. As I shall subsequently argue, the usual attempts by theologians today to interpret the Christian witness to God typically lead to an impasse from which the conventional philosophical wisdom, both old and new, provides no possibility of escape. My conviction, however, is that a way out of this impasse *is* provided by just the kind of philosophical theology that Heidegger here seems to propose. Hence, if this conviction can be proved correct, an attempt to understand his proposal may claim a theological importance more than sufficient to justify undertaking it.

In what follows, then, I shall be engaged in two main tasks: first, to interpret Heidegger's footnote by drawing out its several implications in its larger context in *Sein und Zeit* as a whole; and, second, to show that what he there proposes as a philosophical interpretation of God's eternity has a unique relevance for the attempts of Christian theologians to develop an adequate doctrine of God for our time.

1

I begin by inquiring as to the purely formal meaning of a philosophical interpretation of God, given Heidegger's general method and approach in this work. Since Heidegger nowhere directly speaks to this question, one can seek an answer to it only by the indirect route of seeing how principles otherwise employed in his analysis might also be applied to the task of a philosophical theology. That this does not throw open the door to a merely subjective interpretation of Heidegger's thought, but rather enables one to find an answer to the question whose legitimacy can be defended, should become evident from the course of the argument itself.

In general, Heidegger understands the task of philosophy to be that of formal ontological analysis. Unlike the special sciences, which are directed toward understanding some particular being or region of beings (*das Seiende*), philosophy has as its ultimate objective a completely general ontology, or an understanding of the meaning of being as such (*das Sein*). Provisionally, this task requires a "fundamental-ontological" analysis of human existence (*Dasein* or *Existenz*) as the being that has a unique ontic and ontological priority. Even so, the purpose of this preliminary analysis does not reside in itself, as though philosophy's objective could be exhausted by simply providing an anthropology. Rather, human existence is made the object of inquiry primarily in order, on this basis, to answer the ultimate philosophical question of the meaning of being itself. Furthermore, even as existentialist analysis, philosophy's function is formal and ontological, not material and ontic. This is why Heidegger distinguishes between the "existentialist" (*existenzial*) understanding that is the proper business of philosophy and the "existential" (*existenziell*) understanding that is uniquely the concern of each existing person.

It seems evident, then, that the special task of a philosophical theology which would proceed in accordance with these general principles of method could only be to offer a formal ontological analysis of the being of God. The question to be asked by such a theology would not be the "existential" question of God, which every man must be supposed to ask in asking about his own "authenticity" (*Eigentlichkeit*),[6] but rather a more purely theoretical question about God, which would parallel in this inquiry the "existentialist" question that philosophy properly addresses to human existence. This implies, in turn, that the object of philosophical theology would not be the divine "existence" (*Existenz*), but, in some sense of the word, the divine "existentiality" (*Existenzialität*), the basic structure or essence that determines "the godness of God," even as existentiality in the human case is the ontological structure determining the man-ness of man.

The import of such a view is that the task of philosophical theology would in no way conflict with, but rather provide a necessary complement to, the task of a confessional theology grounded in faith in a special revelation. Just as there can be, in principle, no opposition between a philosophical analysis of human existence and a theological explication of the particular self-understanding of Christian faith, so there also could be no incompatibility between a proper

[6] See Rudolf Bultmann, *Glauben und Verstehen,* Vol. II, Tübingen: J. C. B. Mohr, 1952, pp. 231 f. (English translation by J. C. G. Greig in Rudolf Bultmann, *Essays, Philosophical and Theological,* London: SCM Press Ltd., 1955, pp. 256 ff.).

philosophical construction of the being of God and a theological witness to God's concrete action as revealed in Jesus Christ. On the contrary, such a construction would provide the only possible means for bearing a *theological* witness to God's action, as distinct from the witness of preaching and personal confession.[7] The prerequisite of any adequate theological statement is a conceptuality which, in the given historical situation, is at once appropriate to faith itself and genuinely understandable. Therefore, if faith as self-understanding is by its very nature also an understanding of God and his gracious action, no theological explication of faith can be adequate apart from the concepts that a proper philosophical theology alone is in a position to provide.

A possible objection to this interpretation of Heidegger is that it presupposes a strict analogy between the being of man and the being of God—even to the extent of holding that the same distinction in the case of man between essential structure (existentiality) and the concrete actualization of that structure (existence) must also be affirmed in the case of God. To this I reply that Heidegger himself presupposes just such an analogy in speaking of God's more primal temporality. As Heidegger otherwise uses the term, "primal temporality" (*ursprüngliche Zeitlichkeit*) is distinguished both from the "within-timeness" (*Innerzeitigkeit*), which is the derived mode of being temporal appropriate to mere objects or "presence-on-hand" (*Vorhandenheit*), and from the actual occurrence of "primal time" (*ursprüngliche Zeit*) as the "temporalizing of temporality" (*Zeitigung der Zeitlichkeit*). Such usage clearly implies that the relation between primal temporality and the event of primal time itself exactly parallels—and, in fact, is but another way of expressing—the relation between existentiality and existence. Therefore, it is not at all surprising that Heidegger can define the existentiality of existence as "care" (*Sorge*) and can then say that the meaning of authentic care is disclosed as temporality.

Yet, granting that Heidegger does thus assume a strict analogy between the being of man and the being of God, one must still become clear about just what this analogy involves. At the risk of oversimplifying Heidegger's meaning and restating it in somewhat different terms, I submit one understands the analogy he intends by taking into account two main considerations.

[7] See Bultmann's discussion of the difference between theology and preaching in Schubert M. Ogden (ed.), *Existence and Faith: Shorter Writings of Rudolf Bultmann,* New York: Meridian Books, Inc., 1960, pp. 97 ff.

First, in affirming that the eternity of God is to be construed as his more primal temporality, Heidegger necessarily implies that God's being, like man's, is in some sense a "being-in-the-world" (*In-der-Welt-sein*). According to Heidegger, man is completely misunderstood unless it is recognized that real internal relatedness to others, both human and nonhuman, is not an accident of his being but its essential structure.[8] The Cartesian notion of the self as a worldless ego whose possiblity of relating to others is in principle uncertain can only be regarded as a basic misreading of the phenomenological data. Man's very being is his being with others, and the possibility of any particular relation is always guaranteed by the fact of his primal relatedness. Nor is the character of this relatedness adequately understood as the mere theoretical knowing whose importance has been so overrated in the classical philosophical tradition. Man's relation to his world is not primarily the disinterested registration of bare data in consciousness, but an active participation in others of an essentially practical and emotional kind. Indeed, Heidegger holds, the only term by which man's "being-in" (*In-Sein*) can be comprehensively described is the eminently nontheoretical term "care." And it is just this care, this real affective relation to others, that constitutes the existentiality or essential structure of human existence.

By analogy, then, God must be understood as essentially related to a world of others in whose being he actively participates by reason of a similar basic structure of care. To the question of just what is comprised within God's world, the only answer, as shall be more fully explained hereafter, is the totality of beings both present and past who are individually distinguishable from God himself. Here, however, the point to notice is that Heidegger's concepts of "temporality" and "care" are logically so related that God can be construed as temporal only by also construing his being as care, and thus as essentially a being-in-the-world with others, in real internal relation to them.

In affirming God's temporality, therefore, Heidegger departs quite radically from the classical Western tradition in philosophical theology. The hallmark of this tradition has always been its denial that

---

[8] On the distinction implied here between internal and external relations, see Charles Hartshorne, *The Divine Relativity: A Social Conception of God,* New Haven: Yale University Press, 1948, pp. 60–115. That this distinction may be legitimately invoked in interpreting Heidegger is confirmed later in the argument, where it is disclosed as grounded in Heidegger's basic distinction between primal and derived temporality.

God is in any sense structurally related to beings other than himself. As the *"causa sui,"* whose being is utterly "from itself" (*a se*), God's only relation to the world is the wholly external relation of the metaphysical Absolute. Naturally, in the versions of the tradition where the influence of distinctively Christian experience has been more than merely token, this denial of God's real relatedness has not been unequivocal. Recognizing that the God of Holy Scripture is undeniably a God who is related to his creatures, theologians have generally allowed that relational concepts may be predicated of deity, provided they are understood analogically instead of literally. The difficulty, however, is that, on conventional metaphysical premises, to say that God is not literally related to the world could only mean that he is literally not related to it; and so the classical *analogia entis,* like traditional theism in general, has been continually caught in incoherence and self-contradiction. But, in proposing that the being of God be conceived as temporality, Heidegger breaks away from such a theism. He opens the way to a view of God himself as essentially being in relation to other beings, and therefore as radically different from the Absolute of the metaphysical tradition.

Likewise implied in the analogy Heidegger proposes is that God, no less than man, has a past and a future, as well as a present in the general sense conveyed by the term "primal temporality." It is usually recognized that one of Heidegger's most important contributions to philosophy is the clarification of the phenomenon of time to which a considerable part of *Sein und Zeit* is devoted. The guiding insight of this clarification is that our everyday experience of time, in which the so-called "vulgar" concept of time has its basis, is not original but derived, itself grounded in a more primal temporality. Building on a foundation first laid by Augustine in his discussion of time in the *Confessions,* Heidegger argues that the truly primary time of our experience is not the "within-timeness" in which we order the objects of our ordinary external perceptions, but the time constituted by our experiencing itself, as actual occurrence. Precisely as care, human existence has a relation not only to the being of others, but also to itself: to its past through memory, and, even more important, to its own future possibilities by anticipation. Heidegger maintains, indeed, that it is only by virtue of a relation to his future, and thence also to his past, that man has any world, any present relation to others, at all. Only because we continually project ourselves into the future in terms of some specific range of possibilities inherited from our past do we participate in the ordered whole of "significance" (*Bedeut-*

samkeit) that makes up our phenomenal world. Hence, when it is conceived in its primal meaning, the present is not an extensionless instant within our experience, but the decisive "moment" (*Augenblick*) in which our experience itself occurs and is constituted. As such, the present extends beyond itself into both the past and the future and is, in fact, the unification of these other modes or "ecstasies" (*Ekstasen*) of time. Thus primal temporality is the structure of our own being as experiencing selves, in whose successive occasions of experience this structure is continually temporalized in the form of ever new syntheses of anticipated future and remembered past into ordered wholes of significance.

Consequently, if temporality is to be predicated also of God in some sense, this can mean nothing less than that he, too, is an experiencing self who anticipates the future and remembers the past and whose successive occasions of present experience are themselves temporal occurrences. In affirming this, of course, Heidegger once more comes into sharp opposition to the classical theological tradition. As he points out in the footnote, the traditional concept of God as eternal belongs to the general orientation of classical philosophy to the vulgar understanding of time, which is derived from our ordinary perception of objects as located within the field of our phenomenal world. On this understanding, the present is an extensionless instant or "now" (*Jetzt*), and time as a whole is the endless continuum of such instants in which the now is, so to speak, constantly moving as one instant follows upon another. By reference, then, to this conception of time as its "moving image," eternity is defined as the "stationary now," or as sheer nontemporality or timelessness. When traditional theologians speak of God's eternity, it is to just such utter timelessness, such complete absence of temporal distinctions, that they in reality refer. True, at this point also, their absolute negation of a basic concept with reference to God is more or less ambiguous. Analogically, at least, God is conventionally conceived as having a will or purpose and still other perfections that imply temporal distinctions. And yet, once again, such analogical speaking is completely emptied of meaning by the nonanalogical denial that the being of God is in any sense temporal being. The concept of his eternity is so understood that it can only mean the literal negation or exclusion of the distinctions that the concept of temporality entails. For Heidegger, on the other hand, the logical relations between the concepts of "temporality" and "eternity" are not those of mutual negation and exclusion, but are wholly positive and mutually implicative. We can rightly conceive God's eternity, he holds, only by construing it as in a certain sense precisely his temporality.

With this, however, one comes to the second consideration that is crucial for understanding Heidegger's meaning. Throughout the preceding discussion, I have assumed, for reasons which have been partially explained, that the relation between man and God which Heidegger affirms is an analogical relation. So far, the argument has sought to show the least that must be implied if this analogy is to have any meaning. Thus I have said that, if the being of God is to be construed somehow as a more primal temporality, this can mean no less than that God, like man, essentially exists as being-in-the-world, with real internal relations to others, and that, as this kind of a caring, experiencing self, his successive occasions of present experience each involve the same kind of relations to the future and the past exhibited by our own occasions of experience as men. Yet, if this were all one were to say, he would fail to interpret the relation between man and God as the *analogical* relation Heidegger evidently intends. By its very meaning, an analogy implies a difference as well as a similarity between the two analogues it serves to relate. In consequence, if God's being is to be construed as analogous to the being of man, this must mean that God's essential structure is not only the same as man's, but also, in some significant respect, different from it. This, however, is just what Heidegger asserts in proposing that God's eternity be construed not simply as temporality, but as a temporality which is "infinite" (*unendlich*).[9] My purpose now is to clarify the implications of this important qualification.

As Heidegger views him, the distinctive thing about man is not his temporality, but his "finitude" (*Endlichkeit*). Man is not only being-in-the-world, in relation to others and to his own future and the past; his is also a being circumscribed by definite limits and therefore encompassed by what he himself is not. Thus, for example, his temporality is itself temporally conditioned or determined. In the first place, he is not his own ground or beginning, but finds himself

[9] It should be noted that, in this context, Heidegger places the word "infinite" in quotation marks. The reason for this, clearly, is that "infinite" is otherwise used by him solely in connection with the vulgar concept of time, to refer to the "endless" continuum of nows that constitutes "within-timeness." Like the other terms having to do with time, "infinite" has a different meaning, depending on whether it is understood in relation to the derived time of our external perception or the primal time of our experience as selves. The following interpretation assumes that it is the latter meaning which Heidegger naturally intends.

"thrown" (*geworfen*) into the world, and hence as having come from a source beyond himself. His birth is the constant reminder that there once was when he was not, and the fact of this "nothing" (*Nichts*) sets an impassable limit to his being as a man. Nor is this precedent nothing the only temporal limit that presses itself upon him. He is determined, in the second place, by the subsequent nothing of death, beyond which he knows he shall be no more. In fact, Heidegger insists, it is just as "being toward death" (*Sein zum Tode*), as the resolute affirmation of the finitude in time which death so powerfully discloses, that man realizes his possibility of authentic existence. Because the temporality that defines his being is itself in principle temporally finite and limited, he can be who he truly is only in the full consciousness of this finitude and the deliberate acceptance of his temporal limitations.

In the case of God, however, what is distinctive is the complete absence of just such temporal finitude and limitation. Heidegger's statement that God's is an infinite temporality can only mean that, radically otherwise than with man, God's temporality is not itself temporally determined, so that there is neither a time when God was not yet nor a time when he shall be no more. Unlike man's, God's being has neither begun nor will it end, and the past and future to which he is related in each successive occasion of his present experience can be nothing less than a literally limitless past and future.

Because this is so, Heidegger's departure from the theological tradition, however radical, does not involve a complete denial of its claims. For him, too, there is a qualitative difference, a distinction not merely in fact but in principle, between the finite being of man and the infinite being of God. Heidegger's difference from the tradition, however, is that he defines God's distinctiveness not as an utter negation of temporality, but as its eminent exemplification. God's eternity is not sheer timelessness, but an infinite fullness of time, for which our own finite temporality provides a real but hardly univocal likeness. This means that Heidegger's implied reformulation of the *analogia entis* is not, like its classical precedent, involved in essential incoherence. Perfections entailing temporal distinctions may be predicated of God without being emptied of meaning by contradictory negations; and the assertion of God's qualitative distinction from finite beings does not exclude, but positively implies, the meaningfulness of such predication.

But man's finitude, as Heidegger sees it, is not only the limitation of his temporality in time; his being is also radically limited in space. Man's world, as comprising the other beings to which he is essentially and really related, never coincides with the totality of beings as such, but is always a restricted phenomenal field bounded by an external environment. The reason for this, as noted earlier, is that man's having a world at all is grounded not in his openness to possibility as such, but in his being necessarily confined to some specific range of possibilities inherited from his finite past and projected into his finite future. Thus man's relatedness to others is itself relative. He does not participate in them fully, as they are in themselves, but is in principle required to encounter them under the perspectives imposed by his own particular projects of self-understanding. Naturally, in his average, everyday existence, man is not fully conscious of this spatial limitation of his world and, in fact, hides from himself the situational character of the "truth" (*Wahrheit*) constituted by his highly restricted encounters with others. He treats other things and persons as the mere objects of his own finite appreciations, and so "falls" (*verfällt*) or succumbs to his world by absolutizing its limitations. As authentic existence, however, man acknowledges that the truth in which he stands is always a relative truth, and he holds himself open for ever new encounters with the others whose being in themselves transcends their being for him as objects in his world. Although as a man, he must continue to exist within his world and may always succumb to a new bondage to it, his authenticity consists in being dialectically free from it, and therefore free for both himself and the other beings that make up the environment beyond him.

Yet, in this respect, too, Heidegger's qualification of the divine temporality as infinite marks God's qualitative difference from man. While God's being, like man's, is being-in-the-world, in real relation to others, God's relatedness to others is radically unlike man's in being itself not merely relative, but wholly absolute. *That* God is related to other beings is itself relative to nothing beyond God himself, but is grounded solely in his own complete openness to possibility or to the future simply as such. Consequently, God's world can comprise nothing less than the sum total of all beings other than himself, both present and past, and his only environment is the wholly internal environment encompassed by his not merely finite but infinite care. Moreover, the truth constituted by God's encounter with his world is not simply some relative truth, but *the* truth—truth in its absolute and definitive meaning. The final measure of all things as they are in themselves is precisely their being in and for God's infinite care; and the ordered whole of significance that in each present constitutes his actual world is the ultimate integrity of all the significance there is.

Once again, we see that Heidegger's opposition to the theological tradition, sharp as it is, is not the unqualified opposition of an extreme contrary. In his view, also, God is in principle different from man by being in a strict sense nonrelative or absolute. But whereas, for the tradition, God's absoluteness entails the denial of his real relation to others, for Heidegger, it is just God's eminent relatedness, his real relation to *all,* instead of merely to some others, that defines his being as absolute. The one thing in God that is strictly independent, relative to no other being whatever, is his essential structure as eminent being-in-the-world, eminent being in real relation to others, and thus in genuine dependence upon them. Of such limitless relativity and dependence our own limited being-in-the-world is, in truth, but the faintest image. And yet it is in just this image that the perfections of God which are so distinctive of Holy Scripture and of the witness of Christian faith have their analogical basis. On Heidegger's proposal, these perfections are not contradicted by God's infinity or absoluteness, but are disclosed as expressing its essential meaning.

From this, as from the whole of the preceding argument, it should now also be clear why Heidegger must regard it as at best uncertain whether the traditional *via negationis et eminentiae* can still provide a valid theological method. On the interpretation of his proposal presented here, he points to a rather different theory and practice of analogy from those of the theological tradition. It was noted that the difficulty with the traditional way of analogy, as with the whole classical theistic position of which it is a part, is the implicit and often explicit contradiction between the two elements of which it is composed. Some of the positive perfections predicated of God by the way of eminence are in reality emptied of meaning by the absolute denials arrived at by the way of negation. Hence, while pretending to pursue a middle way between anthropomorphism and agnosticism, the classical way of analogy really succeeds in avoiding neither, but merely trades on both of them as occasion may demand.

The reason for this is that the traditional *via negationis* leads to the literal denial in God not merely of the limitations of finitude, but also of what, as Heidegger shows, are positive perfections inherent in the meaning of being as such and also implied by many of the predications of the way of eminence—namely, primal temporality and real internal relatedness to others. Such denial cannot but seem arbitrary until one recognizes with Heidegger that the *via negationis,* like the *via eminentiae* and the whole metaphysical outlook to which they belong, is oriented not to the primal phenomenon of our own existence as experiencing selves, but to the derived phenomenon of the objective world as the field of our ordinary sense perception. Given this orientation, temporality can mean only the succession of wholly externally related instants, and relatedness to others, merely simple location in relation to an external environment. In consequence, to speak of an infinite or eminent temporality and relatedness can only be a stark *contradictio in adiecto,* and God's qualitative uniqueness can be defined solely by negating all temporal distinctions and relation to others. But since the usual anthropomorphic portrayal of God arrived at by the way of eminence is itself oriented to the same derived phenomenon, and thus assumes the same meanings for temporality and relatedness, such negation can only entail its complete denial or contradiction. Hence the familiar situation where the personal God portrayed in the mythological language of Scripture is demythologized in terms of a metaphysical construction of infinite being that utterly empties such language of meaning.

On Heidegger's proposal, however, this situation is fundamentally transcended, and the direction is pointed to a theory and practice of analogy beyond the *via negationis et eminentiae.* Because Heidegger's basic ontological orientation is not to the objective world of ordinary perception, but to the more primal phenomenon of human existence, finitude is seen by him to consist not in temporality and relatedness as such, but in the limited mode of these perfections appropriate to our own being as men. In their truly primal forms, temporality and relational structure are constitutive of being itself, and God's uniqueness is to be construed not simply by denying them, but by conceiving them in their infinite mode through the negation of their limitations as we experience them in ourselves. The way to this goal, however, can hardly be less different than the goal itself. Although the method of analogy implied by Heidegger has certain clear parallels to the classical method, there is no mistaking its essential distinction. On his view, one may indeed continue to speak of both eminence and negation, but only in a quite new and different sense from that of the theological tradition.

2

If this interpretation of Heidegger's footnote is correct, I believe one can only conclude that what he proposes there has a most important bearing on the discussion currently going on in Christian theology. To make clear the reasons for this conviction, I must now venture a brief and perforce schematic characterization of this discussion so far as it has to do with the central task of developing an adequate interpretation of the Christian witness to God in our situation.

The usual attempts by theologians today to treat the problem of God represent one or the other of two general positions. The first of these is the position of classical theism, which has been present in the church ever since the age of the Fathers, and the union they effected between the faith witnessed to in Holy Scripture and the metaphysics of classical antiquity. The method of this theism has consistently been some form of the traditional *via negationis et eminentiae,* and its most characteristic assertions have always involved the denial that God is in any literal sense temporal or really related to the world. In our time, probably few important theologians hold to this position in its classical medieval purity. Among Protestants, at any rate, the influence of postclassical forms of philosophy has been great enough to effect certain minor transformations and refinements. Thus, in Britain, for instance, in the work of Ian Ramsey and others, this classical theism is in process of being restated by means of resources provided by the quite modern philosophy of linguistic analysis.[10] In America, Paul Tillich has written a brilliant new chapter in the same long history with a position that clearly bears the marks of the German philosophy of the nineteenth century and, to a lesser extent, of contemporary existentialism.[11] Yet, even in such modern treatments as Ramsey's and Tillich's, the characteristic features of classical theology are still easily discernible. With whatever qualifications, they, too, affirm a nontemporalistic theism.

The other main position in the current discussion is both more distinctively modern and less readily described. Its possible philosophical bases are more varied, and it assumes several somewhat different forms. Typical of them all, however, is a sharp rejection of classical theism with its way of analogy and a deep conviction as to the reality and significance of time and history that can hardly be

[10] See especially Ian Ramsey, *Religious Language,* London: SCM Press Ltd., 1957; also Basil Mitchell (ed.), *Faith and Logic: Oxford Essays in Philosophical Theology,* London: George Allen & Unwin Ltd., 1957; and Anthony Flew and Alasdair Macintyre (eds.), *New Essays in Philosophical Theology,* London: SCM Press Ltd., 1955.

[11] See especially *Systematic Theology,* Vol. I, Chicago: The University of Chicago Press, 1951, pp. 163–289.

reconciled with classical metaphysics. On the Continent, the chief expression of this general view is the theology whose principal conceptual resource has been existentialist philosophy, either in Heidegger's form or in some other. This theology shares a general suspicion of all metaphysics and "natural theology" and seeks to interpret statements about God as either wholly or primarily statements about human existence, that is, as expressive of a certain possibility of existential self-understanding. In the Anglo-Saxon countries, a quite similar view is often held by theologians who have been strongly influenced by analytic philosophy. Here the rejection of metaphysics and the way of analogy is justified not only by pointing to the inherent contradictions in their traditional forms, but also by appealing to an empiricist criterion of meaning and truth that makes any metaphysics or theological analogy in principle impossible. On this positivistic basis, then, theological utterances are characteristically interpreted as not really assertions at all, but as expressing a "blik"[12] or "an intention to behave in a certain way"[13]—both of which notions are probably quite close in meaning to some uses of the existentialist concept "self-understanding."

The most provocative statement of this view yet to appear is that of the theologian, Paul M. van Buren, in *The Secular Meaning of the Gospel*.[14] In virtually the same terms as R. B. Braithwaite, van Buren holds that ostensible theological assertions about God and his action are really expressions of a human "historical perspective," which is somehow causally connected with the "story" of the life, death, and resurrection of Jesus of Nazareth as the story of man's radical freedom. So, for example, the real meaning of the utterance, "God is love," is said to be something like, "I, the person making the utterance, intend to lead a life of loving service to my fellows." The advantage of such an interpretation, van Buren argues, is not only that it fully respects the narrow limits of modern man's empiricism, but that it also for the first time makes really clear the wholly human, ethical, and so "secular" meaning of the Christian witness itself.

Van Buren's view is clearly extreme, and probably few theologians who share his appreciation for analytic philosophy would be willing to draw such radical conclusions. But the significance of his book is

[12] See R. M. Hare in Anthony Flew and Alasdair Macintyre (eds.), *op. cit.*, pp. 99–103.

[13] See R. B. Braithwaite, *An Empiricist's View of the Nature of Religious Belief*, Cambridge: Cambridge University Press, 1955, pp. 32 f.

[14] New York: The Macmillan Co., 1963.

to have made fully explicit the nontheistic tendency implicit in many of the attempts to deal with the problem of God from this second main position. To be sure, there are other such attempts where this tendency is stoutly resisted. Rudolf Bultmann, notably, has for some time asserted the indispensability of some kind of theological analogy and, in one of his latest writings, has set forth a clear, though certainly not classical, theistic interpretation of the idea of God.[15] But even Bultmann's view is not fully secured against a misunderstanding of its intention.[16] Even when it is obviously qualified, the second position is not sufficiently distinguished from a non- or merely quasi-theistic temporalism.

It should be clear from even this brief characterization of the usual theological alternatives why the contemporary discussion of the doctrine of God so inevitably leads to a typical impasse. On the one hand, those who represent the position of classical theism can explicate Christian faith's reference to a transcendent God only by denying or seriously obscuring the reality and significance of temporality. On the other hand, the spokesmen for the more modern view succeed in doing justice to temporality, and thus to man and his historicity, only by denying or failing adequately to explicate the certainty of faith in its eternal ground. It is no doubt only in the most extreme expressions of the two positions that this impasse becomes obvious. In most views, it tends to be hidden, and we witness the familiar spectacle of classical theists trying to adjust to the demands of temporality, and of modern temporalists inconsistently appealing to the God of traditional theism. In neither case are we offered anything like a real third alternative, but are left to choose either the sacrifice of time and man to God's eternity or the abandonment of God and infinity for the temporality of man. On occasion, indeed, as with van Buren, this

---

[15] "Der Gottesgedanke und der moderne Mensch," *Zeitschrift für Theologie und Kirche*, December, 1963, pp. 335–48. In the work of Gerhard Ebeling also, there are many clear evidences of a neoclassical theistic intention. See, e.g., *The Nature of Faith*, trans. R. G. Smith, Philadelphia: Muhlenberg Press, 1961, pp. 72–83; and *Word and Faith*, trans. J. W. Leitch, Philadelphia: Fortress Press, 1963, pp. 98–161, 191–200, 354–62. On the other hand, the work of Herbert Braun (see especially *Gesammelte Studien zum Neuen Testament und seiner Umwelt*, Tübingen: J. C. B. Mohr, 1962, pp. 297 f., 325–41) occasionally seems to reflect a position not too unlike van Buren's. Bultmann, to be sure, interprets Braun's intention as quite close to his own (see *ibid.*, p. 347, n. 45), and this is probably the better interpretation.

[16] See my essay in William L. Reese and Eugene Freeman (eds.), *Process and Divinity: The Hartshorne Festschrift*, La Salle, Ill.: Open Court Publishing Co., 1964, pp. 493–513.

tragic choice is actually put to us, and the real poverty of our situation is revealed.

Yet it is from just this situation, this choice which even the most extreme view can hardly accept without qualification, that Heidegger's thesis of the temporality of God provides a real avenue of escape. Unlike those who would merely qualify the two extremes, Heidegger goes to the root of the problem and makes clear in principle why they are not our only real alternatives. By construing being itself, and thus even God, as essentially temporal, he affirms all that the temporalist himself can possibly affirm and, at the same time, implies a method of analogy free from the contradictions which justify rejecting the traditional method. In doing this, however, Heidegger also does what the temporalist either cannot or does not do—namely, shows both that and how God can be construed philosophically, and so at least outlines a genuinely philosophical theology.

From the classical standpoint, of course, Heidegger's third alternative will almost certainly be regarded as fatally compromised by its concessions to modernity. His radical temporalism will be seen as the denial of essential Christian truth, and his avoidance of contradiction will be dismissed as a rationalistic dissolution of unavoidable "mystery." But to this I can only reply that Christian faith has no stake in unnecessary logical confusion, even when such confusion is piously called mystery, and that, far from being the denial of this faith, a deep conviction as to the essential significance of temporality is in reality one of its chief fruits. As Friedrich Gogarten and others have shown, our distinctively modern sense of the importance of the secular, and thus of time and history, cannot be understood except against the background of the Reformation concept of faith with its stress on man's paradoxical freedom from the world and responsibility for it.[17] Nor is the fundamental insight that God himself is essentially temporal and related to others an invention of Heidegger and certain other modern philosophers. It is, rather, the central discovery implicit in the witness of Holy Scripture, and its *locus classicus* is the Old and New Testaments. One thinks, for example, of Jesus' summary of the law in Mark 12:28–34, where the God who is witnessed to is so intimately related to the self and the neighbor that a proper love of them is implicitly contained in the whole and unre-

[17] See Friedrich Gogarten, *Verhängnis und Hoffnung der Neuzeit, Die Säkularisierung als theologisches Problem,* Stuttgart: Friedrich Vorwerk Verlag, 2d ed., 1958.

served love of him. Or, as an equally striking expression, there is the portrayal of the Last Judgment in Matt. 25:31–46, to which Bultmann has recently referred as the most impressive of all the testimonies to what the sculptor Ernst Barlach called "the metamorphoses of God."[18]

Therefore, when Heidegger asserts God's temporality, this is no mere concession to the modern temper, but the restatement in formal ontological terms of the understanding of God implicit in Holy Scripture. This is the deeper reason, indeed, for regarding Pöggeler's view of the general theological background of Heidegger's thought as also confirmed here. The chief evidence of such theological influence is that the temporal God of whom Heidegger speaks as a philosopher is the same God who was experienced and known in primitive Christian faith.

But, if Heidegger's proposal seems certain to raise questions in the minds of classical theists, I fear the same will be true of those who represent the other main position in contemporary theology. From their standpoint, his view will almost surely appear as a falling back into metaphysics and natural theology which can at best have a negative theological relevance. And yet here, too, the critics' most likely objections can be met. If Heidegger's proposal involves metaphysics and even natural theology, they are nevertheless radically different from what has traditionally gone under those names, and it will not do to obscure the distinction by the indiscriminate denunciations of metaphysics so often heard from representatives of this position. I have pointed out how Heidegger's analogical statements about God are sufficiently free from the usual contradictions to escape "the death of a thousand qualifications" that awaits all assertions made by the traditional method of analogy.[19] Moreover, the God of whom he speaks, far from being irrelevant to our ethical and secular decisions, is most intimately involved in them and is, in fact, the ground of their ultimate significance. Because God himself is essentially being-in-the-world, in real internal relation to us and to all other beings, the final context of our finite decisions is God's own eternal life, and we can at last render really intelligible our conviction as to their infinite importance. Finally, the common claim that the God of Christian faith is not the *deus philosophorum* is also deprived of its force by Heidegger's proposal. If this claim means that the being of God is not that of

---

[18] "Der Gottesgedanke und der moderne Mensch," *Zeitschrift für Theologie und Kirche,* December, 1963, p. 348.

[19] See Anthony Flew and Alasdair Macintyre (eds.), *op. cit.,* pp. 96 ff.

the metaphysical Absolute, but the being of One who is genuinely and eminently personal, then this is the very thing Heidegger himself tells us. If, on the other hand, the point of the claim is that faith in God is something different from a philosophical interpretation of God's essential being, then this, too, as we have seen, is fully taken into account in Heidegger's view. As a matter of fact, by conceiving God as infinite temporality, he provides the only possible basis for making just this distinction in a clear and self-consistent way.

Hence I can only conclude that the proposal Heidegger makes in this remarkable footnote in *Sein und Zeit* has a unique importance for our present theological situation. This does not mean that I regard these few sentences as the only or even the most adequate form in which some such proposal has been made. So far as I can tell, Heidegger himself nowhere really develops the view he outlines there, and it is even possible that the so-called "later" phase of his thought entails its repudiation. In any case, there are other contemporary philosophers —most notably, Alfred North Whitehead and Charles Hartshorne— for whom such a view is not confined to a footnote, but is carefully expounded in the setting of a fully developed neoclassical metaphysics. Even so, I am convinced that the profound truth of the temporality of God is something we as theologians are all sooner or later going to have to learn, and that Heidegger's footnote is able to teach us that truth. In this connection, I cannot but recall the words of Gogarten in a similar context: "Needless to say, it does not have to be Heidegger from whom one learns this. If one thinks he can learn it better elsewhere, all well and good. But, in one way or another, learned it must be."[20]

[20] Friedrich Gogarten, *Entmythologisierung und Kirche,* Stuttgart: Friedrich Vorwerk Verlag, 2d ed., 1953, p. 57, n. (English translation by N. H. Smith in Friedrich Gogarten, *Demythologizing and History,* London: SCM Press Ltd., 1955, p. 52, n. 1).

VI

Y

What Sense Does It Make

to Say,

"God Acts in History"?

The question is often asked, "Can one make sense of the statement, 'God acts in history'?" Here I would like to reformulate the question and ask instead, "What sense does it make to say, 'God acts in history'?" Since the differences between the two questions are slight, I need to explain why I nevertheless think them important.

First of all, the question as I have formulated it already assumes an affirmative answer to the original question; and this assumption seems appropriate to the present discussion. I certainly do not want to presume too much, and I recognize there are many for whom the original question may seem better just because it does not make this assumption. But, for my part, the real issue is not *whether* the statement "God acts in history" makes sense, but *what* sense it makes. Furthermore, it belongs to the very nature of the theologian's work that the possibility of speaking of God's acting in history is not the question he must consider. It is true that he would not ask even the reformulated question unless such speaking were in some sense problematic. He asks this question only because he recognizes that not all the ways in which his fathers in the faith have spoken of God's action are relevant possibilities for men today. Indeed, it is probably just because some one or other of these traditional ways has now shown itself to be no longer relevant that he, too, is tempted to ask whether one can really speak of God's acting at all. But he ought to resist this temptation—so long, at least, as he continues to profess the

164

Christian faith and, at some level or other, engages in trying to explicate that faith in an adequate Christian theology. Thus precision in formulating the question I have to consider seems to me to require the changes I have made.

But there is a second reason for these changes. If I understand the lesson to be learned from what Frederick Ferré has called "contemporary linguistic philosophy,"[1] the question whether "God acts in history" *can* make sense is a somewhat old-fashioned question. According to Ferré, the development of linguistic philosophy falls into two more or less distinct phases: a first phase characterized by "verificational analysis" and a more recent phase in which the emphasis has been on "functional analysis."[2] In the earlier period, which was dominated by the logical positivists and their so-called "verification principle," the question under discussion was precisely whether theological statements can make sense; and the positivists gave a resoundingly negative answer to the question. But subsequent discussion has made clear that their answer was based less on a careful analysis of the actual uses of religious and theological language than on certain *a priori* assumptions that reflected, as one historian has written, "an extreme respect for science and mathematics" and "an extreme distaste for metaphysics."[3] Later linguistic philosophers, by contrast, have tended to proceed more cautiously. Instead of asking whether theological statements *can* make sense, they have attempted to determine what sense such statements in fact *do* make by analyzing their function in actual religious and theological speech. If this shift in approach is, as I believe, fortunate, it presumably has a bearing on the procedure of the theologian. It suggests he will do better not to pronounce on the question *whether* "God acts in history" makes sense, except insofar as an attempt to show *what* sense it makes implies an answer to that question. If his attempt to explain the sense of the statement is successful, then, of course, one can make sense of it; for *ab esse ad posse valet consequentia*. If, on the other hand, his attempt should fail, the possibility will still exist for someone else to show that, and how, the statement makes sense.

The following discussion is divided into two main parts. In the first, I shall try to clarify the problem as I understand it and indicate

[1] *Language, Logic, and God,* New York: Harper & Row, 1961, p. vii.
[2] *Ibid.,* pp. 8, 58.
[3] G. J. Warnock, *English Philosophy Since 1900,* London: Oxford University Press, 1958, p. 44.

briefly the more important resources available for solving it. In the second, I shall attempt to point the way to a constructive solution.

1

It may be claimed without exaggeration that no Protestant theologian of our century has given more sustained and self-conscious attention to the meaning of theological statements than Rudolf Bultmann. Unlike many of his contemporaries, Bultmann has continued to be sensitive to the difficulties posed by traditional theological language for anyone whose outlook has been shaped by the scientific world picture and a distinctively modern understanding of human existence. One could wish, perhaps, that Bultmann's resources for dealing with these difficulties were not so exclusively limited to those of Continental theology and philosophy and that he was more knowledgeable than he is of the work done on the logic of theological language by Anglo-Saxon philosophers and theologians. Certainly for any of us who live in the Anglo-Saxon world and are sympathetic with Bultmann's basic approach, there is an obligation, which I myself feel with increasing intensity, to enter into discussion with English-speaking thinkers who are concerned primarily to clarify the meaning of theological language. But, granting the limitations of Bultmann's work, I would insist that the meaning of theological statements has been the focus of all his systematic efforts and that his contribution toward defining this problem and attempting to solve it is of fundamental importance for the rest of us who also have the problem.

As is well known, Bultmann maintains that the language of Christian theology, both in Holy Scripture and in the church's tradition, is for the most part and in its central elements "mythical" or "mythological" language. By this he means that the statements in which theology has usually spoken of God and his action in history have the same "objectifying" character as the statements of empirical science. Although the "intention" of such mythological statements—or, as the functional analyst would say, their "use" or function—is quite different from that of scientific statements, their linguistic form is essentially the same. Like scientific statements, they "objectify" the existential reality of which they speak and thus represent it in terms of space, time, causality, and substance—or, in a word, in the Kantian forms of sensibility and categories of understanding that Bultmann takes to be determinative for all empirical knowledge. The result is that God and his action are represented as though God were but one more secondary cause in the chain of secondary causes and his action but one more action alongside those of other causal agents.[4]

It should be clear from even this brief summary that Bultmann does not so define "myth" (or "mythology") as to make it inclusive of all analogical discourse about God.[5] He holds, rather, that "myth" refers to only one way in which God may be spoken about in language otherwise used to speak of the nondivine. As we shall see further below, he distinguishes a "mythological" way of speaking of God and his action from another way that he refers to as "analogy"; and this distinction can be understood only if the restricted scope of his definition of "myth" is carefully observed. The specific difference of myth is not that it speaks of God in terms also applicable to the nondivine, but that its terms are "objectifying" in a manner appropriate only to ordinary empirical knowledge and its refinement by the various special sciences.

Bultmann maintains that such mythological language makes for a double difficulty. First, because mythological statements have the linguistic form of scientific statements, they are open to scientific criticism, with results that are devastating. Given the thoroughgoing development of scientific thinking as we find it in the method of modern natural science, mythology seems to be merely a primitive attempt to think scientifically which is no longer credible or relevant. The scientist, as Laplace said, has no need of the "God hypothesis" to perform his particular task. His continuum of secondary causes does not include the cause represented by myth as God, nor does he reckon with the action of such a being in his scientific explanations. Because this critical attitude toward myth has come to determine our whole contemporary cultural consciousness, the problem inevitably arises—for those of us who share in that consciousness—how the statement "God acts in history" makes any sense. We realize that it certainly cannot make *scientific* sense, since the logic of scientific discourse simply leaves no room for it in its traditional mythological form.

But there is a second and, Bultmann argues, more fundamental difficulty. It may be equally doubted whether mythological statements make *theological* sense—or, better said, whether they are an appro-

---

[4] See, e.g., Rudolf Bultmann, "On the Problem of Demythologizing," *Journal of Religion,* April, 1962, pp. 96–102.

[5] See my discussion in *Christ Without Myth: A Study Based on the Theology of Rudolf Bultmann,* New York: Harper & Row, 1961, pp. 24–31, 90–93, 146 ff., 166–70.

priate way of expressing the sense or meaning that theological statements are supposed to express. Just because mythology objectifies God and his action and thus represents them in the terms and categories appropriate solely to empirical knowledge, it seriously misrepresents the divine transcendence as understood by Christian faith. Instead of preserving "the infinite qualitative difference" between God and the world, myth so represents God that he seems to be but one more item within the world. Thus, for example, the mythological way of speaking of God as the Creator represents his creative act as though it were simply the temporally prior action in the whole series of causal actions. Myth thereby obscures faith's understanding that God's act as Creator is presupposed by *all* actions in the series, including the temporally first, if, indeed, there ever was any first action. Similarly, the mythological representation of God as the Redeemer or Consummator (in the manner, say, of apocalyptic eschatology) pictures his action as though it were the temporally last in the causal series. Myth thus fails to make clear that God's redemptive action fulfills or consummates *all* actions, including the temporally last, insofar as one may meaningfully speak of a last action.

Bultmann insists that the first difficulty of myth's evident incompatibility with the thinking of science but provides the occasion for focusing this more fundamental difficulty of myth's inappropriateness as the language of Christian faith. It forces us to ask for the true meaning of theological statements, and whether there is not some other, nonmythological way in which their meaning can be expressed.[6]

Bultmann's answers to these questions are given in his project of "existentialist interpretation." He holds that the true meaning of theological statements is not scientific but "existential" and that the existentialist analysis of the early Martin Heidegger provides an alternative conceptuality in which this meaning can be given nonmythological expression.

In holding that theological statements really have an existential intention or use, Bultmann means that they function to present a certain possibility for understanding human existence, summoning us directly or indirectly to realize this possibility. This is the true intention, he argues, even of the mythological statements, which, on the face of it, seem to have a scientific or pseudoscientific use. Although such statements have the linguistic form of objectifying assertions,

6 See Rudolf Bultmann, *Jesus Christ and Mythology,* New York: Charles Scribner's Sons, 1958, pp. 83 ff.

their function is not to provide scientific information, but to express an understanding of man's existence as a historical being who must continually decide how he is to understand himself in the world. Thus, to take the same examples considered above, the mythological statement that God is the Creator is "in its fundamental intention not the statement of a cosmological theory that seeks to explain the origin of the world, but rather man's confession to God as his Lord—the Lord to whom the world belongs, whose power and care sustain and preserve it, and to whom man himself owes obedience."[7] To affirm that God is Creator, then, is in reality to affirm a certain possibility for understanding one's historical existence; it is to affirm the utter dependence of one's self and his world on the existential reality of God's power and love, which are the ultimate ground of all created things. Likewise, the real use of mythological statements about God's final redemption of the world is very different from that, say, of modern scientific theories about the eventual "running down" of the physical universe. Their true intention, Bultmann says, is to remind us that "the fulfillment of life cannot be the result of human effort, but is rather a gift from beyond, a gift of God's grace."[8] Hence, to affirm such statements is really to affirm an understanding of one's existence in which one renounces every attempt at self-contrived security and utterly opens himself to the security of God's love, wherein all things find an ultimate acceptance.

Bultmann proposes to solve the problem of the meaning or sense of all theological statements in the way illustrated by these two examples. He believes that the intention of such statements is throughout existential and that the task of theology is to recognize this and to give their intention appropriate expression. As indicated above, he regards Heidegger's existentialist analysis as making available the philosophical concepts in which this may be done. The reason for this is that Heidegger has provided a conceptually clear and precise analysis of the phenomenon of human existence, which quite avoids objectifying this phenomenon either in the manner of mythology or in the manner of the special sciences.

My position is that the problem of theological meaning is the

[7] Rudolf Bultmann, *Das Urchristentum im Rahmen der antiken Religionen,* Zürich: Artemis Verlag, 1949, p. 11 (English translation by R. H. Fuller in Rudolf Bultmann, *Primitive Christianity in Its Contemporary Setting,* New York: Meridian Books, Inc., 1956, p. 15).

[8] *Glauben und Verstehen,* Vol. III, Tübingen: J. C. B. Mohr, 2d ed., 1962, p. 88.

general problem Bultmann clarifies and that his proposed solution to it is essentially the correct solution. I, too, would say that the use of theological statements is existential and that the sense of the statement "God acts in history" is therefore an existential sense. And yet, while agreeing with Bultmann's analysis of the general problem and the direction of his proposal for solving it, I would urge that his solution itself is problematic, so that the problems it raises define, as it were, the specific differences of the general problem as I myself understand it. In particular, his solution poses two problems that must also be taken into account and solved in any tenable answer to the question of this essay.

There is, first, what I will call somewhat hesitatingly the one-sidedly existentialist character of his solution. As the term "existentialist interpretation" already suggests, Bultmann proposes to treat all theological statements as statements about man and his possibilities for understanding his existence. Thus, in prefacing the interpretation of Paul in his *Theology of the New Testament,* he argues that, for Paul, "every assertion about God is simultaneously an assertion about man and vice versa" and that, therefore, "Paul's theology can best be treated as his doctrine of man."[9] The difficulty with this argument is that its conclusion is one-sided. If the premise is correct—that, for Paul, all statements about God are statements about man *and vice versa*—then one could just as well conclude that Paul's theology can best be presented as the doctrine of *God*. But Bultmann is reluctant to accept this second conclusion. For reasons I cannot give here,[10] he displays a marked unwillingness to speak directly of God and his action and prefers instead to speak of them only indirectly by speaking of man and his possibilities of self-understanding. Add to this, then, his repeated defenses of the theological adequacy of Heidegger's existentialist analysis, in which God does not so much as figure, and what I mean by his one-sided existentialism will be obvious.[11]

Other critics have remarked this same one-sidedness and have even gone so far as to say that Bultmann so interprets Christian faith that it is in danger of becoming indistinguishable from a merely human

9 *Theology of the New Testament,* trans. Kendrick Grobel, New York: Charles Scribner's Sons, 1951, p. 191.

10 See, however, my essay in William L. Reese and Eugene Freeman (eds.), *Process and Divinity: The Hartshorne Festschrift,* La Salle, Ill.: Open Court Publishing Co., 1964, pp. 493–513.

11 One such defense of Heidegger's philosophy is made in *Jesus Christ and Mythology,* pp. 57 ff.

self-understanding utterly lacking in any divine basis or object.[12] But this is to go too far. Both in practice and in theory, Bultmann makes clear that he has no intention of reducing faith simply to a human attitude or perspective. His view may fairly be said to be one-sided and less than fully secure against a reductive or restrictive existentialism. Yet the existentialist interpretation he actually practices and, to a limited extent, also theoretically justifies is ampler than it sometimes seems to be from certain of his statements.

The chief evidence of this is the attention he has given in his more recent writings, beginning with his reply to his critics of 1952, to what he speaks of as "analogy."[13] Although he unfortunately fails to develop exactly what he means by "analogy," he does state that, while mythology can have no place in an existentialist theology, analogical speaking of God can and must have a place in it. Furthermore, he makes clear that the specific difference of analogy from mythology is that it represents God, not in the objectifying categories of empirical knowledge, but in the nonobjectifying "existentials" (*Existenzialien*) of Heidegger's philosophy. Analogy thus represents God's action as analogous to human action and the relation between God and man as analogous to the relation of men with one another. In this way, analogy, unlike mythology, preserves God's hiddenness or transcendence because it represents him as "a personal being acting on persons."[14]

In brief, Bultmann's theory of analogy, however fragmentary and undeveloped, makes clear that he has no intention of excluding by his existentialist interpretation a direct speaking of God and his action such as Christian faith requires. Demythologizing there must be, and it must be radical and thoroughgoing. But the positive alternative to mythology is not existentialist interpretation alone, but existentialist interpretation *plus* analogy—or, better said, existentialist interpretation as inclusive of an analogical speaking of God and his action.

Nevertheless, because Bultmann's treatment of analogy is so frag-

---

[12] See, e.g., John Macquarrie, *An Existentialist Theology: A Comparison of Heidegger and Bultmann,* London: SCM Press Ltd., 1955, especially pp. 240–46.

[13] H. W. Bartsch (ed.), *Kerygma und Mythos,* Vol. II, Hamburg: Herbert Reich-Evangelischer Verlag, 1952, pp. 196 f. (English translation by R. H. Fuller in H. W. Bartsch [ed.], *Kerygma and Myth,* New York: Harper & Row, 2d ed., 1961, pp. 196 f.). Cf. *Jesus Christ and Mythology,* pp. 60–70; and "On the Problem of Demythologizing," *Journal of Religion,* April, 1962, p. 101. Cf. also my discussion in *Christ Without Myth,* pp. 90–93, 146 f., 169 f.

[14] *Jesus Christ and Mythology,* p. 70; cf. p. 68.

mentary and because his aversion to direct speaking of God is so marked, his position does have a certain one-sidedness that requires correction. And here is where I see the great importance of Charles Hartshorne's philosophical theology. I believe it can be shown that Hartshorne's dipolar view of God provides a virtually exact counterpart to Heidegger's existentialist analysis of man. By attempting to take seriously "the religious idea of God" and working out a conception of the divine in strict analogy to personal existence, Hartshorne presents in its fullness what is barely more than postulated in Bultmann's fragmentary remarks on analogy. He thus provides a means for correcting Bultmann's one-sided existentialism by offering a precise philosophical conceptuality in which God as well as man can be appropriately spoken about in nonmythological terms. My view is that Bultmann's existentialist solution to the problem of the meaning of theological statements can be fully justified, in accordance with his own intention in proposing it, only when Heidegger's existentialist analysis is complemented or supplemented by something like Hartshorne's dipolar theism.[15]

I have spoken of Bultmann's existentialist one-sidedness only with certain misgivings. This is because I profoundly share his conviction that all theological statements are, directly or indirectly, existential statements and that there are serious dangers in speaking as though only *some* such statements are existential, while others have to do not with man but with God and his action. I fear my proposal just now to supplement Bultmann's position with Hartshorne's—or, rather, to bring the two positions together into one integrated position—is open to just this misunderstanding. I would stress, therefore, that, in calling for the correction of Bultmann's one-sided existentialism by Hartshorne's fully developed theism, I in no way intend to abandon the position that *all* theological statements are existential statements. That no such abandonment is logically required seems evident to me because, for Hartshorne, no less than for Bultmann, to speak of God and his action here and now is also always to speak of man and his possibilities of self-understanding, and, of course, *vice versa*.[16]

The second problem posed by Bultmann's project of existentialist

[15] This view is more fully worked out in the essay referred to above in n. 10.

[16] See, e.g., Hartshorne's statement that "self-knowledge and knowledge of God are apparently inseparable" and that "neither is clear unless both are somehow clear" ("The Idea of God—Literal or Analogical?" *Christian Scholar*, June, 1956, p. 136).

interpretation—or, rather, by his own execution of that project—arises from his failure consistently to carry it out. I have argued at length elsewhere[17] that he stops short of a thoroughgoing existentialist interpretation of theological statements in the central matter of christology. In the manner of the radically "christocentric" theology that is one main strand in the Protestant tradition, he claims that authentic human existence is factually possible solely in consequence of God's unique act in Jesus Christ. Although all men simply as men have the "possibility in principle" of authentic life, this possibility becomes a "possibility in fact" for them exclusively in the event of Jesus' crucifixion, or in the proclamation of the Christian church in which that event is again and again re-presented. But, as I have sought to show, this claim as such is mythological, by Bultmann's own definition, and therefore stands in need of demythologizing, which is to say, existentialist interpretation.

In one sense, Bultmann himself recognizes this, and his existentialist interpretation of the christological statements of the New Testament and of the theological tradition is an attempt to express the existential meaning of Jesus Christ. Yet he refuses to accept the implication that the significance of Jesus is simply that he decisively manifests or re-presents man's universal possibility of authentic existence in and under the love of God. Jesus not only decisively *reveals* God's love, he claims, but actually *constitutes* it as an event, so that apart from him (or the witness of the church that proclaims him), man cannot actually realize his authentic life.

In making this claim, however, Bultmann falls back into the very mythology he wants to overcome. By saying that God acts to redeem mankind *only* in the history of Jesus Christ, he subjects God's action as the Redeemer to the objectifying categories of space and time and thus mythologizes it. Therefore, I argue, the only course open to one who wishes to follow Bultmann in his intention is to carry out his existentialist interpretation with a consistency he himself fails to display. The claim "only in Jesus Christ" must be interpreted to mean, not that God acts to redeem only in the history of Jesus and in no other history, but that the only God who redeems any history—*although he in fact redeems every history*—is the God whose redemptive action is decisively re-presented in the word that Jesus speaks and is.

But this position obviously has its own complex of problems and,

[17] *Christ Without Myth*, pp. 111–26.

in particular, raises the question of the sense, if any, in which one can still say with the historic Christian community that the event of Jesus Christ is the decisive act of God. Since I understand this question to be the crux of the problem before us here, it is toward answering it that the second and constructive part of the essay must be directed.

2

If one proposes to deal with the sense of theological statements in the way I have indicated, he is immediately faced with the question of analogy. It is well known that this question has been and still is perhaps the most complex and difficult question the theologian faces. Its difficulty is felt with particular force today because it is widely believed by contemporary philosophers and theologians that the classical theory of analogy cannot be maintained, since it fails to solve the problem it purports to solve. Intended to provide a middle way between univocality and equivocality—or between anthropomorphism and agnosticism—it actually does nothing but oscillate uneasily between the two extremes, caught in an inescapable dilemma.[18] Thus Ferré argues persuasively that "it is no longer possible . . . to hold that the logic of analogy, as it has normally been interpreted, is cogent" and proposes that it be reassigned a purely "formal" instead of a "material" function in "the manifold logic of theism."[19]

While recognizing the complexity and difficulty of this question, I, too, hold that the classical theory of analogy is untenable. Instead of solving the problem it is intended to solve, it but reflects and perpetuates the problem in the way its modern critics have so often pointed out. But I also hold that the problematic character of the classical theory of analogy is entirely of a piece with the problems posed by classical theism generally and is, indeed, but a particularly clear evidence of the indefensibility of this theological position. Because classical theism is the impossible attempt to synthesize the personalistic view of God of Holy Scripture with the substance ontology of classical Greek philosophy, the theory of analogy it develops to rationalize its procedures cannot but be an inconsistent and untenable theory.

Still, to grant that the classical theory of analogy is untenable is not to concede the untenability of all theories of analogy—any more than

[18] See, e.g., Frederick C. Copleston, *Contemporary Philosophy*, London: Burns & Oates, 1956, p. 96.
[19] *Op. cit.*, pp. 76 f., 154.

to reject a classical theistic position as indefensible is to say that no theistic position can be defended. On the contrary, Hartshorne has amply demonstrated that a consistent logic of analogy can be developed and that the ancient dilemma of anthropomorphism and agnosticism can be resolved without in any way prejudicing the claims of Christian faith.[20] That he does this only by taking the dilemma by the horns and working out a frankly "anthropomorphic" view of God must be admitted. But he also convincingly shows that the traditional prejudices against such a view spring, not from commitment to the understanding of God attested by Scripture (with which understanding, on the contrary, this view is perfectly compatible), but rather from the tacit assumption of the premises of classical metaphysics.[21]

The crucial insight of the neoclassical theism Hartshorne has pioneered in developing is that God is to be conceived in strict analogy with the human self or person. The force of the word "strict" is that God, as Whitehead says, is not to be treated as an exception to metaphysical principles, but rather is to be understood as exemplifying them.[22] Thus, for example, if to be a self is possible only by being related to and dependent on others, and most directly on the others that constitute one's body, then God also can be conceived only as related to and dependent on the others that constitute his body, which is to say, the whole world of created beings. On the other hand, the word "analogy" reminds us that God is not a self in univocally the same sense as man—that, as Whitehead puts it, God is not simply *an* exemplification of metaphysical principles, but is their *"chief"* exemplification.[23] So, whereas the human self is effectively related only to a very few others—indeed, only to a very few others within the intimate world of its own body—the divine Self is effectively related to *all* others in such a way that there are no gradations

[20] In addition to Hartshorne's essay referred to above in n. 16, see his arguments in *Man's Vision of God and the Logic of Theism*, New York: Harper & Brothers, 1941, especially pp. 174–205, and *The Logic of Perfection and Other Essays in Neoclassical Metaphysics*, La Salle, Ill.: Open Court Publishing Co., 1962, especially pp. 133–47.

[21] See especially *Man's Vision of God*, pp. 85–141.

[22] Alfred North Whitehead, *Process and Reality: An Essay in Cosmology*, New York: The Macmillan Co., 1929, p. 521. Another way of explaining what is meant by "strict" is made clear by Hartshorne when he argues that there must be a literal as well as an analogical sense in which fundamental concepts refer to God ("The Idea of God—Literal or Analogical?" *Christian Scholar*, June, 1956, p. 136).

[23] *Op. cit.*, p. 521.

of intimacy of the various creatures to it. God is not located in a particular space and time, but rather is omnipresent and eternal, in the sense that he is directly present to all spaces and times and they to him.

Or, to take another illustration of the same point, God's dependence on his world, which is a real and not merely verbal dependence, is by no means simply the same as man's dependence on his world or body. We are dependent on our bodies not only for whether we shall be in this actual state or that, but also for whether we shall be in any actual state at all. Ours is, we may say, a dependence both for actuality and for existence. In the case of God, however, there is no existential dependence, but only an actual dependence. *That* God is, in some actual state or other, or in relation to some actual world, is dependent on nothing whatever and is in the strictest sense necessary. The only thing that is contingent (and that only in part) is *what* God is, what actual state of the literally infinite number of states possible for him is in fact actualized; and this depends both on his own contingent or free decisions and on the free decisions of the creatures who constitute his world.[24]

But, if God is thus to be conceived in strict analogy to the human self, his action must be understood in strict analogy to the action of man. In saying this, however, one must take pains to clarify exactly what is meant by man's action. We ordinarily understand a human act to be a specific word or deed whereby, through the instrumentality of the body and its various members, the self undertakes to carry out its particular purposes or projects. Thus I may be said to be acting in any attempt by means of the written word to communicate my understanding of the issues of the present discussion. And yet this ordinary meaning of the words "human act" is certainly not their only or even primary meaning. Both Heidegger and Hartshorne, each

---

[24] It is just this distinction between actuality and existence, and so between actual and existential dependence, that those who express an exaggerated fear of "anthropomorphism" commonly fail to recognize. When Paul Tillich argues, for instance, that "a God who is not able to anticipate every possible future is dependent on an absolute accident and cannot be the foundation of an ultimate courage" (*Systematic Theology*, Vol. I, Chicago: The University of Chicago Press, 1951, pp. 275 f.), he completely ignores this distinction and so is forced to realize one legitimate theological motive (the absoluteness of God's existence) only by sacrificing another (the relativity of God's actuality). For a discussion of the theological importance of the distinction as it is clarified in Whitehead's philosophy, see Charles Hartshorne, *Reality as Social Process: Studies in Metaphysics and Religion*, Glencoe, Ill.: The Free Press, 1953, pp. 204-7.

in a different way, remind us that human action is also to be understood in another and more fundamental sense as the action whereby the self as such is constituted. Behind all its public acts of word and deed there are the self's own private purposes or projects, which are themselves matters of action or decision. Indeed, it is only because the self first acts to constitute itself, to respond to its world, and to decide its own inner being that it "acts" at all in the more ordinary meaning of the word; all its outer acts of word and deed are but ways of expressing and implementing the inner decisions whereby it constitutes itself as a self.

These decisions by which the human self acts to constitute its own inner being may take one or the other of two basic forms—or, as we may also say, the self is always confronted with two basic possibilities for understanding itself in relation to its world.[25] Either it can open itself to its world and make its decisions by sensitively responding to all the influences that bear upon it, or it may close itself against its world and make its decisions on the basis of a much more restricted sensitivity than is actually possible for it. In other words, man can act either as a self who loves and thus participates as fully and completely as he can in his own being and in the being of others, or he can act as a self who hates and thus is estranged both from the more intimate world of his own bodily life and the larger world of fellow selves and creatures. In the first case, all his outward acts of word and deed will be in function of the inner act whereby he constitutes himself as one who loves—just as in the second case, by contrast, all his "acts" in the more ordinary sense of the word will but express or implement the primal act of a self who hates.

Now, if God's action is to be understood by strict analogy to the action of man, what is meant by man's action is, first of all, this inner act whereby the human self as such is constituted, and constituted, moreover, as a self who loves. According to the central claim of the Christian witness of faith, the being of God is a being of "pure unbounded love" (Charles Wesley). I take this to imply that the primary meaning of God's action is the act whereby, in each new present, he constitutes himself as God by participating fully and completely in the world of his creatures, thereby laying the ground for the next stage of the creative process. Because his love, unlike ours, is pure and unbounded, his relation to his creatures and theirs to him is direct and immediate. The closest analogy—and it is but an

[25] Cf. Rudolf Bultmann, *Glauben und Verstehen,* Vol. I, Tübingen: J. C. B. Mohr, 2d ed., 1954, pp. 222 f.

analogy—is our relation to our own bodily states, especially the states of our brains. Whereas we can act on other persons and be acted on by them only through highly indirect means such as spoken words and bodily actions, the interaction that takes place between our selves or minds and our own brain cells is much more intimate and direct. We respond with virtual immediacy to the impulses that come from our brains, and it is over our brains (or their individual cells) that our decisions as selves or minds exercise a virtually direct power or control. I hold with Hartshorne that the interaction between God and the world must be understood analogously to this interaction between our own minds and bodies—with the difference that the former interaction takes place, not between God and a selected portion of his world (analogous to our own brain cells and central nervous system), but between God and the whole world of his creatures. Because his love or power of participation in the being of others is literally boundless, there are no gradations in intimacy of the creatures to him, and so there can be nothing in him corresponding to our nervous system or sense organs. The whole world is, as it were, his sense organ, and his interaction with every creature is unimaginably immediate and direct.

It is in terms of this conception, in which God's action is conceived by strict analogy to man's, that I believe one may appropriately interpret the Christian faith in God as Creator and Redeemer and the traditional theological statements in which that faith has found expression. On this conception, to say that God acts as the Creator is not merely to say that both I and my world are utterly dependent on his power and love and that I am bound to be obedient to his will as it pertains to myself and my world. That this existential meaning is the *indirect* meaning of the statement is to be readily granted. But what it *directly* says is that the ultimate ground of every actual state of the world is not just the individual decisions of the creatures who constitute its antecedent states, but rather these decisions as responded to by God's own decision of pure unbounded love. In a similar way, to say that God acts as Redeemer is to say more than that I now have the possibility of that radical freedom from myself and openness to my world that constitutes the authentic existence of love. It is also to say—and that directly—that the final destiny both of myself and of all my fellow creatures is to contribute ourselves not only to the self-creation of the subsequent worlds of creatures, but also to the self-creation of God, who accepts us without condition into his own everlasting life, where we have a final standing or security that can nevermore be lost.

I cannot now explore the ramifications of this basic conception or show how it might be used to provide a nonmythological interpretation of all the claims implicit in the Christian understanding of God. But I hope even this brief outline will make clear what is meant by saying that an adequate existentialist interpretation of theological statements must be understood to include an analogical speaking of God and his action. I have tried to show that, although all theological statements directly or indirectly have an existential significance, the direct reference of *some* theological statements is not to man and his possibilities of decision, but to God and his action as Creator and Redeemer.

I now turn directly to the question, "What sense does it make to say, 'God acts in history'?" It may appear that the line of thought just developed is a strange preparation for answering this question. The force of the preceding argument is to affirm that God's action, in its fundamental sense, is not an action in history at all. Although his action as Creator is related to history—indeed, is the action in which all historical events are ultimately grounded—his creative action as such is not an action *in* history, but an action that *transcends* it—just as, by analogy, our own inner decisions as selves are not simply identical with any of our outer acts of word and deed, but rather transcend or lie behind them as the decisions in which our words and deeds are grounded and to which they give expression. Likewise, God's action as the Redeemer cannot be simply identified with any particular historical event or events. As the act whereby he ever and again actualizes his own divine essence by responding in love to all the creatures in his world, it is an act that transcends the world as the world's ultimate consequence—just as, again by analogy, the acts whereby we constitute our own selves by responding to our worlds can never be identified with any of the things within these worlds to which we respond. Yet, if this conception is valid, it may seem to make any statement that God acts *within* history impossible. Does it not, in fact, completely rule out all such statements by representing God's act as something necessarily timeless and unhistorical?

I respond, in the first place, by suggesting that such words as "timeless" and "unhistorical" do not conduce to clarity in grasping the fundamental issue. If the viewpoint set forth here is correct, there is a real sense—namely, an analogical sense—in which God as well as man is a temporal and historical being. Because God is to be understood in strict analogy to the human self or person, one must distinguish in him, no less than in man, between what he essentially is and the contingent acts or states in which his essence is again and again actualized. God is not the timeless Absolute of classical metaphysics, who may be said to act only in some Pickwickian sense that bears no real analogy to anything we know as action. Instead, he is the living dynamic God of Holy Scripture, to whom the temporal distinctions of past, present, and future may be properly applied and whose being is the eminent instance of historical being. And yet, because God's historicity is an *eminent* historicity, it must never be confused with the ordinary historicity of man or of the other creatures. God acts, and he acts in the strict sense of the word; but his action is *his* action, and it cannot be simply identified with the action of ordinary historical beings.

Is there no sense, then, in which God may be meaningfully said to act *in* history? There are, I believe, two senses in which this may be said.

If we recall the basic insight that God is to be conceived by strict analogy to the human self and that, in particular, his relation to the world is to be viewed as analogous to our own relation to our bodies, then we may say that every creature is to some extent God's act—just as, by analogy, all our bodily actions are to some extent our actions as selves. There is, to be sure, a certain freedom on the part of the creatures so that they are the result not only of God's action but also of their own; in part, at least, they are self-created. Still, this creaturely freedom has definite limits ultimately grounded in God's own free decisions, and in this sense every creature has its basis in God's creative action. Although the acts whereby God actualizes his essence are his acts and not the acts of the creatures, each creature is what it is only by partly reflecting or expressing in its being God's free decisions.

This is the first sense in which God may be meaningfully said to act in history. But there is also a second sense in which this may be said, and with it we come to the crux of our problem.

It is the distinct prerogative of the uniquely human being that it not only is, but also knows or understands that it is. Man has the capacity of consciousness or of self-consciousness, with the result that he is uniquely the creature of meaning. He is able to understand himself and his fellow creatures and the divine reality in which they have their origin and end and, through his thought and language, is able to bring all this to unique expression. As *logos* himself, he is able to grasp the *logos* of reality as such and to represent it through symbolic speech and action.

This capacity to discern meaning and to give it symbolic expression is what lies behind the whole complex phenomenon of human culture. Thus it also lies behind the particular cultural expression ordinarily designated "religion." What constitutes religion as one form of culture alongside of others is man's attempt to express the ultimate meaning of his existence by grasping the divine *logos* that he encounters in his experience and re-presenting it through appropriate symbolic means. All the various historical religions are so many such attempts, and each of them implicitly or explicitly makes the claim that through it man is decisively confronted with the word that reveals the ultimate truth about his existence.

This is to say that man as the being who can understand his existence and express its meaning symbolically through word and deed can, at least in principle, also re-present or speak for the divine. Insofar as what comes to expression through his speech and action is the gift and demand signified by God's transcendent action as Creator and Redeemer, he re-presents not only his own understanding of God's action, but, through it, the reality of God's action itself. As a matter of fact, one may even say that, in this case, man's action actually *is* God's action—just as, in our case, our outer acts of word and deed may be said to be ours just because or insofar as they give (or are understood to give) expression to the inner actions whereby we constitute our existence as selves.

In one sense, of course, all our bodily actions, including the actions of all our organs and cells, are our actions because they are to some extent the result of the inner decisions by which we actualize our selves or persons. And we have just seen that there is something analogous to this in the case of God, that every creature in his body or world is to some extent his action because it is created by him by being ultimately grounded in the decisions through which he realizes his own divine essence. Yet I think we all recognize that, although all our actions are equally ours, some of them are peculiarly ours in a way that the others are not, especially in our relations with other persons. This is particularly true of those distinctively human actions in which, through word and deed, we give symbolic expression to our own inner beings and understandings. Such actions are, as we say, our "characteristic" actions, since, in them or through them, the persons we are, are uniquely re-presented or revealed to others. Each of us is known to other persons through such acts, and all the other things that we may be and do are interpreted by our fellows in terms of what they understand to be typically *our* statements and actions.

Thus, to take a specific example, my understanding of my wife, and of myself in relation to her, is based upon certain of her words and deeds in a way that it is not based on the many other things that she is and says and does. Who she is for me is who I understand her to be in terms of certain quite particular events, having a "once-for-all" historical character, that I take to be revelatory of her person and attitude as they relate to me. It is true that my understanding of her is to some extent constantly changing in the light of new "revelations" of her being and that I can never be absolutely certain she really is as I understand her to be. Even so, not everything she says and does is equally important in revealing her to me, and I always think of her in terms of certain actions that are hers in a sense that the other things she does are not.

It is because we all commonly understand one another in this way that we are occasionally even led to deny that someone has done something he has in fact done because the action in question is understood to be so untypical or out of character. Thus it is not unusual to find ourselves saying such things as, "Why, John wouldn't do that!"

In short, some of our outer acts of word and deed either are in fact or at least are understood to be *our* acts in a way that others are not. Because certain of our actions give peculiarly apt expression to what we are (or are rightly or wrongly believed to be by others), these actions *are* our actions (or are believed to be our actions) in a special sense.

A strictly analogous statement can be made about the actions of God. Although every creature, as we have seen, is in one sense his act, certain creaturely happenings may be said to be his act in another and quite special sense. Wherever or insofar as an event in history manifests God's characteristic action as Creator and Redeemer, it actually *is* his act in a sense in which other historical events are not.

It will be obvious from what has been said that the possibility of being such a special act of God is peculiarly open to those uniquely human events in which man expresses his understanding of the ultimate meaning of his existence through symbolic speech and action. Because man, at least in principle, can grasp and express the ultimate truth about his life, his words and deeds always carry within themselves, so to speak, the possibility of becoming an act of God. It is also possible, naturally, that they will not become God's act, that the understanding to which they give expression will not re-present the divine *logos* or will re-present it only in a fragmentary or distorted way. The existence of the several historical religions is a constant reminder that this possibility is in fact actualized; for given the quite different and conflicting understandings of existence expressed in these religions, they cannot all be true and so cannot all be genuine revelations or acts of God. But wherever or insofar as particular religious symbols appropriately re-present God's action as Creator and Redeemer, they actually are or become his act in a sense strictly analogous to the sense in which some of our own symbolic actions are our acts in a way others are not.

Of course, it is not such intentionally symbolic actions alone that have the possibility of being special acts of God. Any event, whether intended by anyone as symbolic or not, can become such an act of God insofar as it is received by someone as a symbol of God's creative and redemptive action. Because man is distinctively the creature of meaning, there is no event he experiences that cannot become for him such a symbol. The objective ground of this possibility is that, by the "analogy of being" (*analogia entis*), not only man himself, but also every event or creature is in some sense the image or reflection of the transcendent God and therefore expresses God's being and action in its own creaturely nature. It may be argued that one can discern this symbolic meaning in any event only in the light of some intentionally symbolic action such as a human word or deed through which the meaning of God's action is re-presented. The truth in this argument is that man is the creature of meaning and his encounter with reality and understanding of it are ordinarily mediated by such intentionally symbolic structures as concepts and language. But it would be wrong to assign such intentional symbols any absolute priority. After all, they themselves are the products of man's immediate encounter with reality, and so are not original but derived. If we must decide the question of priority as between the symbolic meaning of events themselves and the intentionally symbolic meaning of our own words and deeds, the former is undoubtedly prior. The various religions, like human culture generally, all have the character of a response to something more original than themselves. They are human attempts in face of the actual events of existence to discern the divine word or meaning of which these events are understood to be the symbols.

And yet, because man is the creature of meaning and ordinarily understands and expresses his existence through the intentionally symbolic actions of human words and deeds, such actions are uniquely adapted to become acts of God. Therefore, what is meant when we say that God acts *in* history is primarily that there are certain distinctively human words and deeds in which his characteristic action as Creator and Redeemer is appropriately re-presented or revealed. We mean that there are some human actions, some specific attempts to express the ultimate truth of our existence through symbolic words and deeds, that are vastly more than merely human actions. Because through them nothing less than the transcendent action of God himself is re-presented, they are also acts of God, that is, they *are* acts of God analogously to the way in which our outer acts *are* our acts insofar as they re-present our own characteristic decisions as selves or persons.

Against this background, I may now answer the question raised at the end of the first part of the essay. I asked there how one can overcome Bultmann's own inconsistency in carrying out his project of existentialist interpretation while still affirming with the Christian community that the history of Jesus of Nazareth is the decisive act of God.[26] If the preceding argument is correct, to say of any historical event that it is the "decisive" act of God can only mean that, in it, in distinction from all other historical events, the ultimate truth about our existence before God is normatively re-presented or revealed. The decisiveness of the event, in other words, lies in its power to decide between all the different and conflicting historical claims to reveal the divine *logos* or meaning everywhere discernible to our experience. In this sense, a decisive act of God is the "revelation of revelations" or, in Paul Tillich's word, the "final" revelation that provides the criterion by which all putative revelations are at once judged and fulfilled.[27]

---

[26] In the remainder of the discussion, I am particularly mindful of the criticism directed to me in different ways in the reviews of *Christ Without Myth* by Rudolf Bultmann (*Journal of Religion*, July, 1962, pp. 225 ff.) and James M. Robinson (*Christian Advocate*, February 1, 1962, pp. 11 f., and *Union Seminary Quarterly Review*, May, 1962, pp. 359–62). I trust the following argument makes clear that, although, like any other Christian theologian, I naturally affirm Jesus Christ to be the decisive act of God, I understand this affirmation in a sufficiently different sense from Bultmann and Robinson to avoid any inconsistency with thoroughgoing demythologizing and existentialist interpretation.

[27] See *Systematic Theology*, Vol. I, pp. 132–37.

That any event ever becomes such a decisive act of God is, naturally, also a function of its being received and understood by someone as having decisive revelatory power. A revelation is not only a revelation *of something* (or someone), but also a revelation *to somebody*—just as analogously, in the example above, certain of my wife's words and deeds reveal her being for me both because they in fact express her inner attitude toward me and because I receive them as having such expressive power by understanding her and myself in relation to her in the way they concretely make possible. Indeed, this second or "subjective" component in the revelatory correlation is existentially fundamental. No event can become a decisive act of God for us unless we receive it as determinative of our self-understanding; and, as has been indicated, we may receive events as thus decisive, and so as final revelations of God's being and action, which in fact do not re-present his gift and demand as they actually confront us. This is the reason Luther can say in the statement so often quoted from the *Large Catechism* that "the trust and the faith of the heart alone make both God and an idol. . . . For these two belong together, faith and God. That to which your heart clings and entrusts itself is, I say, really your God."[28]

On the other hand, Luther also recognizes that there is a "wrong" as well as a "right" faith and that it is only when "your faith and trust are right" that "your God is the true God."[29] What constitutes such "right" faith he subsequently explains when he says that God "wishes to turn us away from everything else, and to draw us to himself, because he is the one eternal good."[30] In other words, there is an "objective" as well as a "subjective" component in the revelatory correlation, and this means that an event is a decisive revelation of God only insofar as it truly re-presents the existential gift and demand of "the one eternal good." This it can do only to the extent that its form or structure is such that the possibility of self-understanding it expresses is in fact the true or authentic understanding of human existence.

To say with the Christian community, then, that *Jesus* is the decisive act of God is to say that in him, in his outer acts of symbolic word and deed, there is expressed *that* understanding of human

[28] Theodore G. Tappert (ed.), *The Book of Concord,* Philadelphia: Muhlenberg Press, 1959, p. 365.
[29] *Ibid.*
[30] *Ibid.,* p. 366.

existence which is, in fact, the ultimate truth about our life before God; that the ultimate reality with which we and all men have to do is God the sovereign Creator and Redeemer, and that in understanding ourselves in terms of the gift and demand of his love, we realize our authentic existence as men.

Presupposed by this argument is the conviction that the entire reality of Jesus' history—at any rate, as it is presented to us in the Gospels—is simply a transparent means of representing a certain possibility for understanding human existence.[31] Not only Jesus' preaching and acts of healing, but also his fellowship with sinners and (perhaps unintentionally) his eventual death on the cross are so many ways of expressing symbolically an understanding of our existence *coram deo*. They are a single witness to the truth that all things have their ultimate beginning and end solely in God's pure unbounded love and that it is in giving ourselves wholly into the keeping of that love, by surrendering all other securities, that we realize our authentic life. In relation to this understanding of human existence and to the one task of giving it appropriate symbolic expression through word and deed, everything in Jesus' history is strictly instrumental. He knows no other work than to reveal the love of the Father in all its radical meaning as gift and demand, and he neither makes nor tolerates any claims other than those that this love itself makes or implies (cf., e.g., Luke 11:27 f.; Mark 3:31–35; Matt. 7:21).

But if this understanding of existence that Jesus re-presents is true, if we really are created and redeemed by God's sovereign love, then, in a real sense, Jesus himself *is* God's decisive act in human history. For in him, in the word that he speaks and is, God's action as Creator and Redeemer is expressed with utter decisiveness; and this can only mean, for the reasons given above, that he actually *is* God's decisive act.

We may also say, of course, that if Jesus is God's decisive act, then the ultimate truth about our existence—indeed, about every man's existence—is that we are created and redeemed by God's love, and that in abandoning ourselves wholly to him we realize our true life. It is the nature of the decision of Christian faith that it resolves this hypothetical statement into a categorical confession by affirming its

[31] This conviction is illuminated and supported by the results of the so-called "new quest of the historical Jesus." See James M. Robinson, *A New Quest of the Historical Jesus,* London: SCM Press Ltd., 1959; also my essay, "Bultmann and the 'New Quest,'" *Journal of Bible and Religion,* July, 1962, pp. 209–18.

antecedent and thus also affirming its consequent. My conviction, to which this discussion has tried to give support, is that both of these affirmations are valid and may be so understood as to make sense. So far from being incompatible, the two statements that God's act is, in one sense, not a historical act at all, while, in another sense, it is precisely the act of Jesus' history, mutually require and support one another. Just when we take with complete seriousness the utter transcendence of God's action as sovereign Creator and Redeemer, the historical event of Jesus' life and ministry is seen to be God's decisive act in human history. For the whole meaning of this event is to express or reveal God's transcendent love as the sole basis of our authentic existence; and just in this fact it stands before us as itself God's act in a sense that we both can and must affirm.[32]

---

[32] Cf. Gerhard Ebeling, *Wort und Glaube,* Tübingen: J. C. B. Mohr, 1960, p. 343 (English translation by J. W. Leitch in Gerhard Ebeling, *Word and Faith,* Philadelphia: Fortress Press, 1963, p. 327): "That man fails in the right use of the word in relation to his fellow man, and thus also in relation to God, makes the question of the word a burning question. What is the true, necessary, healing, justifying, and therefore unambiguous and crystal clear word, which, because it accords with man's destiny, corresponds to God? What is the word through which one man can impart God to another, so that God comes to man and man to God? That salvation is to be expected from God alone and that it is to be expected from the word alone, and that therefore it is both wholly of God and wholly of man—these statements are not paradoxes or oddities" (my translation).

VII

Y

What Does It Mean to Affirm,
"Jesus Christ Is Lord"?

Before we attempt to answer this question, it is necessary to clarify just what is being asked.

We must note, first of all, that it is the sort of question which could call for one or the other of two different kinds of answer. On the one hand, we might interpret it primarily as a historical (or descriptive) question, directed toward learning what Christians in the past have in fact meant when they have affirmed that Jesus Christ is Lord. On the other hand, we might ask it more in a systematic (or normative) sense, as a question about what Christians ought to affirm, if they are to be responsible to their faith, even if in fact they have not always done so, or have done so only more or less inadequately. My purpose in this essay is to consider the question in the second sense. I intend the discussion to be a contribution to the present task of systematic theology, which, summarily defined, is the task of stating in an adequate conceptual form in our particular situation the understanding of God, man, and the world re-presented in the witness of faith of Jesus Christ.

If we are not to misconceive this task, however, we should remind ourselves of one of the peculiarities of the systematic theologian's responsibility. The theologian, even as systematic thinker, is never his own man, but rather exists for the purpose of expressing as adequately as he can the faith of the historic Christian community. To be sure, his function is different from that of the historian. He is not there simply to repeat what others in the past have said in speaking on behalf of the church of their particular time and place. Nor is the systematic task yet begun even when the historian conceives his own responsibility to involve an inescapable critical moment. Even though the historical theologian as historian may also do something more than simply transmit tradition—namely, engage in the critical analysis (*Sachkritik*) of tradition, interpreting what its various statements "say" in terms of what they "mean"[1]—the proper task of the systematic theologian still transcends such strictly historical responsibility. What he must seek to do is to present a new critico-constructive interpretation of the witness of Christian faith that will enable the church to speak adequately in the present historical situation.[2] Nevertheless, the systematic theologian of today is bound together with all the theologians of yesterday at least in having a common question and a common task. Furthermore, if he is responsible, he knows his own answer to this question can be taken seriously only if he is constantly willing to be guided in formulating it by all those who have gone before him.

Consequently, if I propose to discuss our question here not as a historical theologian, but rather systematically, I do not intend to disregard the unavoidably communal character of the theological enterprise. On the contrary, I intend to speak within and, indeed, on behalf of the catholic Christian church. And if perforce I must go a different way from those who have gone before me (at least some of them!), I trust this will not be done arbitrarily or without cause—as should be evidenced by a willingness to listen respectfully and receptively to whatever comment or criticism may be forthcoming from all the others who are engaged in this same theological task. And when I say *are* engaged, I mean to speak comprehensively. I agree completely with Karl Barth that we cannot follow the rule in theology, *De mortuis nihil nisi bene.* We cannot follow this rule "simply because the theologians [of the past] are not dead. 'In Him they all have life,' in the greatness and within the limitations in which they once lived. . . . And thus they live, excitingly enough, also for

[1] Classical examples of such interpretation are provided by the exegetical and historical writings of Rudolf Bultmann. See especially *Das Evangelium des Johannes,* Göttingen: Vandenhoeck & Ruprecht, 13th ed., 1953; *Theology of the New Testament,* trans. Kendrick Grobel, New York: Charles Scribner's Sons, 1951, 1955; and *Das Urchristentum im Rahmen der antiken Religionen,* Zürich: Artemis-Verlag, 1949 (English translation by R. H. Fuller in Rudolf Bultmann, *Primitive Christianity in Its Contemporary Setting,* New York: Meridian Books, Inc., 1956).

[2] It is one of the great services of Paul Tillich to have clearly focused this as the distinctive moment of the systematic task. See *Systematic Theology,* Vol. I, Chicago: The University of Chicago Press, 1951, pp. 3–8.

us. They will not cease to speak to us. And we cannot cease to listen to them."[3]

This is true *a fortiori* of the theological voices that speak in Holy Scripture, especially in the New Testament. If to be a responsible theologian means to listen attentively to all the voices of the theological past, this holds with particular force of the canonical theologians. The seriousness of our own systematic concern must be evidenced by gratefully receiving whatever guidance may be available to us from the New Testament. Our answer to the common question must indeed be our own, and it may even be that we will find it necessary to depart from some of the things said by the New Testament theologians. Yet the responsibility of our own systematic undertaking turns on our willingness to listen with utter respect to the original witness of the New Testament as we formulate the question and try to answer it.

The second clarification our question calls for has to do with our motives in asking it. I suspect our main motive is that many of us today are desperately concerned to hear an answer to the question which will actually *mean* something to us. In other words, I assume we are impatient with theological statements (not only historical theological statements, but even systematic ones) that do not really mean anything to us at all because they are framed in terms we no longer understand. I do not mean simply that we have become impatient with the jargonistic predilection of the professional theologian. That, unfortunately, seems to be an occupational hazard, which no theologian had better claim to have overcome. What I have in mind is something worse (and there is something worse!) than using technical language in nontechnical contexts—namely, the widespread habit of using the technical or even nontechnical language of the church's past to speak to men today in the present.

I stated earlier that the task of the systematic theologian is to express adequately in a particular historical situation the Christian understanding of human existence. I did not stress then, however, that one criterion of theological adequacy is that the understanding of faith be formulated "understandably." The theologian defaults in his responsibility if he does not make an earnest effort to state the eternal word of the Christian gospel in a way that will seem both meaningful and true to men who live in the particular time in and for which he has his theological vocation. This means that the contemporary

[3] *The Humanity of God,* trans. J. N. Thomas and Thomas Wieser, Richmond: John Knox Press, 1960, pp. 32 f.

theologian must recognize that men today by and large no longer express their understandings of the meaning of existence in the mythological language of the classical theological tradition. It is not so much that they do not have the same understandings of existence as men of the past as that they do not express their understandings in the same kind of terms. Hence what is needed from theology is a thoroughgoing attempt to translate the meaning of the church's traditional witness into terms in which contemporary men either do or can most readily understand their life as human beings.

And this need is, as it were, reinforced by the very character of this witness itself. Contrary to a prevalent and perennial misunderstanding, Christian faith is not fundamentally a matter of intellectual assent to theoretical truths or belief in doctrinal propositions. To be sure, faith does imply definite assertions about the reality encountered in our experience, and these assertions can be formulated reflectively only as an integral system of beliefs. But simply to affirm these beliefs theoretically, without being transformed by them in one's total existence as a self, is far from realizing what the church has always meant by "faith." This is because "faith," in its most basic sense, properly refers to a certain understanding of one's existence as a self, whose burden and greatness is continually to have to decide how he is to understand and lead his own unique life. What confronts us in the church's witness is not primarily a world view that commands our intellectual assent, but a specific possibility for understanding our lives as men in history, which demands of us a free, personal decision. Just this fact, however, is more or less seriously obscured by the mythological language in which this witness has traditionally been presented. Hence the deeper reason for trying to restate the Christian witness in other, nonmythological terms is the reason that follows from the other criterion of theological adequacy—that the meaning of faith shall also be stated "appropriately," in terms that do not obscure, but transparently express its fundamentally existential character. What is demanded of theology—and of us today even more so, since the resources for meeting the demand are now at hand—is the kind of christology implied by Luther when he says that Christ is properly preached only "when that Christian liberty which he bestows is rightly taught"[4] or by Melanchthon's famous statement, *Hoc est Christum cognoscere, eius beneficia cognoscere*.

It is with a view toward meeting this demand and the need of men

[4] *Luther's Works*, Vol. XXXI, ed. Harold J. Grimm, Philadelphia: Muhlenberg Press, 1957, p. 357.

such as myself for an understandable statement of the lordship of Christ that I reraise this central theological question. My intention is to engage in what Rudolf Bultmann has spoken of as an "existentialist interpretation" of the claim that "Jesus Christ is Lord."[5] I would like so to exhibit the meaning of this affirmation that we today will indeed understand what it means and that the personal decision it summons each of us to make will be clearly posed and can be conscientiously made. As to procedure, I propose simply to accept the guidance offered us by the following statement of the Apostle Paul's: "We know that an idol has no real existence and that there is no God but one. For although there may be so-called gods in heaven or on earth—as indeed there are many 'gods' and many 'lords'—yet for us there is one God, the Father, from whom are all things and for whom we exist, and one Lord, Jesus Christ, through whom are all things and through whom we exist" (I Cor. 8:4–6). I will consider three topics suggested by these sentences and, in so doing, present an answer to our question that at least seeks to meet the criteria just set forth.

1. THE REALITY OF GOD AND THE POSSIBILITY OF "SO-CALLED GODS"

The first thing about Paul's statement that attracts attention is his acknowledgment that "there may be so-called gods in heaven or on earth." This acknowledgment naturally raises the question as to the reason for this "may be." What are the conditions of the possibility that "so-called gods" may in fact exist—a fact Paul himself explicitly attests in the next phrase in the statement?

In order to answer this question, we must begin by speaking not of the possibility of so-called gods, but of the reality of God and his original revelation to mankind. In this respect, we are in no different position from that of Paul himself; even as he clearly speaks of the

---

[5] See especially H. W. Bartsch (ed.), *Kerygma und Mythos,* Vol. I, Hamburg: Herbert Reich-Evangelischer Verlag, 2d ed., 1951, pp. 15–48 (English translation by R. H. Fuller in H. W. Bartsch [ed.], *Kerygma and Myth,* New York: Harper & Row, 2d ed., 1961, pp. 1–44). Cf. also Bultmann's attempt to interpret this affirmation in Walter Leibrecht (ed.), *Religion and Culture: Essays in Honor of Paul Tillich,* New York: Harper & Brothers, 1959, pp. 240 f.

possibility of so-called gods on the basis of his understanding of the one true God and his original self-disclosure, so we, too, must proceed to our answer to the question in exactly the same way.

For the witness of Christian faith, the most important thing about man is that he always exists in the presence of God as a free and responsible self, whose final purpose is to reciprocate God's unconditioned love for him by a love that is in its own way unconditioned. It is true that Christian faith affirms that the whole of nature and history is likewise the beneficiary of God's love, that all creatures are his creatures and so have in him their only ultimate source and end. But it is of the essence of the Christian witness to attest to the uniqueness of *man's* relation to God. Unlike any of the other creatures (so far, at least, as we have the right to say), man is, in John Wesley's phrase, "capable of God." This is what is meant when traditional theology speaks of man's being created "in God's image." He is uniquely gifted with the strange power of self-awareness and thus can become the sole recipient of God's universal self-disclosure in and through all of nature and history.

Like all the other creatures, man has his own appointed end in the total scheme of God's creative purposes; and, as is true of them also, this end is none other than the maximum realization of all his distinctive possibilities, in realizing which he fulfills his existence as a creature. And yet, unlike his fellow creatures, man has the freedom and responsibility of himself affirming or trying to deny his creaturely destiny. Because of his capacity to be self-aware, he may either consent to his creaturehood in confident obedience or else attempt to escape from it by in effect pretending to be his own creator. He is constantly faced with the question of who or what he authentically is and therefore must continually give an answer to this existential question by the way he understands himself in his world. His own authentic being as a self confronts him in the double form of promise and demand. Something he must always choose as the underlying basis of his existence, some "center of value" or meaning that makes possible the moment-by-moment decisions he is forced to make in his encounters with other persons and with what befalls him in his own particular destiny. In short, as Christian faith understands him, every man has an inextinguishable knowledge of God, in the sense of the ultimate reality which is the final source and end of all things, but for which men alone have the freedom and the responsibility to exist.

This is what Paul evidently has in mind when he speaks of God as the One "from whom are all things and for whom we exist." Man simply as man always lives before this God, and his own authentic being as a creature of the Creator constantly confronts him as the "commandment which promises life" (Rom. 7:10). Each of us at the center of his selfhood is always aware of the One who is the beginning and end of all created things and for or against whom we as men uniquely have the possibility of deciding (cf. Rom. 1:18 ff.). Unlike our fellow creatures, we are not simply given our existence before God—to be from him and through him—but rather have the freedom and responsibility of ourselves choosing whether we shall exist *for* God or not (cf. Rom. 1:20 f.). All of us know there is some final source of being and meaning; this much is the inalienable gift of God's original revelation to us in "the things that have been made." Yet what is to be invested with these divine predicates is left to our own freedom to decide. Although each of us knows infallibly *that* something ultimate is both promised to him and demanded of him, he himself must determine "without excuse" *what* it is that possesses such ultimate significance.[6]

This is not to say, obviously, that Paul supposes man has the power to decide whether or not God exists as the ultimate ground and end of all being. In one sense, the reality of God has nothing whatever to do with our decision. God *is,* and he is whether anyone affirms him or not. Yet, in another sense, he only is *for me,* in his proper work as my gracious Creator, when I myself, in my own freedom, choose to exist for him in authentic creaturehood. This is the meaning of Luther's well-known statement in his *Large Catechism* that "the trust and the faith of the heart alone make both God and an idol. . . . For these two belong together, faith and God. That to which your heart clings and entrusts itself is, I say, really your God."[7] Luther's point, like Paul's, is that the meaning of the term "God," at least in relation to man, is "God *for* man." God is, indeed, God *over* everything, the other creatures as well as mankind. But, in relation to man, he also wills to be the God *for* or *of* man, the One whom each of us freely and responsibly acknowledges as the ultimate source and end of his

[6] See Bultmann's discussion in *Theology of the New Testament,* Vol. I, pp. 227–32; also what Paul Tillich says in *Dynamics of Faith,* New York: Harper & Row, 1957, pp. 16 ff., regarding the elements of "certainty" and "uncertainty" in man's relation to the ultimate.

[7] Theodore G. Tappert (ed.), *The Book of Concord,* Philadelphia: Muhlenberg Press, 1959, p. 365.

particular life.[8] In this sense, Luther says, "these two belong together, faith and God."

In this light it becomes clear why, in order to explain the possibility of so-called gods, we first had to speak of the reality of the one true God and his original self-disclosure to human existence. Precisely because man as man exists before God and constantly receives his original revelation, man not only has the possibility of authentic faith in God, but also the possibility of inauthentic or idolatrous faith in so-called gods. Unless God, "ever since the creation of the world," revealed "his eternal power and deity" in "the things that have been made," so that man as free and self-aware person could always receive this original revelation, man would know nothing of ultimate demand or ultimate promise, and thus could not even be an idolater. Here again, we may appeal to Luther, who tells us in his *Lectures on Romans* that even those who worship idols or, in the terms of Paul's statement, so-called gods, can do so only because they have an inobscurable knowledge of God's eternal power and deity, which they then mistakenly attribute to some nondivine object or objects.[9]

Yet something more is obviously required for there to be so-called gods than man's existing before the one true God as a free and responsible self who knows of the ultimate demand and promise that God signifies for his life. What is needed, clearly, is some other reality or realities that can become the mistaken subject of the divine predicates that man comes to know through God's original self-revelation. Paul's definition of God as he "from whom are all things" points in the direction of such realities. Man's original knowledge of God is always given only "in, with, and under" his knowledge of "all things," that is, the world, the totality of created beings in dynamic relation with which man alone has his own creaturely existence.[10] Consequently, it is always possible for him mistakenly to invest some one or the other of the realities within the world with the ultimacy that properly belongs solely to God himself. Strictly speaking, it is less that man can simply identify such creaturely things with God

[8] See also Emil Brunner, *Truth as Encounter,* trans. A. W. Loos, David Cairns, and T. H. L. Parker, Philadelphia: The Westminster Press, 1964, pp. 94 f.

[9] *Lectures on Romans,* ed. and trans. Wilhelm Pauck, Philadelphia: The Westminster Press, 1961, pp. 22 ff.

[10] See John Baillie, *Our Knowledge of God,* New York: Charles Scribner's Sons, 2d ed., 1959, pp. 178 f.

than that he can regard them as having a unique and indispensable significance as symbols or sacraments of God's presence. But, be this as it may, because man lives out his days in the midst of a world of fellow creatures, there is an indefinite number of possible realities that may become so-called gods for him, things that he invests with ultimate significance by making them integral to the ground of his self-understanding.

For my present purpose, this brief analysis of the possibility of religion must be sufficient. I am mainly interested in establishing two important points. First, what is meant by the term "god" in its purely formal existential sense (which includes not only the one true God, but also all so-called gods) is whatever functions for anyone as the ultimate ground of his existence as a self. To have a "god" is to have something that lays upon one an ultimate demand—namely, that one surrender everything else for the sake of this particular thing—and also holds out to one an ultimate promise—namely, of bringing him to his authentic existence as a human being provided he meets this demand. Then, second, the reason "there may be so-called gods in heaven or on earth" is that man is continually endowed with the freedom to invest any of the things in the world with the divine significance that, in reality and for the witness of Christian faith, belongs to God the Father alone. Man has the possibility of treating some creaturely thing that is in no sense really ultimate as though it were ultimate—as though it could somehow account for both the final obligation and the final hope of his life.

2. THE ACTUALITY OF "MANY GODS AND MANY LORDS"

Paul not only affirms the *possibility* of so-called gods; he also affirms that such gods *actually exist*: "as indeed there are many 'gods' and many 'lords'." Earlier, to be sure, he tells us that "an idol has no real existence and that there is no God but one." But that the contradiction is merely apparent should be clear from the preceding discussion. The purely formal meaning of the term "god" (and essentially the same thing may be said of "lord") is whatever constitutes for someone the ultimate ground of his self-understanding as a person, or, in other terms, the reality that places him under an ultimate demand and offers him the promise of finally fulfilling his life as a man. In this sense, whatever a man chooses to invest with ultimacy in relation to his own existence is *his* "god" or "lord."

This does not mean that everything men thus choose to regard as their god or lord really is so. On the contrary, it is possible that they in fact choose to live in terms of realities that in themselves are not divine at all, that are not the reality from and through which all things exist and thus also that for and through which man is to live his life. Indeed, Paul's conviction is that just this possibility is ever and again actualized in the human community, and this is what he means when he says that there are indeed many gods and many lords. Everywhere there are men who understand the ultimate meaning of their existence as grounded in some other reality—in fact, several such realities—than the one true God alone. Paul knows, naturally, that these realities are not truly ultimate, and this is why he can say that they have no real existence and are merely so-called gods. But he also knows that men nevertheless may and do regard them as though they were gods. As a matter of fact, his whole understanding of man's predicament rests on his belief that each of us is to some extent constantly engaged in just this kind of empty and idolatrous worship (cf. Rom. 1:20–32). Whether we find the ultimate meaning of our life in "images resembling mortal man or birds or animals or reptiles" or, rather, in what William James called "the bitch goddess success," who dominates so many of our lives today, we are in effect worshiping at the shrine of some so-called god or lord that has no real existence as the divinity we take it to be through our idolatrous devotion.

Of course, when Paul speaks of many gods and many lords, he is speaking in terms of the mythological understanding of reality he characteristically shares with the rest of the ancient world of which he is a part. He undoubtedly pictures earth and heaven as peopled with a motley of supernatural beings, headed up, finally, by Satan, who can become the objects of men's idolatrous worship (cf. I Cor. 7:5; II Cor. 4:3 f.; Gal. 4:8 ff.). There are, for example, demonic powers at work in man's sensual nature and vital impulses. There are also the more sublime spirits of the heavens that have the power to control sublunary happenings (cf. I Cor. 2:6 ff.). Likewise, there are powers of life and fertility that account for the whole creative process of nature, and still other beings who set the norms for human thought and action (cf. Gal. 3:19 f.). All such powers, Paul assumes, make claims on man and hold out promises to him if he will but accept their claims; and so they readily become the objects of his misplaced devotion to God.

We today no longer share such a mythological picture of ourselves and of the world, and there is something at once tragic and comic about theologies that try to pretend otherwise. But there cannot be the least question that the existential reality underlying this picture is as much a reality now as it ever was in the time of Paul. Does not each of us know only too well what it means to devote himself to some worldly power—his own health or reputation, the prestige and prosperity of his community or nation, the products of his cultural creativity, his race, or some person or institution—that he invests with ultimate significance? The question is rhetorical and but enables us today to understand the force of Paul's assertion that there are indeed many gods and many lords. We all know that there are as many gods and lords as there are idolatrous faiths such as our own.

I stated above, parenthetically, that the same analysis made of the term "god" could also be made of the term "lord." But since it is the latter term that is central in the formulation of our main question, it is necessary to add a word or two more concerning its meaning.

In general, the word "lord" means one who has both the power and the authority to claim obedience from another—another who in rendering such obedience acknowledges himself to be his lord's "slave" or "subject." Thus the term corresponding to the Greek word κύριος, which we translate with our word "lord," is δοῦλος, best translated as "slave" or "subject." In the field of religion, in which, quite naturally, the word "lord" also comes to be employed, it means the one to whom a man extends an *ultimate* (or unconditional) obedience, and from whom, by the same token, he also expects an ultimate fulfillment. And this relational meaning of the term is of the essence; for, as Bultmann points out, "lord" "indicates the respective deity not primarily in his divine majesty and power, but in his 'master' relation to the speaker (the corresponding term for the worshiper is 'slave' . . .)."[11] Therefore, when Paul speaks of "many lords," what he primarily has in mind are all the realities in fact regarded by men as having ultimate power and authority over their existence and in relation to which, therefore, they understand themselves to be slaves or subjects.

[11] *Theology of the New Testament,* Vol. I, p. 125. See also the extended discussion by Werner Foerster and Gottfried Quell in *Bible Key Words,* Vol. VIII, trans. H. P. Kingdom, London: Adam and Charles Black, 1958, especially pp. xiii f., 1–35, 82–110.

To be sure, it is quite likely that here, as well as in other passages in his letters, Paul is specifically thinking of the various mystery religions in which different deities were worshipped as lords through sacramental rites, including frequently baptismal baths and sacred meals. This is borne out by his apparently thinking of the term "lord" as designating some subordinate divine being, for which the term "god" would not be strictly appropriate. Thus, in the next verse, which we will need to consider more carefully below, he speaks of "one God, the Father, *from* whom are all things" and of "one Lord, Jesus Christ, *through* whom are all things," thereby assigning to the Lord a merely mediating reality in relation to the ultimate source of things in God himself. Technically, at least, this distinction seems to point in the direction of the same kind of "subordinationism" which elsewhere characterizes Paul's explicit statements regarding the relation of "Lord" to "God" and which was the stock in trade of the typical theology underlying most of the mystery cults.[12] And yet, even if such "subordinationism" seems to characterize Paul's view and thus suggests that it is of the many lords of the mystery cults that he is speaking, we can surely infer that his thought also has reference to the many other lords men actually worship. We in no way illegitimately extend his meaning if we proceed on the basis of the general definition of "lord" previously clarified and claim that what he means when he says "there are many 'gods' and many 'lords'" is the actuality of mankind's various idolatrous faiths. Wherever a man endows some merely creaturely thing with the ultimate power and authority to claim and fulfill his life, there we have the actuality of many gods and many lords in one of its instantiations. And, as I have said, each of us should be able to recognize from his own firsthand experience just what this actuality is.

3. FOR US—"ONE GOD, THE FATHER," AND "ONE LORD, JESUS CHRIST"

It is against this background of the possibility and the actuality of idolatrous faith in many gods and many lords that Paul offers the

[12] See Rudolf Bultmann, *Das Urchristentum im Rahmen der antiken Religionen,* pp. 173–80, 196 f. (Eng. trans., pp. 156–61, 176 f.); also *Theology of the New Testament,* Vol. I, pp. 125 ff.

following succinct formulation of the Christian witness: "Yet for us there is one God, the Father, from whom are all things and for whom we exist, and one Lord, Jesus Christ, through whom are all things and through whom we exist." Paul is speaking here, of course, on behalf of the Christian community; and he says simply that, for those who belong to this community, the so-called gods of mankind have no real existence as divine powers, because *for them,* for Christians, there is no god but God the Father, and no lord but the Lord Jesus Christ. If the preceding analysis is correct, to join Paul in saying this would be to affirm that the reality ultimately determining our own existence both as promise and as demand is the reality signified by the words "God the Father and the Lord Jesus Christ." But what reality is signified by these words? Clearly, we need to know not only the *formal* meaning of the Christian witness, but its *material* meaning as well.

As soon as one asks this further question, however, he is faced with a problem to which I have already briefly referred, but which we must now consider more fully. This is the problem of whether Paul really intends to affirm what appears to be a "subordinationist" understanding of Jesus Christ in relation to God the Father. If one simply adheres to Paul's explicit formulation, he seems to take for granted that the Lord Jesus Christ is a second divine being alongside of and subordinate to the ultimate divine reality he refers to as God the Father. And there is ample support throughout the rest of his letters to sustain this impression. Consider, for example, a passage like II Cor. 11:31, where God is expressly said to be the πατήρ (father) of the κύριος (lord). The same conception is also apparently expressed in the salutations of the various letters, where Paul regularly speaks of "God our Father and the Lord Jesus Christ" (Rom. 1:7; I Cor. 1:3; II Cor. 1:2; Gal. 1:1; Phil. 1:2; I Thess. 1:1; Philem. 3). One may further refer to Phil. 2:11, where it is said that Jesus Christ is confessed as Lord "to the glory of God the Father." Thus the evidence is clear that, if we take Paul's explicit formulation as a technically precise statement, Bultmann is correct in saying that Paul would have to be considered a "subordinationist" in his christology.[13]

And yet Bultmann has also convincingly shown that this is just

---

[13] *Glauben und Verstehen,* Vol. II, Tübingen: J. C. B. Mohr, 1952, pp. 250 ff. (English translation by J. C. G. Greig in Rudolf Bultmann, *Essays, Philosophical and Theological,* London: SCM Press Ltd., 1955, pp. 277 ff.).

how we ought *not* to take Paul's formulation.[14] In passage after passage in his letters, θέος (God) and κύριος (lord) are either explicitly or implicitly completely synonymous terms (cf., e.g., Rom. 5:15 with II Cor. 8:9; or I Cor. 3:10 with Rom. 1:5; or II Cor. 6:4 with I Cor. 3:5); and he time and again assigns to the Father and the Lord indifferently the same essential functions (cf., e.g., I Thess. 3:13 and Rom. 3:5 with I Thess. 2:19 and I Cor. 4:5).[15] It seems fairly certain, then, that when Paul affirms that Jesus Christ is Lord, while it is God who is our Father, he does not really intend to affirm either two divine beings as the object of Christian faith or to assert what is, strictly speaking, a "subordinationist" christology. It is true that he is always more or less aware that the divine reality he knows in Jesus Christ is by no means present exclusively in this one decisive disclosure (cf., e.g., Rom. 1:20, 3:21, 4:1–25; I Cor. 10:4; Gal. 3:6 ff.); and he never forgets that in some sense the specifically Christian dispensation must eventually come to an end, so that, as he puts it, God alone "may be all in all" (I Cor. 15:28). Still, in his view, the reality signified by the words "God our Father" is, in the last analysis, one and the same with the reality designated as "our Lord Jesus Christ"—or, better expressed, what it means to have God as our Father is existentially the same as having Jesus Christ as our Lord.

Yet how can this be so? The only way to answer this question is to clarify further what is meant by "God the Father" and "the Lord Jesus Christ." But to do this, we have to go beyond what is immediately presented in the statement from I Corinthians that has so far guided our thinking. In fact, we have to make explicit what Paul simply takes for granted in this statement. I am confident we rightly grasp his intention, however, if we say that "God the Father" for him signifies the covenant God of Israel who has disclosed himself in Israel's history, and thence through the law and the prophets, to be the God of a unique promise and demand. By the *promise* of God, Paul understands God's free and unconditioned offer of his love as the only proper ground for man's understanding of his authenticity (cf. especially Rom. 4:1–25); and by God's *demand* he understands the command that men shall understand themselves solely in terms of this promise and thereby be freed to fulfill the law, which is all

[14] *Ibid.*, pp. 253–57 (Eng. trans., pp. 281–86).
[15] *Ibid.*, pp. 253 f. (Eng. trans. pp. 281 f.). It may also be noted that the mediating role explicitly assigned to the Lord in I Cor. 8:6 is assumed by God himself in Rom. 11:36.

summed up in the one sentence, "You shall love your neighbor as yourself" (Rom. 13:8 ff.; cf. Gal. 5:14, 6:2).

Paul is convinced, to be sure, that Israel has not been obedient to its revelation of God's promise and demand as this has been represented to it through the law and the prophets (Romans 2–3). Instead of submitting to the free acceptance of God's love, the Jews have sought to establish their own righteousness by a merely formal or external obedience to the commandments of the law (cf. Rom. 10:2 ff.). Even so, whenever Paul speaks of God, he unquestionably means the covenant God of Israel, whose significance for man is the promise and demand of pure unbounded love. And when he says that, for us as Christians, there is no God but "God the Father," it is precisely *this* God to whom he refers.

The crucial point, however, is that the phrase "one Lord, Jesus Christ" has for Paul exactly the same existential significance. I realize, of course, that Paul's christology is, in one respect, a very complex matter that requires considerable careful analysis to be adequately interpreted. But, in another respect, his thought about Christ is so astonishingly simple that no one need long remain uncertain of its meaning. Clearly, the underlying intention of all his christological formulations is to affirm that the history of Jesus of Nazareth is the decisive re-presentation to all mankind of the same promise and demand re-presented by the Old Testament revelation (cf. Rom. 3:21)—and, beyond that, also attested by the whole of creation and man's conscience as well (cf. Rom. 1:18 ff., 2:15).[16] Thus by "the Lord Jesus Christ" he means essentially the actual announcement in a single human life of the promise and demand of unconditioned love, which alone has the power and authority to command every man's ultimate allegiance. This is borne out by the designation of the theme of his preaching as "Christ crucified" (I Cor. 1:23), which is to say, the event of the cross understood in the light of the resurrection. It is precisely in the event of Jesus' crucifixion that God has announced to the world the radical demand of his love that men must die to every form of self-contrived security and idolatrous faith in which they involve themselves. And the significance of Jesus' resurrection is that, whenever this death to self takes place, the promise of "a new creation" in and under that same reconciling love thereupon begins to be fulfilled (cf. II Cor. 5:17).

In short, the real function of all the mythological language in

16 See C. H. Dodd, "Natural Law in the Bible," *Theology*, May, 1946, pp. 130–33; June, 1946, 161–67.

which Paul formulates his christology is to express one basic claim: the human word that speaks to men in the event of Jesus, and thence in the kerygma and sacraments of the church (cf. II Cor. 5:18 ff.; Rom. 6:4; I Cor. 11:26), is the same word always addressed to them in God's original revelation, as well as through "the oracles of God" with which Israel in particular has been entrusted (Rom. 3:2). Therefore, when Paul says that, for us as Christians, there is "one Lord, Jesus Christ," what he means is that the one promise and demand under which we live out our lives is "the love of God in Christ Jesus our Lord" (Rom. 8:38), which is concretely re-presented to us in the witness of the Christian community.[17]

Thus, if we take seriously the guidance offered us by Paul, to affirm that Jesus Christ is Lord means both something positive and something negative. It means positively that the human word of promise and demand addressed to us in Jesus Christ is infinitely more than a merely human word and, in fact, has the divine power and authority to claim our ultimate allegiance and thereby also to bring our lives to their authentic fulfillment. And it means negatively that no other promise and demand have this same divine significance.

Of course, this negative implication is not to be understood as though the word spoken in Jesus Christ were any different word from that which always confronts men in their actual existence before God and is particularly re-presented through "the law and the prophets." On the contrary, the whole point of what Paul would teach us is that it is precisely the *same* word, albeit here spoken, in the particular human life of Jesus of Nazareth, with all the force of final revelation. The real meaning of the exclusiveness of Jesus Christ's lordship is not that divine lordship is exercised solely in that particular life, but rather that wherever such lordship is exercised—and that, naturally, is everywhere: "through whom are *all* things"—it can take no other form than the same promise and demand re-presented *for us* in Jesus.[18]

Thus to affirm that Jesus Christ is Lord is to affirm that the final promise in which we place our confidence is none of the many promises of the so-called gods of heaven and earth, but solely the promise of God's unending love to all who will but receive it.

[17] See especially Bultmann's discussion in Schubert M. Ogden (ed.), *Existence and Faith: Shorter Writings of Rudolf Bultmann,* New York: Meridian Books, Inc., 1960, pp. 197–201.

[18] See my argument in *Christ Without Myth: A Study Based on the Theology of Rudolf Bultmann,* New York: Harper & Row, 1961, pp. 127–64.

Likewise to affirm that Jesus Christ is Lord is to affirm that no demand may ultimately claim us except the one demand that we accept God's love for us and thereby be freed to fulfill his command to love all the others whom he also already loves. *To affirm this promise and this demand is the real meaning of affirming the lordship of Jesus Christ.*

Ideally, what should be done now is to spell out the implications of this affirmation for the Christian's life in the church and in the world. But this is a task that falls outside the limits of the present essay. I hope I have succeeded in making clear, however, that because Jesus Christ is Lord, Christians—and, indeed, all mankind—have both a hope and an obligation that no other lordship entails. Because *Jesus Christ* is Lord, the horizon of our expectations is not bound by the various hopes this world sets before us. We ultimately depend neither on social and economic success nor on a happy issue to our several undertakings as the cultural creatures we are—whether in science and philosophy, art and technology, or social and political action. Nor, I would add, does our final confidence in the worth of our life hang on the possibility of our own moral perfection or the perfectibility of our species in its long, slow climb toward a more decent human life. Rather, beyond all such earthly hopes, which it is far from my intention to degrade, we have an ultimate hope in the sovereign love of God, apart from which any other promise we can imagine is finally lacking in significance. In the words of Isaac Watts, "His mercies shall endure/ When this vain world shall be no more." By the same token, we also stand under an obligation that none of the many gods and lords of heaven and earth is great enough to impose. Because *Jesus Christ* is Lord, ours can never be a merely formal obedience to moral precepts, and much less can we fulfill our responsibility by simply realizing a decent bourgeois virtue. Rather, the final claim by which we are bound is the radical claim of self-sacrificing love that, again in Watts' words, demands our soul, our life, our all. Only when we first accede to the demand to affirm all beings even as God himself affirms them can we correctly assess both the rights and the limits of all the other claims that also constantly confront us.

I have assumed throughout the essay that the meaning of the term "affirmation" and its cognates appropriate to the present discussion is its *existential* meaning. But, like all terms having to do with knowledge, this word also has another, primarily *theoretical* sense; and, as I had occasion briefly to note, this theoretical sense also has a proper place even in the field of faith and theology. Nevertheless, the affirmation whose meaning I have tried to interpret is fundamentally an affirmation that each of us must make not only with his mind and lips, but with his "heart," with the whole weight of his existence as a self through a free, personal decision. And this means that all I have said has been—or, at least, has been intended to be—that "indirect" kind of preaching which no authentic theology can avoid being.

VIII

Υ

The Promise of Faith

It is striking that no theological questions seem to be of such wide-spread popular interest as those which are properly called "eschato-logical." Time and again, I have noted that university audiences, like lay groups in the churches, include many who assume that religion means nothing if not some way of dealing with the problems of death and of man's final destiny. Yet it is, I think, a common experience for contemporary theologians to find such problems particularly hard to handle. Whereas in the case of the other articles of faith, we suppose we are on relatively solid ground and have some confidence about how to proceed, when we come to the article of death and the other so-called "last things," many of us tend to falter and act as though we had suddenly stepped onto an area where nothing can be very certain. Thus, in the statements of faith and understanding submitted each year by my theological students, eschatology is consistently treated with less insight and more obvious embarrassment for want of something to say than any other doctrinal area. And it is significant that the vast bulk of the time I spend in discussions with these students is usually devoted, in one way or another, to clarifying eschatological questions.

But it is not only among apprentice theologians that eschatology is commonly a knotty problem. The same is true of the journeymen and masters as well, as is evident from the paucity of adequate treatments of eschatology by mature theologians. No one, at least in the English-speaking world, has recently written in this area more often or with greater insight than Reinhold Niebuhr. His recurrent theme for over a generation has been "the nature and destiny of man," and he has succeeded in convincing most of his fellow theologians that tradi-tional eschatological symbols have a meaning and importance that an earlier liberal theology either overlooked or falsely interpreted. And yet there are good reasons, I believe, why Emil Brunner says "it would be difficult to determine just what Reinhold Niebuhr means by his . . . crucial concept of the Biblical 'eschatological symbol.' "[1] Niebuhr clearly has no intention of simply eliminating biblical eschatology, but rather stresses that eschatological symbols are to be taken seriously as symbols. "But," Brunner asks, "what kind of reality lies hidden beneath these symbols? Is it an everlasting life, for which we should hope in the hour of death? Is it the fulfillment of the Biblical expectation of the kingdom of God? . . . To what extent there stands behind Niebuhr's 'eschatological symbols' a *reality,* and what kind of reality—or whether perhaps these eschatological symbols are merely 'regulative principles' in the Kantian sense—these are questions on which we should like to have him make a definitive pronouncement."[2]

From this it should be clear why the layman in theology *a fortiori* is so frequently puzzled over discussions of the last things, not only by Niebuhr, but by many other contemporary theologians as well. Reading or listening to what Protestant theologians today usually have to say on such matters, the layman often wonders, for example, whether these thinkers really do believe in life after death or not. He realizes that, if they hold such a belief, it almost certainly has a different character from the more conventional belief that most men still accept or reject. But what troubles him is that he is not at all sure as to the exact nature and scope of the difference. The theologians are frank to tell him that the conventional belief is a "symbol" or "myth." And yet, as even their fellow theologians attest, it is not easy to know from their frequently hazy interpretations just what the traditional belief is a symbol of and whether recognition of it as mythical leads one to deny, finally, what at least seems to be its obvious meaning.

If we inquire as to the reasons for this state of affairs in current discussions of eschatology, different things may come to mind. Thus one suggestion is that theologians suppose, with many of their contemporaries, that questions as to the final destiny of man or the ultimate meaning of the natural-historical process are in principl difficult questions, any answers to which are bound to raise serious problems. We commonly recognize today that the very nature of death is to set a limit or boundary to our finite existence, and hence

[1] Charles W. Kegley and Robert W. Bretall (eds.), *Reinhold Niebuhr: His Religious, Social, and Political Thought,* New York: The Macmillan Co., 1956, p. 31.

[2] *Ibid.,* p. 32.

to all our experience and knowledge as well. We feel that it is simply not given to us—to *any* of us—to speak with authority about issues that transcend our qualifications to speak. We have no question that men have always and everywhere attempted to see beyond the limits of finitude and, by their myths and theories, have sought to account for the reassurance that death makes so poignantly urgent. But can there be any doubt that all these myths and theories (of immortality, resurrection, reincarnation, etc.) are simply all-too-human attempts to shed a little light on the final mystery of man's existence—a mystery about which, just because it is a mystery, none of us really knows very much? Is not all the talk about immortality and resurrection, as a contemporary philosopher has said, "the desperate (for some) or the confident (for others) affirmation by 'one-who-must-die' that he *matters*"?[3] And has not the problem always been (even where it was not recognized) whether this affirmation can be more than sheer desperation and really a matter of confidence, given no more than any of us can honestly know?

But beyond this, as it were, perennial problem that the questions of eschatology may be thought to pose, there is the fact that most of us today, including, presumably, theologians, are modern men in a modern world, to whom the eschatological symbols of the past no longer seem credible or even meaningful. In consequence of the astonishing triumphs of science and technology, the outlook of Western men is now so determined that the mythological elements in the church's traditional eschatology have lost all clear meaning. And this is true for vast numbers of persons who have only an indirect part in the ongoing process of scientific research and are quite unsophisticated about science's method and procedures. Even the ordinary man in the street increasingly finds it hard to look forward to the imminent or eventual end of the world, with Christ's returning on the clouds to consign men to a final destiny in some transhistorical heaven or hell. For many, to be sure, the vivid images of the old apocalyptic have sometimes seemed to speak with a new power in face of the possible nuclear holocaust that so profoundly disturbs the peace of our technological civilization. But even a moment's reflection leaves no doubt that the annihilation of man by the "ultimate" weapons of a global civil war is something utterly different from the end of the world so graphically portrayed in Christian mythology. Then, so far as such matters as heaven and hell and the last judgment

[3] Frederick Ferré, *Language, Logic, and God*, New York: Harper & Row, 1961, p. 123.

are concerned, we simply do not know what to make of them when they are presented to us in their conventional mythological forms, with no attempt to interpret their meaning. Instinctively we find ourselves asking, "But where is this heaven (or hell) you talk about?" and "What sense is there in speaking of an 'end' of the natural process?"

There are doubtless other reasons that help explain why eschatology is experienced by many theologians today as peculiarly problematic. But perhaps it will be agreed that the two reasons I have specified are the most important. Eschatological questions strike many of us as particularly difficult both because they seem to ask about matters that quite transcend our capacity to know and to speak and because we find that the traditional symbols in which these questions have been answered no longer have any clear meaning.

If there is agreement about this, however, I should hope we might also agree about something else. I am convinced that neither of these reasons would have quite the force we often suppose it to have were we to remember and take seriously one basic point: the one and only theme of all theological thinking and speaking is the theme of faith. The task of theology, properly understood, is to explicate Christian faith, and thus to set forth the understanding of existence—of ourselves, our fellow creatures, and the God whose love embraces us all—which faith itself involves or implies. Yet, if this is theology's task, and if eschatology is held to be a legitimate part of that task, the only conclusion is that the theme of eschatology, also, is somehow the one theme of faith; that our eschatological questions and answers offer but one more way in which the meaning and scope of Christian faith itself are explained and made clear.

I hold that eschatology *is* a proper part of an adequate Christian theology and that this is so because the theme of eschatology is *the promise of faith,* the promise which is given in and with faith itself and for which the experience of faith alone provides the basis and warrants. The common suppositions that eschatological reflection has to do with matters which transcend faith's present experience and that these matters can be symbolized only in ways that conflict with the scientific world picture—these suppositions can be seriously entertained only so long as we misunderstand either the nature of such reflection or the nature of faith itself, or, possibly, both. If we are not to think of eschatology as a kind of pseudo science in which we build guesses and hunches about the future into a structure no more secure than its weakest part; or, if we are not to reduce faith to a loose collection of independent articles of belief so that it becomes "like a shop offering all kinds of goods for sale, according to need and taste,"[4] then we must be clear that eschatology is an integral part of the one task of theological reflection and that the only theme of such reflection, and thus of eschatology, is faith and the reality of God which faith knows and affirms.

Once we are clear about this, however, we are also freed from the special difficulties that eschatology supposedly entails. We may grant, no doubt, that a theologian's reflections on the last things do provide something like a test case, a good opportunity to determine the coherence and adequacy (or the lack thereof) of his general theological position. But we dare not suppose that the last things raise special problems that are somehow quite different from the problems everywhere raised by faith and its claims. The problems of eschatology are really the problems of theology generally; and the key to their solution is that particular form of faith in the reality of God which Christian theology is charged with making clear and explicit.

This is to say that the last things can never be properly understood as things that have a certain future place, proximate or remote, on the time-line of the individual's personal destiny or of the natural-historical process as a whole. Being really and truly *last* things, that is, *ultimate* things, things constituting the most essential reality of *all* places on the time-line, they are always and only matters of the present—though, of course, of *every* present. Just as the reality of God as the Creator is not something belonging to the past of nature and history, but is their ever-present primordial ground, so the reality of God as Judge and Redeemer is not a particular event of the future, but the ever-present final consequence of each passing moment in the stream of time. Hence, from the standpoint of Christian faith itself, none of the traditional eschatological symbols may be thought to refer to things or events in principle beyond our present experience and knowledge. This is because their real reference is always to the abiding structure and meaning of our actual existence here and now, which faith presently understands. They are, we must say, ways of symbolizing or re-presenting the promise implied by the reality of God, which promise is known and affirmed by Christian faith whenever it becomes actual.

In saying this, we also remove any ground for the other alleged difficulty in dealing with eschatological questions. Once it is recog-

---

[4] Gerhard Ebeling, *The Nature of Faith,* trans. R. G. Smith, Philadelphia: Muhlenberg Press, 1961, p. 151.

nized that the traditional symbols of eschatology are really ways of re-presenting the promise of faith in God, the undeniable fact that they are now seen to be meaningless by the standards of empirical science no longer poses an insoluble problem. Rightly understood, all talk of heaven and hell, the last judgment, the resurrection of the body, and the life everlasting is not *scientific* talk at all. Rather, it is *mythological* talk, whose use and, therefore, meaning is to re-present an understanding of human existence. It symbolizes the essential structure and meaning of life as each of us immediately experiences them and as they are decisively understood and clarified by the witness of Christian faith.[5]

Some such approach to eschatology has long since been agreed upon by a fair number of Protestant theologians. But, as was remarked above, their interpretations of eschatological symbols typically display a certain haziness or lack of conceptual clarity, which tends to obscure some important differences between them. Therefore, before proceeding to offer my own interpretation of the promise of faith, I want to clarify my approach still further by sharpening the issues between it and certain of its near relatives on the contemporary scene.

The first of these is the kind of position set forth in an early book of John A. T. Robinson, *In the End, God . . . : A Study of the Christian Doctrine of the Last Things.*[6] Robinson maintains, very much as has been maintained here, that "the eschatological statements of the Bible are of [a] 'mythical' nature, in precisely the same way as its narratives of the Creation and Fall. They are neither inerrant prophecies of the future nor pious guess-work. They are necessary transpositions into the key of the hereafter of sure knowledge of God and His relation to men given in the revelatory encounter of present historical event."[7] Hence Robinson rightly emphasizes that all eschatological assertions are "ultimate convictions about *God*," that they "can finally be reduced to, and their validity tested by, sentences beginning: 'In the end, God . . .'"[8]

It is clear from the outset, however, that Robinson has his own peculiar way of understanding these points of basic agreement. Thus, in contrasting theology's employment of myth with that of science, he

[5] See above, pp. 104–7, 114–19.
[6] London: James Clarke & Co. Ltd., 1950.
[7] *Ibid.*, p. 35.
[8] *Ibid.*, pp. 30 f.

says that theology "uses it for the purpose of translating its [*sc.* theology's] fundamental understanding of God, given and verified in present experience, into terms of the primal and ultimate, where it [*sc.* theology's understanding of God] *must* apply and yet where direct evidence is, in the nature of the case, unobtainable."[9] One infers that the reason direct evidence cannot be obtained for theology's assertions about creation or the last things is that they refer in both cases to events in principle beyond our present experience and knowledge. To be sure, the God who acts in the events *is* presently known; and statements about the "primal" and the "ultimate" are really "translations" or "transpositions" of that present knowledge. But Robinson speaks of the transpositions as "necessary," and this is apparently because he holds creation and the last things themselves to be realities either of the past or of the future.

That he does in fact hold this view is confirmed by his subsequent discussion. He repeatedly speaks, without the least sign of regarding such phrases as only mythical, of "the final state of history," "the last time," "a supervening state of fruition," "the chronological moment of the end," "the climax of the world-process," and "the moment of consummation," commenting in connection with the latter, "Whether it takes a thousand years or one day is all the same to God."[10] Further, he states explicitly that the myths of creation and of the last things can serve their purpose "to interpret present realities in all their primal and eschatological quality . . . only if they depict, not abstract truths, but events, and events which run back into the past and out into the future."[11] In keeping with this general statement, he has the following to say about the last things in particular: "Judgment Day is a dramatised, idealised picture of every day. And yet it is not simply every day. The Parousia and the Judgment are not merely cross-sections. They must also be represented . . . as realities which consummate as well as transect the historical process. For the process as a whole has a movement and has a meaning: it 'works up' to a goal."[12]

Now I do not question that the motives which have led Robinson to this particular approach to eschatology are legitimate. It is quite

[9] *Ibid.*, p. 34.

[10] *Ibid.*, pp. 36, 37, 44, 50, 69, and 49. Cf. also his statement: "Of course, *something* must actually happen to the individual, just as the world must end in one way and not another" (p. 90).

[11] *Ibid.*, pp. 67 f.

[12] *Ibid.*, p. 69.

evident that the faith to which witness is borne in Holy Scripture has something important at stake in his insistence that not only the present moment, but the whole of nature and history as well, is of ultimate significance. Just as the church could never fully express its faith in God as Creator except through its doctrine of *creatio ex nihilo a deo,* so it also has never been able to re-present its assurance of God's redemption except by the equally problematic doctrine of "the resurrection of the body." Both doctrines serve the identical purposes of asserting the sole sovereignty of God as the ground and end of whatever is or is even possible, and of denying, against all forms of metaphysical dualism, that there can be anything at all which is not subject to his sovereignty. But these are the very purposes Robinson also intends to serve by his interpretation of eschatology—to the point, even, of finally embracing the risks of a complete universalism.[13] He correctly recognizes that the promise of faith can be adequately explicated only as entailing the belief that *all* the stages in the natural-historical process find their ultimate end, even as they have their primal ground, in the encompassing reality of God's love.

But *this* belief in no way requires the claim Robinson mistakenly associates with it—that there sometime will be, nay even must be, a last stage of the cosmic process. To suppose that the promise of faith in itself requires us to make any such claim is as wrong as to hold that faith in God as the Creator implies that the world process sometime had a first stage. It is true that the doctrine of *creatio ex nihilo* has traditionally been interpreted as expressing this implication. Yet, as Thomas Aquinas made clear, the conventional interpretation has no warrant in the idea of creation as such. "It belongs to the idea of eternity to have no principle of duration; but it does not belong to the idea of creation to have a principle of duration, but only a principle of origin—unless creation be accepted as it is accepted by faith."[14] The reason Aquinas allows for the final qualification is that the exegesis of the scriptural myth of creation which he took to be valid interpreted it as affirming a beginning of the world in time. But more recent investigations of the nature of mythical language have successfully challenged that exegesis. We are now able to understand that the use of myth is throughout existential and that the creation

[13] See *ibid.,* pp. 99–123.
[14] *Questiones Disputatae,* ed. P. Bazzi *et al.,* Rome: Marietti Editori Ltd., 9th ed., 1953, p. 82 (*De potentia,* 3, 14, *ad* 8).

myth, therefore, intends to illumine the essential structure and meaning of our life in the present, and does not refer to some more or less remote event in the past. Because this is so, however, there is no reason to assume with Robinson that the scriptural myths of the last things include any reference to a "final state of history" in the near or distant future. They do indeed mean to affirm something that will also be true of the future, even as the creation myth expresses a truth that also holds good of the past. But this is so because their real reference is to the essential constitution of *every present moment* in and under God's sovereign love. Just as the myth and doctrine of creation affirm primarily that the one essential *cause* of each moment is God's boundless love for it, so the first intention of the myths explicated by eschatology is to re-present that same love as each moment's one essential *effect*. This intention, however, in no way begs the question whether the series of present moments must have a temporal end, any more than the meaning of creation assumes that it had to have a temporal beginning. Indeed, on a proper analysis of what is meant by "redemption," there is an exact parallel to what Aquinas says about the idea of creation: It does not belong to the idea of redemption that the world have an end of duration, but only an end of ultimate significance.

The weakness of Robinson's position, in short, is that it fails consistently to demythologize the Christian myths about the last things. The result, as in all cases of such inconsistency, is that Robinson never succeeds in overcoming a double difficulty. First, he fails to free himself from making claims about a final stage of the cosmic process, despite the fact that such claims are in no sense warranted by Christian faith itself and must be regarded as, at the very least, extremely problematic on any other possible grounds. Certainly science can offer no support for them, since judgment on this type of claim lies outside the jurisdiction of a scientific mode of verification. But hardly less certain is that metaphysics also could never verify them. What could possibly be meant by a last (or first) moment of time? Does not the very meaning of "moment" require that the referent of the term anticipate its objectification in some subsequent moments (or remember some precedent moments which it itself presently objectifies)? And can one coherently conceive even a divine or necessary consciousness which would not necessarily have *some* contingent objects? But more important, in a way, is the second difficulty in Robinson's position. He also fails to make clear that the only meaning of eschatological myths, as of all myths, is existential;

that they are in all cases symbols of faith and, therefore, have no other intention than to illumine our life here and now in each present in face of the reality and promise of God.

The foregoing discussion has already given indication of a deep indebtedness to Rudolf Bultmann in the approach here proposed to the problems of eschatology. I would now acknowledge this indebtedness by stating explicitly that, in this area, as in most others, I have found Bultmann to be our best contemporary guide. By his general method of "existentialist interpretation," he has provided a way (or, at any rate, the outlines of a way) to interpret eschatological myths consistently and radically as symbols of the promise of faith. The great merit of this approach, as I have suggested, is that it alone can free us from the difficulties posed by the mythological form of traditional eschatological doctrine and, at the same time, enable us to see the integral relation of eschatology to theology's one essential task.

But, in thus acknowledging my close relation to Bultmann's basic approach, I would also dissociate myself from a certain misunderstanding of his approach that I have sometimes encountered among those who think of themselves as his followers. In putting the matter this way, my point is not to exonerate Bultmann of all responsibility for the misunderstanding, since it seems clear to me, as it has to numbers of his other critics, that his own view is often stated sufficiently one-sidedly to give the misunderstanding a certain plausibility. I do contend, however, that it is a *mis*understanding, which can be supported from his writings only by disregarding some of their most important parts. What, then, is this misunderstanding?

I can best answer this question by pointing out how the central eschatological symbol "resurrection" is sometimes interpreted by so-called existentialist theologians. According to certain interpreters, the meaning of this symbol is simply to re-present a possibility of self-understanding, or of understanding one's existence before God and in relation to one's neighbors and fellow creatures. To be "raised up" on this interpretation means that one comes to have a true or authentic self-understanding; that he realizes in his own individual life the existential knowledge of God and of self and others in God which is made concretely possible by the witness of faith. The correlate to "resurrection," then, is "death"—not, however, in the ordinary sense of the cessation or termination of one's subjective participation in being, but in the sense of a false or inauthentic understanding of one's existence. In this sense, "death" really means the same as "sin," for what is properly meant by "sin" is precisely a distorted existential knowledge of God and of one's neighbor and self in God. Although the inauthentic man may be said to be alive in the ordinary sense of "life," since he does subjectively participate in being to some degree or at some level, he cannot be said to be *truly* alive (or, as our American idiom has it, "really livin' "). Because he participates fully neither in God nor in himself and his fellows, he does not enjoy the fullness of subjectivity that is actually possible for him and is literally not what he might be. Consequently, should he ever come to an authentic understanding of himself, wherein he does fully participate in being, the change is veritably a change from death to life. He who was dead is now alive; and, in his new authentic self-understanding, he is, as the New Testament expresses it, "a new creation" (II Cor. 5:17; Gal. 6:15).

There cannot be the least doubt that such an interpretation lays hold of one fundamental motive in the New Testament's own use of the symbol "resurrection." If we consider the letters of Paul, for example—especially, say, Romans 6—it is just this meaning of "resurrection" that is again and again expressed and even empha- sized. Jesus' resurrection is affirmed to be also *our* resurrection, and we are summoned to allow ourselves to be crucified with him, thereby abandoning our old, sinful self-understanding and understanding ourselves anew as "alive to God in Christ Jesus" (Rom. 6:11). In the same vein, Paul removes any question that the "new creation" of which he speaks is an existential reality by paralleling it, in one place, with "keeping the commandments of God" (I Cor. 7:19) and, in another, with "faith working through love" (Gal. 5:6). Clearly, for Scripture, just as for this kind of existentialist interpretation, "resur- rection" means the possibility of new and authentic human existence which the decision of faith concretely actualizes.

Yet where I find a real parting of the ways between the New Testament and any such theological interpretation is that the *sole* motive in the meaning of "resurrection" which such interpretation explicates is *but one* of the motives in its use in the New Testament. I can put the difference over-simply in these terms: whereas for this kind of existentialist theology, "resurrection" designates a *human possibility,* for Scripture, it also refers, and, indeed, primarily, to a *divine actuality.* That this is so of the scriptural use of the symbol can be made sufficiently clear by briefly considering what is meant by the New Testament witness that Jesus is the risen Lord.

As Bultmann has correctly pointed out, the striking thing about the

New Testament kerygma is that "the cross and the resurrection belong together as a unity."[15] Jesus is never witnessed to in either the Gospels or the Epistles in such a way that the significance of his life and death could be discerned only by the circuitous route of historical reconstruction. Instead, he is always proclaimed as the crucified one who is at the same time *christus kyrios,* the risen and exalted Lord of all mankind. This is to say that the witness to Jesus is always borne from the standpoint of the Easter faith of the first disciples, by which the decisive existential significance of his crucifixion is already understood and affirmed. Because this is so, there is no mistaking that the New Testament's talk of Jesus' resurrection is, as Bultmann says, "the expression of the significance of the cross."[16] In its witness to Jesus as the risen Lord, the early church is quite obviously making use of the symbol "resurrection" to express its own decision of faith—or, as we may say, its own self-understanding in terms of the possibility re-presented to it by the historical Jesus, and supremely by the event of his death. As a matter of fact, this is so clearly a motive in the New Testament's use of the symbol that one may conclude with Bultmann that, insofar as the Easter event itself can be considered an event in history, it is "nothing other than the rise of faith in the risen one in which the proclamation had its origin."[17]

And yet it would be wrong to claim (as Bultmann himself has been falsely accused of doing[18]) that this exhausts the New Testament's meaning when it speaks of Jesus' "resurrection." Bultmann brings this out quite clearly when he says that, for Christian faith today, "just as for the first disciples, the historical event in which the Easter faith originated signifies the self-attestation of the risen one, the act of God in which the salvation-occurrence of the cross is completed."[19] This does not mean, of course, that "the act of God" which the faith of Easter signifies is yet another historical happening in space and time, subsequent to the events of Jesus' life and death. The New

[15] H. W. Bartsch (ed.), *Kerygma und Mythos,* Vol. I, Hamburg: Herbert Reich-Evangelischer Verlag, 2d ed., 1951, p. 44 (English translation by R. H. Fuller in H. W. Bartsch [ed.], *Kerygma and Myth,* New York: Harper & Row, 2d ed., 1961, p. 38).

[16] *Ibid.*

[17] *Ibid.,* p. 46 (Eng. trans., p. 42).

[18] See my reply to Karl Barth's charge to this effect in *Christ Without Myth: A Study Based on the Theology of Rudolf Bultmann,* New York: Harper & Row, 1961, pp. 86 ff.

[19] *Op. cit.,* p. 47 (Eng. trans., p. 42).

Testament's representations of it as though it were such a happening are undeniably mythological and demand to be critically interpreted—and that, primarily for the sake of expressing more appropriately its own distinctive reality as an act of *God*. The crucial point, however, is that the witness of faith, which did originate in history at some time after Jesus' crucifixion, is by no means something completely independent or primary. On the contrary, it is by its very nature the response to another and altogether different "witness" on which it absolutely depends, namely, the *"self*-attestation" of the risen Lord, or, as the New Testament also expresses it, *God's own* testimony to the decisive significance of Jesus and his cross (cf. Rom. 1:4).

In other words, by the New Testament's own account, the significance of Jesus which faith affirms is nothing that the decision of faith itself creates or explains. Rather, the ground of that significance is always and only the prior decision of God to which the Christian's own decision of faith can never be more than the obedient response. Thus it is that the other, and perforce always primary, motive in the kerygma's witness to Jesus as the risen Lord is to refer to the transcendent act of God's love in which Christian faith has its one abiding ground and object. When the New Testament writers speak of Jesus' "resurrection," they do indeed make use of the word as a symbol of their own self-understanding of faith. But, if we are not utterly to miss what they intend to say, we will never infer from this that the word has some merely "noncognitive" meaning, betokening only their own "historical perspective."[20] We will recognize, rather, that just because it is a symbol of faith—namely, of *their* faith—it is also and, more fundamentally, a clear witness to the gracious reality of God.

What is true of the New Testament's speaking of *Jesus'* "resurrection" is also true of its use of the symbol more generally to re-present the redemption of all mankind. The reason for this is that Jesus' resurrection is understood to be also *our* resurrection, so that, as Paul puts it, "in Christ *all* shall be made alive" (I Cor. 15:22). This means that our resurrection is never an authentic understanding of our existence until it is first a gracious action of God, which is real

---

[20] See Paul M. van Buren, *The Secular Meaning of the Gospel*, New York: The Macmillan Co., 1963, especially pp. 126–145. Although van Buren would hardly count himself a follower of Bultmann, his general theological approach expresses in a radical (and thus more consistent) form the same kind of view being considered here as a misunderstanding of Bultmann's position.

quite independently of our self-understanding. God first raises us up, first makes us the objects of his limitless love, and only then do we have the possibility of participating in that "new creation" which his love ever and again makes possible for us and all our fellows. In a word, before resurrection is *our* decision, it is *God's* decision; and our faith does not create the risen life, but simply accepts it as already created by God through Christ and participates in it.

This, as I see it, is without any doubt the consistent teaching of the New Testament. Yet I confess that, in trying to make that teaching clear, one is faced with a definite problem. In holding that "resurrection" properly means more than a possibility of man's self-understanding, one is in danger of misrepresenting the true relation between man and God by seeming to imply that this relation is wholly external for one or the other of its two terms. Rightly understood, God and man are so related that to speak of either in his actual concrete being is really always to speak of both. Consequently, to say that resurrection is a human possibility *is* to say, at least implicitly, that it is also a divine actuality—and *vice versa*. The significance of Bultmann's work is that he has, for the most part, clearly and consistently realized this and has had the courage to draw the consequences that follow from it. But even he, as his critics have rightly stressed, has tended to express the matter in a one-sided "anthropocentric" way; and this is even more obviously the case with those of his followers whose position I have been criticizing. Therefore, in seeking to point up the limits of their interpretation by insisting that "resurrection" as a symbol of faith or self-understanding also refers—and, indeed, primarily—to the gracious action of God, I have doubtless run the risk of stating a "theocentric" position that is equally one-sided.

But this risk, I am convinced, has to be run, even though one should also try so to restate the issue that both falsely anthropocentric and falsely theocentric distortions are avoided. The essential point with which we began—that eschatology is an integral part of the one theological task because its sole theme is the promise of faith—in no way requires one to hold that a symbol like "resurrection" merely expresses the self-understanding of faith as a human decision. On the contrary, because faith by its very nature is always faith *in . . . ,* namely, *in* the God who is disclosed to us in Jesus Christ, "resurrection," like all other eschatological symbols, has to be interpreted as having to do, first of all, not with our decision of faith, but with the divine reality to which our faith always refers.

I would add, in fairness to those whose position I have criticized, that it is possible, and perhaps likely, that few of them intend to eliminate this primary reference of eschatological symbols to the reality and action of God. That their critics so often claim to detect such an intention is due, in part at least, to the critics' own "Babylonian captivity" to the mythological world picture.[21] But the danger in *any* existentialist theology is that it may fail to observe the priorities of Holy Scripture itself. Like certain liberal theologians who insisted that "resurrection" has to do, not with the *quantity* of life, but with its *quality,* existentialists too easily obscure that the symbol's fundamental reference is to neither the quantity nor the quality of *man*'s life, but to the quality of *God*'s life—to the pure unbounded love, the perfect grace and judgment, whereby our creaturely lives in time are alone endowed with everlasting significance.

Hoping to have precluded some possible misunderstandings, I now wish to offer a constructive interpretation of traditional Christian discourse about the last things. The main point I shall make has already been implied in the preceding discussion; but I would now like to develop that point as fully as present limitations allow.

By "the promise of faith," I understand the promise immediately implied in the witness of faith of Jesus Christ that we are all, each and every creature of us, embraced everlastingly by the boundless love of God. For centuries, an appropriate theological explication of this promise, as of Christian faith generally, was made impossible by the prevailing presuppositions of classical metaphysics. Christian theologians simply assumed, as the Greek philosophers had before them, that God could be properly conceived, as distinct from merely imagined or symbolized, only as in all respects absolute and immutable being. As the one truly eminent or perfect reality, he could not possibly be thought to enjoy real internal relations to other beings beyond himself, nor could his nature in any way be understood to involve intrinsic temporal structure. On the contrary, he had to be conceived as the one wholly nonrelational or nonsocial being, whose eternity is a sheer timelessness which is the complete antithesis of our own temporality. That any such conception could have so long dominated the minds of theologians presumably schooled in Holy Scripture is one of the oddities of our intellectual history; and it could

[21] Cf. especially Friedrich Gogarten, *Entmythologisierung und Kirche,* Stuttgart: Friedrich Vorwerk Verlag, 2d ed., 1953 (English translation by N. H. Smith in Friedrich Gogarten, *Demythologizing and History,* London: SCM Press Ltd., 1955).

have happened at all only, because the stark opposition between the God of the philosophers and the Father of Jesus Christ was made to appear anything but obvious by several ingenious attempts to remove it. But the contradiction has remained, and its fateful effects on the whole task of theological reflection are nowhere more evident than in the area of eschatology.

In the first place, insofar as theologians have assumed that God has to be conceived as wholly timeless and absolute being, they have been utterly unable to demythologize the eschatological myths. Whereas the mythical representations in Scripture having to do with God's own being (say, as the heavenly Father or King) could be accommodated within limits to the God conceived by classical metaphysics, this proved quite impossible in the case of the myths having to do with God's action in relation to the world. As we saw earlier, the scriptural account of creation has been traditionally interpreted as referring to a supernatural event in the past, for which metaphysics as such provides no evidence and which is posited solely on the basis of what is mistaken for revelation. The result is that the myth of creation has been left undemythologized, completely uninterpreted in clear conceptual terms. But the same has been even more strikingly true in the case of the myths of the last things. (Aquinas, after all, did make clear that the idea of creation as such is not simply a mythical idea.) Because God has been conceived as utterly unrelated to the natural-historical process, the eschatological myths could not possibly be interpreted as so many symbols for *his* real relation of love for the world as understood by Christian faith. In consequence, these myths, too, have remained conceptually uninterpreted. They have been allowed to appear as though they refer to supernatural events somewhere off in the future, of which neither metaphysics nor, as we now realize, science enables us to form the least clear conception.

But closely related to this first consequence is another, still more fateful: theologians have also been unable to make clear that it is *God himself* who is the only final end, even as he is also the only primal beginning, both of man and of the world. The whole point of the classical conception of God is to deny that he is in any way the concrete end or consequence of the actions of others. He is held to be in every sense the *cause* of other beings, but in no sense their *effect*. Hence, insofar as he can be conceived as the end of the world at all, it is only as the wholly abstract end or ideal, the ultimate teleological principle that, as Aristotle believed, inspires the motions of the whole natural-historical process without being itself in any way moved by them. This means that, on the classical conception of God, the only *concrete* ends realized by the world process are those of man himself and of the other creatures. The implications of this, in turn, for an adequate understanding of faith in God have been correctly pointed out by Charles Hartshorne.

Religion then becomes man's self-service, not genuinely his service of God. For if God can be indebted to no one, can receive value from no one, then to speak of serving him is to indulge in equivocation. Really it must, on that assumption, be only the creature who is to be served or benefitted. God would be the cause or protector of value; but the value caused and protected must be simply ours. On this time-hallowed view, God was the mine and the miner from and by which the wealth was dug; but the ultimate consumer was ourselves. God was the policeman and judge and ruler, but man was the citizen, for whose sake the common-wealth existed.[22]

In short, a fatal weakness of the classical conception of God is that it can give no clear meaning at all to the New Testament's own vision of that "restoration of all things" (Acts 3:21) in which God himself is "all in all" (I Cor. 15:28).

It has recently become clear, however, through the work of Hartshorne and others, that this classical conception of God is neither the only nor the most adequate theistic conception which is available to the metaphysician or philosophical theologian. Given the

---

[22] *The Divine Relativity: A Social Conception of God,* New Haven: Yale University Press, 1948, pp. 58 f. I should perhaps add that I find little but faulty analysis and vestiges of classical metaphysics in the familiar attempts to distinguish "faith" sharply from "religion," when the latter is defined with Hartshorne as "service of God." Gerhard Ebeling, for example, defines "the structure of what we specifically mean by religion" as "the desire to give God something, instead of simply receiving everything from him," and argues that for faith, "we can give to God only that which he already has—his honour, and that this honour is his mercy, and that therefore God can only be honoured by faith" (*op. cit.,* p. 145). Such an argument, I submit, is completely shattered by a New Testament text like Romans 12. Unlike Scripture, Ebeling fails to see that receiving from God and giving to him are *alike* elements in the one reality of "faith working through love," and that *both* elements may take either the authentic form of such faith or the inauthentic form of idolatry. In the nature of the case, there can always be an idolatrous receiving from God as well as an idolatrous giving to him; and, if faith is not dead, but is the "living, busy, active, mighty thing" known to Luther, there must be an authentic giving to God as well as an authentic receiving from him. A similar reply is to be made to the Lundensian theologians, whose basic distinction between "theocentric" and "egocentric" religion betrays the same mistaken analysis and unwitting deference to the God of classical metaphysics. Cf. especially Anders Nygren, *Agape and Eros,* trans. P. S. Watson, London: S.P.C.K., rev. ed., 1953; and Watson's own *Let God Be God! An Interpretation of the Theology of Martin Luther,* London: The Epworth Press, 1947.

starting point and premises of a neoclassical metaphysics, it is as easy to conceive God as the eminent *effect* of all things as to think of him as their eminent *cause*. The reason for this is that the completely general concept of "being affected by the actions of others" is not, as classical metaphysics held, a negative idea, referring only to an imperfection of nondivine beings, but is a wholly positive concept, which obviously admits, if any concept does, of a truly eminent or perfect case. *To be affected by* all things is clearly as unique a property as *to affect* all things, since neither property could conceivably belong to any but a completely perfect or divine being. Indeed, analysis discloses that the two properties can be conceived, if at all, only as the two essentially correlative aspects or poles in one divine life, whose very nature as eminent love is to affect *and* be affected by the nondivine lives of *all* others. Because this is so, the theological task of interpreting the scriptural myths in *conceptual* terms no longer needs to be left uncompleted or so undertaken that it is doomed to fail right from the start. One of the chief proofs of this is the wholly new possibility which a neoclassical theism opens up for at last conceiving the meaning for Christian faith of the eschatological symbols.[23] Now we can make clear in terms of fundamental philosophical concepts why the reality of God's pure unbounded love is itself the whole substance of the promise of faith. The reason, quite simply, is that, in making each of us the object of his boundless love, God accepts us all into his own everlasting life and thereby overcomes both our death and our sin.

By "death" here I do not mean that spiritual death or inauthentic mode of existence to which existentialist theologians often refer by the term. Rather, I mean, first of all, simply that final termination or cessation of our subjective participation in being which one day overtakes each of us and of which we are each always aware. It is the death referred to in the old saying, *mors certa, hora incerta*—death is certain, its hour uncertain. Each of us comes to maturity in the realization that, even as there was a time when he was not, so there will also be a time when he will not be any more. To be sure, most of us do not live in the full light of this realization, but rather seek in various ways to escape its disturbing power. Still, there is perhaps never a moment when we are wholly without it, and, as some

---

[23] See especially Charles Hartshorne, *The Logic of Perfection and Other Essays in Neoclassical Metaphysics*, La Salle, Ill.: Open Court Publishing Co., 1962, pp. 234–62. For an independent statement of an essentially similar position, see Hans Jonas' Ingersoll Lecture, "Immortality and the Modern Temper," *Harvard Theological Review*, January, 1962, pp. 1–20.

philosophers have argued, it is this very awareness of our mortality that endows the moments of our life with vividness and intensity. In this sense, our whole existence is, in Martin Heidegger's phrase, a "being toward death" (*Sein zum Tode*).[24]

Yet, in another sense, "death" does not refer simply to something out ahead of us, certain to happen at some uncertain hour in the future, but also refers to something taking place even now. As another old saying has it, *media in vita in morte sumus*—in the midst of life we are in death. Here and now in every present, we are each involved in that inevitable transience of all our moments of experience which Alfred North Whitehead speaks of as "perpetual perishing."[25] No sooner has the present moment of our participation in being achieved its satisfaction than it slips away from us into the past, whence our poor powers of memory and appreciation are unable to recall it into living immediacy. Nothing happens but it directly falls subject to this ineluctable passing away. All our thoughts and feelings, loves and hates, joys and sorrows, projects and causes are relentlessly carried away from us into the past, where, as they more and more recede from our present, they become all but indistinguishable from nothing. For all any of us can see, if we take into account only creatures such as ourselves, destruction is on exactly the same level as creation, and it is the fate of everything that comes to be to become as though it had never been. "On us and all our race the slow, sure doom falls pitiless and dark."

In my view, it is death in this second sense of transience or "perpetual perishing" that raises the really serious existential question. Even if we suppose that death in the first sense is somehow to be escaped and our lives as subjects endlessly prolonged beyond that

[24] *Sein und Zeit*, Halle: Max Niemeyer Verlag, 1927, pp. 235 ff. Cf. also William Ernest Hocking, *The Meaning of Immortality in Human Experience*, New York: Harper & Brothers, rev. ed., 1957, especially pp. 3–77.

[25] See especially *Process and Reality: An Essay in Cosmology*, New York: The Macmillan Co., 1929, pp. 513 ff. Elsewhere Whitehead comments: "Almost all of *Process and Reality* can be read as an attempt to analyse perishing on the same level as Aristotle's analysis of becoming. The notion of the prehension of the past means that the past is an element which perishes and thereby remains an element in the state beyond, and thus is objectified. That is the whole notion. If you get a general notion of what is meant by perishing, you will have accomplished an apprehension of what you mean by memory and causality, what you mean when you feel that what we are is of infinite importance, because as we perish we are immortal. That is the one key thought around which the whole development of *Process and Reality* is woven . . ." (*Essays in Science and Philosophy*, New York: Philosophical Library, Inc., 1947, p. 89).

uncertain hour, still the deeper problem posed by the "perpetual perishing" of all creaturely things remains to plague us. What profit would it be for us to go on and on living—even to eternity—if the net result of all our having lived were simply nothing; if our successive presents in no way added up to a cumulative accomplishment such as no creature is able to provide either for himself or for his fellows? This is the question that seems to me to expose the profound inadequacy of all the philosophical and theological theories of "subjective immortality," according to which each of us somehow manages (or, on some views, *can* manage) to survive death and continue to exist as an experiencing subject. The deeper problem of mortality, of the incessant passing away of whatever comes to be, is left completely unsolved and, indeed, is even intensified by all such theories. Ludwig Wittgenstein writes: "The temporal immortality of the soul of man, which is to say, its eternal survival even after death, not only is in no way guaranteed, but this assumption above all does not accomplish what it has always been intended to attain. Is a riddle solved because I survive eternally? Is not this eternal life just as much a riddle as the present one? The solution of the riddle of life in space and time lies *outside* space and time."[26]

But the same inability to speak to this problem also flaws all the more modern theories of "objective immortality," according to which each of us influences the other men who come after him and thereby acquires an existence in them beyond the termination of his own subjectivity. What these theories fail to take seriously is that our human posterity is as involved in "perpetual perishing" as we are and, furthermore, is not even remotely able to do justice to what we have been in all its concrete richness.

> And there are some who have no
>   memorial,
> who have perished as though
>   they had not lived;
> they have become as though they
>   had not been born,
> and so have their children after
>   them. (Sirach 44:9)

Can anyone really be comforted solely by the thought that he will live on in the memories and appreciations of poor mortals no more

[26] *Tractatus Logico-Philosophicus,* London: Kegan Paul, Trench, Trubner & Co. Ltd., 1922, p. 184 (my translation).

sensitive than himself? Is the final meaning of my life simply the ever-decreasing impact I make on the other men who come after me?

But, if what faith affirms to be true is true, the problem of death, including its more profound dimension of life's inevitable transience, has a solution. Our final destiny, as Christian faith understands it, is not merely to be loved by our human successors, but also, and infinitely more important, to be loved by the pure unbounded love of God, for whom each of us makes a difference exactly commensurate to what he is and of everlasting significance. Because God's love, radically unlike ours, is pure and unbounded, and because he, therefore, both can and does participate fully in the being of all his creatures, the present moment for him never slips into the past as it does for us. Instead, every moment retains its vividness and intensity forever within his completely perfect love and judgment. He knows all things for just what they are, and he continues to know and cherish them throughout the endless ages of the future in all the richness of their actual being. In other words, because God not only *affects,* but is also *affected by,* whatever exists, all things are in every present quite literally resurrected or restored in his own everlasting life, from which they can nevermore be cast out.

This, I hold, is the promise of faith: that, whatever else may befall us and however long or short may be the span of our lives, either here or hereafter, we are each embraced in every moment within God's boundless love and thereby have the ultimate destiny of endless life in and through him. In this sense, the promise of faith, which is already known to the Christian in his present encounter with Jesus Christ, is the promise of victory over death. Faith knows that the final end or, as it were, the ultimate posterity of the whole creation is none other than God himself, who through his free decision in each moment to accept all things into his life overcomes the "perpetual perishing" of death and all its terrors.

Faith also knows the promise of a final victory over sin, where "sin" means just that spiritual death in which man falls short of his authentic existence in the whole and unreserved love of God and of himself and all things in God. Because faith is faith in a God whose love is without limit and who, therefore, accepts his creatures solely because of his own free decision to do so and not because or even in spite of them, faith also knows that the power of sin itself is finally broken by God's love. Or, better said, faith knows that not even man's sin can set a limit to God's free decision in each new present to love his creatures and to give them to share in his own divine life.

Christian faith does not claim, to be sure, that God's love can in any way coerce man's free response of faith and in that sense overcome sin. It always belongs to man as the free and responsible creature he is to refuse to accept God's acceptance and to continue in the life of unfaith and bondage to sin. God's love, being love, has both the strange power of love and its strange weakness; and it can never compel man to acknowledge it and live in its light and power. But what man can never do, even by his sinning, even, indeed, by his repeated and apparently incorrigible sinning, is to set a limit to the mercies of God. The ground of God's love being wholly in himself, wholly in his own eternal nature to love, his decision in every moment to accept his creatures takes place altogether independently of man's decisions. What is given man to decide is not whether he shall be the object of God's gracious love; that, to the contrary, God alone freely decides. Man's decision is only whether he shall accept God's love for him and thus find himself freed for an authentic existence of returning love for God and for all the others whom God also embraces in his love.

Here is the main point at issue in the earlier discussion of a certain kind of existentialist theology. The danger in any restrictively existentialist interpretation of eschatological symbols is that man's decision of faith or unfaith will be assigned a greater weight than it actually has. I can indeed decide whether to let myself be loved by God and so be freed to share in the "new creation" which that decision opens up for me. But what I can never decide is that I am destined for eternity to be raised up either to salvation or damnation by being incorporated in every present into God's everlasting life. Loved by God we are and ever shall be—and about this, we ourselves can do nothing whatever. Our decision is simply whether we are to accept this eternal destiny and thereby enter upon that new life here and now in the moment which is possible for all who open themselves to God's love. The question facing us, we might say, is not the one that stares at us from the fundamentalist's road signs, "Where will you spend eternity?" but rather, "How and in what ways will you spend time?"

Even so, because the answer to this question is something each of us must make for himself, God's final victory over sin cannot be understood to imply a "universalism" which refuses to give any weight at all to man's decisions. What we are, and so what we shall be forever in the final judgment of God's love, is just what we ourselves decide in the present through our responsible freedom. If we choose to open ourselves to God in faith and in love for him and all those whom he loves, then this is who we are, and this is who we will be known to be eternally in God's wholly righteous judgment. If, on the other hand, we shut ourselves off from God and our fellows and live the cramped, self-centered, and anxious life of the old Adam, then this, too, is who we are and who God, in consequence, will judge us to be even to the farthest reaches of eternity.

And yet, if an uncritical universalism denies the importance of our decisions altogether, traditional notions of a "double destination"— of heaven and hell—have generally been simply another way of giving these decisions more importance than they actually have. Although I may indeed decide to live without *faith* in God's love, I cannot live at all without the *reality* of his love. God as he is known to us in Christ creates all things for himself and takes all things into himself quite apart from any creaturely dispositions whatever. Therefore, even hell, even the anxious closure against God and one's fellows, cannot lie outside God's encompassing love. Those who dwell therein belong to him as surely as those who live in the acceptance of his love and so enjoy the bliss of heaven. Luther once remarked that the devil is God's devil. But it is no less true, as faith understands the matter, that hell is God's hell. As a matter of fact, the very meaning of "hell" is to be bound to God forever without any possibility of separation from him, but also without the faith in his love which is the peace that passes understanding.

In sum, eschatology's traditional problem of universalism and double destination, like the parallel problem in Christian ethics of antinomianism and legalism, is simply a special form of the more fundamental problem of the One and the many, of monism and dualism, which runs throughout the whole of Christian theology and is to be solved only by a neoclassical conception of God. The genius of the Christian understanding of existence is that it is the true and original "center" from which the extreme contraries of monism and dualism in all their several forms are equally departures and distortions. By its very nature, faith so understands both God and the world that their relation is in a profound sense one of identity; for, as pure unbounded love, God indifferently identifies himself with all his creatures and thus overcomes all separation between them and him. But faith also knows that there is another sense in which God and the world are not simply one reality but two, and that God's love is not merely oblivious of the world's differences, but rather fully respects them. Thus, for faith, the final truth is genuinely dialectical or paradoxical: God loves *all things* exactly as they are without condition; and yet God loves all things *exactly as they are,* and thus by his judgment of them provides their one definitive measure.

This, then, is how I propose we should understand the traditional eschatological symbols. I have not attempted to interpret all these symbols here, nor have I considered a number of the problems that even a selective interpretation obviously raises. But I trust I have made clear why the proper use of all discourse about the last things is to explicate the promise implicit in Christian faith itself. Simply because faith in its most essential nature is the sure confidence of God's love for us, it includes the promise of the final overcoming of death and sin that it belongs to God's love to accomplish. It knows that the final destiny of all things to be subjected to the reign of his love, where he is indeed "all in all" (I Cor. 15:28), can never be frustrated by either of man's ancient foes—or, for that matter, by any power whatever. Because the God whom faith knows is, as Luther liked to say, "nothing but love" (*eitel Liebe*), faith also knows that "neither death, nor life, nor angels, nor principalities, nor things present, nor things to come, nor powers, nor height, nor depth, nor anything else in all creation, will be able to separate us from the love of God in Christ Jesus our Lord" (Rom. 8:38 f.).

At the risk of anticlimax, I am constrained to add that the interpretation of the promise of faith presented here leaves completely open whether we somehow manage to survive death and continue to exist as experiencing subjects as is claimed by conventional theories of immortality. Although I recognize it is commonly supposed that Christian faith turns on the validity of some such theory, I must state in all candor and as clearly as possible that I hold this supposition to be mistaken. In the New Testament, once its mythological forms of expression are penetrated to their underlying motif, I see little to justify the supposition, and much that should make us profoundly skeptical toward it. I do not mean by this that it is any part of the New Testament's faith to deny that we somehow survive death and continue our subjective existence. Nor do I myself have any interest in making such a denial. I regard the question of subjective immortality—or, at least, of our subjective survival of death—as an open question; and I hope I could be convinced by relevant evidence and warrants that it should be answered affirmatively, even though I do not now find sufficient reason so to answer it. But what I must refuse to accept, precisely as a Christian theologian, is that belief in our continued subjective existence after death is in some way a necessary article of Christian belief. The only beliefs that are necessary are those that have their basis and warrants in Christian faith itself. And I am quite clear in my own mind that belief in subjective immortality is not to be numbered among such necessary beliefs.

Of course, many theologians have undertaken to argue that it is just our faith in God's love that provides the basis for an affirmation of our subjective survival of death—that, as it is usually put, *if* God really loves us, he will not permit the span of our years to be brought to an end. But, whatever the logical force of such an argument (which is not, I think, very great), it seems to me to betray a profound failure of faith, a lapse into the kind of thinking so severely treated by Paul, by which trust in God's love is made subject to certain conditions and we demand a "sign," some tangible proof, that we may give ourselves wholly into his keeping (cf. I Cor. 1:18–25). It betrays, in a word, a most serious departure from the only really essential point, that there is but one faith with which the whole of theology has to deal and that this faith is directed to one sovereign God who *alone* is the ground of our own and all men's authentic existence. *Soli deo gloria*—to God alone be the glory. That is the watchword of all valid Protestant theology, and it also has an application to the area of eschatology.

This may also be expressed by saying that the good news of Jesus' resurrection is never really heard unless it is heard to be as much an "offence" or "stumbling block" as "the word of the cross" (I Cor. 1:18). Indeed, rightly understood, the triumphant message of the resurrection simply *is* the word of the cross—the word that we live only by dying, and that our true life is not really our life at all but is "hid with Christ in God," in whose unending love for his whole creation we are each given to share (Col. 3:3). The task of eschatology is to see to it that this word is given its appropriate and understandable expression. When that at last is done, it will be time enough to speak of a Christian theology adequate both to the witness of faith and to the needs of our time.

Index

231

God (*Continued*)

as eminent historicity, 180
as eminent reality, 59 f.
as eminently absolute, 48, 60, 141 f., 156
as eminently changing, 59 f., 65
as eminently incarnate, 60
as eminently relative, 47, 48, 54, 60, 64, 65, 141 f., 156
as eminently temporal, 59 f.
as eternal, 60, 61, 63, 65, 154, 176
as final end, 210, 213, 221 f.
as ground of basic confidence, 37 f., 43, 44 f., 47, 64, 140 ff.
as growing, 59 f.
as immanent, 124
as immaterial, 61
as impassive, 61
as including the Absolute, 61
as independent of the world, 62, 156, 176
as infinite care, 150, 155 f.
as infinite temporality, 65, 146, 153–157, 163
as Judge, 210
as knower, 49 f., 133
as necessary existence, 22, 62 f., 121 f., 123 f., 141 f.
as object, 83
as omnipresent, 60, 176
as passive, 64
as personal, 62, 66, 163
as primal beginning, 210, 213, 221
as pure unbounded love, 68, 123, 142, 177, 220, 223, 228 f.
as Redeemer, 124, 168 f., 173, 178 f., 181–187, 210, 213
as Self or Thou, 49, 60, 61, 65, 66, 175 f.
as Subject, 83
as suffering, 53 f.
as transcendent, 76, 106, 168
as unchangeable, 60, 61, 65
as unsurpassable, 59 f.
as wholly other, 68
dipolar conception of, 48, 50, 62, 68, 141, 172
monopolar conception of, 48, 50, 61
perfection of, 59 f., 61, 64

God (*Continued*)

proofs of the existence of, 21 f., 43, 95, 123, 127, 135–142
See also Theism
Gogarten, Friedrich, 6 f., 161, 163, 220
Gollwitzer, Helmut, 26
Goodfield, June, 7
Guilt, 114 ff.

Hare, R. M., 84 f., 88, 159
Hartshorne, Charles, 21, 24, 43, 48, 50, 55, 56, 59 f., 61, 63, 77, 83, 94 ff., 97 f., 124, 125, 150, 163, 172, 175, 176, 178, 222, 223
Heaven, 208 f., 211, 228
Hegel, G. F. W., 52, 61
Heidegger, Martin, 39, 48, 56, 57, 78 ff., 94, 96, 118, 138, 144–163, 168, 169, 170, 171, 172, 176, 224
Hell, 208 f., 211, 228
Hepburn, R. W., 91
Hermeneutics, 50, 67, 77, 82, 90, 96, 117
Herrmann, Wilhelm, 4
Heteronomy, 10
Historical Jesus, the, 186 f., 202, 217
Historicity, 91, 117, 145, 160, 169, 180
Hocking, W. E., 224
Hodges, H. A., 104
Hofmann, Hans, 103
Holy Scripture, 4, 49, 53, 65, 66 f., 68, 99, 120–126, 140 f., 151, 156, 158, 161 f., 190, 213, 216, 220, 222
Hooker, Richard, 1
Humanism, 40, 41, 42, 45 f., 126 ff., 136, 142
Hume, David, 8 f., 94

Idealism, 52, 94
Idolatry, 23 f., 124 f., 192–199, 202, 222
Immortality, 10, 207, 208
objective, 225 f.
subjective, 36, 225, 229 f.

James, William, 29, 37 f., 52, 64, 137 f., 197
Jaspers, Karl, 78, 79 f.